DEADLY DOZEN

Twelve Forgotten

Gunfighters

of the Old West

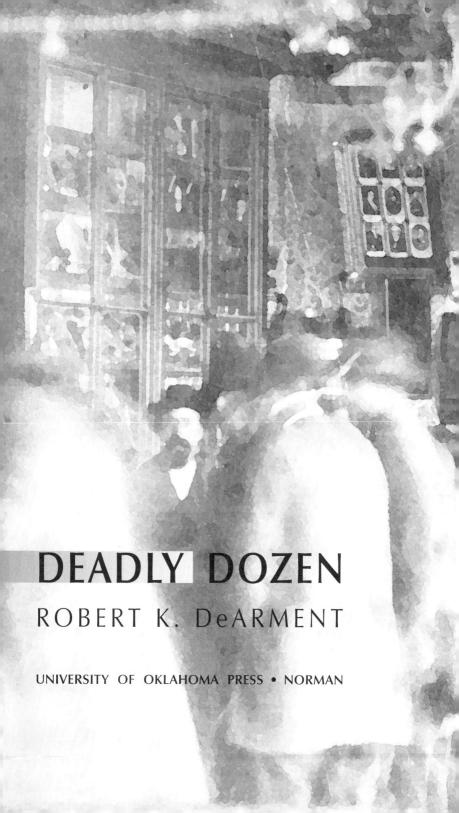

DEADLY DOZEN

ROBERT K. DeARMENT

UNIVERSITY OF OKLAHOMA PRESS • NORMAN

ALSO BY ROBERT K. DEARMENT

Bat Masterson: The Man and the Legend (Norman, 1979)

Knights of the Green Cloth: The Saga of the Frontier Gamblers (Norman, 1982)

George Scarborough: The Life and Death of a Lawman on the Closing Frontier (Norman, 1992)

(ed.) *Early Days in Texas: A Trip to Hell and Heaven* (Norman, 1992)

Alias Frank Canton (Norman, 1996)

Bravo of the Brazos: John Larn of Fort Griffin, Texas (Norman, 2002)

Library of Congress Cataloging-in-Publication Data

DeArment, Robert K., 1925–
Deadly Dozen : twelve forgotten gunfighters of the old West /
Robert K. DeArment.
p. cm.
Includes bibliographical references (p.) and index.
Contents: John Bull—Pat Desmond—Mart Duggan—Milt Yarberry—
Dan Tucker—George Goodell—Bill Standifer—Charley Perry—
Barney Riggs—Dan Bogan—Dave Kemp—Jeff Kidder.
ISBN 0–8061–3559–X (hc : alk. paper)
1. Outlaws—West (U.S.)—Biography. 2. Frontier and pioneer life—
West (U.S.) 3. West (U.S.)—Biography. 4. West (U.S.) History—
1860–1890. 5. West (U.S.)—History—1890–1945. I. Title.

F596.D385 2003
364.3'092'278—dc21
[B]
2003044797

1   2   3   4   5   6   7   8   9   10

Contents

Illustrations

DEADLY DOZEN

Introduction

The power of mass media has firmly established the gunfighter in the collective public consciousness as a stock figure in the story of the settling of the American West. From "penny dreadfuls" and dime novels of the late nineteenth century to elaborate motion picture productions of the late twentieth, the Western gunfighter has been portrayed as a steely-eyed, swift-handed artist of the quick draw, deadly of aim and purpose. Gunfighters of history, Wild Bill Hickok, Wyatt Earp, Billy the Kid, Doc Holliday, and others, have been celebrated in countless publications and cinematic and television productions, and their names are recognized throughout the world. Joining the pantheon of unforgettable gunfighters are many fictional figures, from "the Virginian" of Owen Wister's 1902 novel, to characters created by Hollywood screenwriters who are indelibly etched in the public memory.[1] For two decades the popular television series *Gunsmoke* was introduced by a scene of a towering Marshal Matt Dillon outdrawing and outshooting an adversary on the streets of Dodge City, an image that, probably more than any other, fixed the gunfighter in the public mind.

Gunfighters of the frontier West were generally not called by that name—contemporary newspapers usually referred to them as "shooters" or "shootists," "pistoleers" or "pistoleros," "gunmen," or simply "mankillers." Once he had "killed his man," the Western gunfighter was often called a "badman" by his contemporaries, not necessarily because he was a criminal, but because he was viewed as "a bad man to tangle with." Colorful words like "gunslinger" and "leatherslapper" were inventions of later fiction writers, as was the misrepresentation of the expression "fast on the draw" or "quick on the draw." This originally did not mean swiftness of hand in pulling a pistol, but was applied to the man who easily took offense and reached for his weapon at the least provocation.

Readers of these pages will find no examples of the classic "walk-down" gunfight in a dusty Western street so beloved by Western fiction writers and motion picture and television producers. Gunfights were generally sudden, impromptu affairs, and gunfighters, although desperate, were not stupid. When the fray began, they took every advantage available, including throwing down on an adversary while his gun arm was encumbered by the clutch of his lady friend, or dodging behind anything that might stop a bullet, from a telephone pole to a horse to an innocent female bystander. One of the most dramatic gunfights described in these pages hardly fits the stereotypical Hollywood version. After warily stalking each other on horseback, the combatants dismounted and exchanged long-distance rifle fire. One died.

The first known appearance in print of the term "gunfighter" was in 1874. The *Topeka Daily Commonwealth* in July of that year reprinted a report that a tough fellow showed up in Eureka, California, and loudly proclaimed that he was "a gunfighter from Pioche."[2] A Chicago paper in 1889 used the term in describing the exploits of Dave Neagle, a veteran fighting man of Arizona and California.[3] In 1907 a series of articles entitled "Famous Gun Fighters of the Western Frontier," authored by W. B. "Bat" Masterson, a celebrated pistol-wielder in his own right, appeared in *Human Life*, a popular slick magazine, and did much to bring the expression into common usage. (The two words "gun fighter" were later merged into one.) Masterson's articles also contributed greatly to the later fame of his subjects: Ben Thompson, Wyatt Earp, Luke Short, Doc Holliday, and Bill Tilghman. All have since been memorialized in biographies, and Earp and Holliday especially are firmly established in the popularly accepted hierarchy of six-shooter luminaries. Together with Hickok, Billy the Kid, and John Wesley Hardin, they have all taken their place in the ranks of what historian Richard Maxwell Brown calls "the glorified gunfighters."[4] It is around these relatively few individuals, as Professor Brown points out, that the mythology and legendry of gunfighting have developed in the popular perception.

But throughout the frontier West there were thousands of "grass-roots gunfighters," as Brown has termed them,[5] men skilled in the use of weapons who showed no hesitation in using them against their fellows. Operating on both sides of the law, they were respected and feared in their own localities, but their deeds were not widely publicized. With reputations confined to the grass roots, these men are virtually forgotten today. But their stories have survived, chronicled within four-page frontier newspapers, documented in handwritten records stored in dusty courthouse cellars, and retold and exaggerated by aging contemporaries to wide-eyed grandchildren.

Many were cowboys, particularly drovers from Texas, who regularly packed side arms and earned a wide reputation for reckless bravado. It is not an accident that fully half of the dozen gunfighters whose lives are detailed in this volume spent their formative years in the Lone Star State. As Southerners, most Texans had been influenced by the "subculture of violence" that characterized that region in the nineteenth century, in which an emphasis on manliness was defined by a "code of honor" defended with lethal weapons.[6] This concept was reinforced for Southerners on the frontier by contact with the Plains Indians, whose culture exalted males who would fight to the death to defend "primal honor."[7]

Professional gamblers, who often found it necessary to resort to weapons in the practice of their craft, were well represented in the six-shooter fraternity. Many of the best-remembered gunfighters, including Bat Masterson, Wyatt Earp, Doc Holliday, Ben Thompson, and Luke Short, were professional gamblers. The long career of John Bull, forgotten today but one of the most notorious gambler-gunmen of his time, is considered here.

Outlaws and lawmen, whose basic tool of trade was the six-shooter, and who lived and died by it, dominated the gunfighter ranks; nearly all of the twelve men considered here fell into one—and sometimes both—of these categories.

Perhaps surprisingly, fully a third of the twelve were foreign born. Most were family men, with wives and children. Less surprisingly, at least half died violently.

The men whose stories are recounted here are little known today. They are barely mentioned even in encyclopedias and studies devoted to the subject.[8] But all of them led exciting lives during stirring times in a fascinating region. They were representative of a breed that has long disappeared, but whose memory continues to intrigue lovers of action all over the world.

— I —

JOHN BULL
(1836–1929)

"A desperate man when excited"

On August 25, 1862, two determined-looking men rode into a little mining camp called Gold Creek in Montana Territory. The leader, a small man with dark eyes and coal-black beard, was armed with a double-barreled shotgun and a Colt's navy revolver. He said his name was John Bull and that he and Fox, his companion, were on the trail of thieves who had stolen six valuable horses in Elk City, Idaho. The miners told him that three strangers answering the description of the thieves had arrived in camp a few days before with six horses. The newcomers, giving their names as C. W. Spillman, William Arnett, and B. F. Jermagin, had opened a Spanish monte game in a tent saloon.

Bull, Fox, and a group of miners went after the suspects. Spillman, described in the journal of James Stuart, one of the miners, as a "rather quiet, reserved, pleasant young man," was collared without incident. Miners guarded him while Bull, Fox, Stuart, and others sought out Arnett and Jermagin. They found them running their monte game. "Arnett was dealing and Jermagin was 'lookout' for him," Stuart wrote in his journal that night. Brandishing his shotgun, Bull stepped into the tent saloon "and ordered them to 'throw up their hands.' Arnett, who kept his Colt's navy revolver lying in his lap ready for business, instantly grabbed it, but before he could raise it, Bull shot him through the breast with a heavy charge of buckshot, killing him instantly. Jermagin ran into a corner of the room, exclaiming, 'Don't shoot, don't shoot, I give up.' He and Spillman were then tied and placed under guard till morning." When the miners buried Arnett the next day they found the monte cards in his left hand and the pistol in his right gripped so tightly in his dead fingers that they could not be removed, so they lowered him into the grave still clutching the tools of his trade.

The miners convened a court to hear the case. Jermagin convinced a jury that he had no part in the horse theft, that he had joined Arnett and Spillman on the trail, and his only crime was one of bad association. He was acquitted and ordered to leave the camp. The jury convicted Spillman and sentenced him to death. An hour later the miners carried out the execution and buried the "pleasant young man" beside Arnett.[1]

The incident on Gold Creek is notable for several firsts. According to Montana pioneers Granville Stuart and N. P. Langford, the monte game in the tent saloon was the first professional gambling operation in the territory, and the hanging of Spillman was the first execution.[2] It is also the first record we have of John Bull, a gunman who over the next forty years would be known and feared throughout the West as one of the deadliest.

John Edwin Bull was born in England in 1836.[3] Nothing is known of his early life or when he came to the United States. He was twenty-five years old and already a seasoned boom camp veteran when he joined the 1861 rush to the Elk Creek Basin, one of many stampedes he would experience. It is unlikely that Bull ever panned a creek or swung a pick in a mine; it was as a professional gambler that he appeared in a succession of boom camps over the next four decades.

We hear of him next in 1866 at Virginia City, Nevada, where he teamed up in a gambling operation with a colorful character known as "Farmer" Peel. Like Bull, Langford M. Peel was an Englishman by birth. Ten years older than his countryman, and already a well-known frontier personality, Peel's nickname "Farmer" evidently resulted from the Westerners' strong sense of irony. They called this tall, dangerous fighting man "Farmer" for the same reason they called a bald-headed man "Curly." Arriving in the States at an early age, Peel joined the American army in 1843 when he was seventeen. After serving a five-year enlistment as a bugler in Company B of the First Dragoons, he took a promotion to sergeant and signed up for another five years. During his ten years in the army Peel married and had a son whom he named after his first sergeant. He served throughout the Mexican War and distinguished himself in a number of frontier Indian-fighting engagements. In 1846 at Coon Creek, Kansas, he was one of twenty dragoons attacked by a large war party. Before being driven off, the Indians killed or wounded a dozen soldiers. Peel personally killed three warriors in this fight. In the fall of 1849 he was at Fort Kearny, Nebraska, where he participated in several sharp skirmishes with Pawnee war parties and downed three more Indians. In 1853 he and three other soldiers were cut off from their buffalo-hunting camp by fifty Indians, but managed to fight off the warriors.[4]

After leaving the army Peel established a home for his family at Leavenworth, Kansas, but returned to the frontier, this time as a professional gambler. For the next fourteen years he was one of the most widely known figures in the boomtowns of the West, renowned both as a gambler and a deadly gunman. A tall, well-built man with blond hair and beard and chilly blue eyes, Peel could quickly turn violent when provoked.

In 1858 at Salt Lake City, Utah, he tangled with a faro dealer named Oliver Rucker. The two gamblers drew pistols and opened fire. Both were hit and fell to the floor where they continued to shoot until their weapons were empty. With three bullets in his body, Peel crawled over to Rucker and drove a Bowie knife into his heart. Believing he was dying himself, Peel gasped out to bystanders: "I've got a wife in Leavenworth City. Write and tell her I fit to the last minute; eye, and I fit to the last minute."[5]

Against all odds Peel recovered. He spent several years in the mining camps of California before turning up in booming Virginia City, Nevada, where he declared himself "chief" of the Comstock sporting crowd. Mark Twain, at the time a young newsman in Virginia City, later described the phenomenon of the desperado "chief": "In a new mining district . . . a person is not respected until he had 'killed his man.' That was the very expression used. If an unknown individual arrived, they did not inquire if he was capable, honest, industrious, but—had he killed his man? . . . It was tedious work struggling up to a position of influence with bloodless hands, but when a man came with the blood of half a dozen men on his soul, his worth was recognized at once and his acquaintance sought. In Nevada, for a time, the lawyer, the editor, the banker, the chief desperado, the chief gambler, and the saloon-keeper, occupied the same level of society, and it was the highest."[6] A desperado known as "El Dorado Johnny" Dennis rashly challenged Peel's claim to the title of "chief" and became one of the six victims Peel reportedly dispatched in Nevada.

John Bull's professional association with Langford Peel placed him well up in the Virginia City sporting hierarchy. Mark Twain would remember Bull, however, primarily because of a practical joke the gambler played on him. On a cold night in November 1866 Twain and his agent were walking back to Virginia City after the writer had delivered a lecture at Gold Hill, a neighboring camp. Suddenly six masked and elaborately disguised men leaped from the darkness. Brandishing pistols, they demanded Twain's money or his life. The highwaymen relieved Twain of $125 in coin and a gold watch valued at more than three hundred dollars. Twain described the leader as "small and spry," but, with the disguise, did not recognize John Bull.

Two days later Twain was boarding a stagecoach for California when Bull and his cohorts appeared and with feigned formality presented him with his stolen belongings and the masks and disguises they had worn. Alfred Doten, who witnessed the scene, noted in his journal that "Mark was considerably taken down [and] talked to the boys quite profanely till the stage drove off. Rather heavy on Mark. They were only trying, however, to play even on him for some of his practical jokes in former times."[7]

Twain later admitted that the incident cured him of his penchant for pranks. "Since then," he said, "I play no practical jokes on people and generally lose my temper when one is played on me."[8]

A few months after this affair, Bull and Peel moved their gambling operation to new fields. They were at Belmont, Nevada, and then Salt Lake City, where they had a disagreement and briefly severed their partnership. By the summer of 1867 they had apparently resolved their differences and were teamed again in a gambling enterprise at Helena, Montana. On the night of July 22, 1867, the partners were seated together in a game at Greer Brothers' Exchange Saloon when the smoldering discord was somehow rekindled. The two men jumped to their feet, shouting insults. Peel slapped Bull in the face with his left hand and reached for his gun with his right. Bull threw up his arms,

An illustration from Mark Twain's *Roughing It* depicts the practical joke holdup of Twain by John Bull and confederates. From the author's collection.

protesting that he was unarmed. Peel told him to go and heel himself and come back fighting.

Bull retreated to his rooms where he sat down and composed letters to his family and friends. He spelled out directions for the disposition of his property in the event of his death. Then he carefully oiled and loaded his six-shooter.

For some time after the eruption in the Exchange Saloon Peel kept a wary eye on the door and his six-gun within easy reach. When Bull failed to appear he relaxed, convinced that the little gambler lacked the sand to face him in a gunfight. Finally, he checked out of the game and sauntered down the street to the gambling saloon of Ed Chase, three doors away. There he met faro dealer Belle Neil, his current mistress. Belle took Peel's right arm and the couple stepped out of Chase's into Helena's Main Street.

Suddenly John Bull was there. Without warning he turned loose his six-gun. Peel staggered, struck by a bullet. He tried to reach for the pistol in his pocket, but Belle, screaming, clutched his arm in a tight grip. Bull fired again and Peel collapsed. According to one witness, Bull then walked up to Peel and deliberately fired a bullet into his head, making certain he was dead.[9]

News of the shooting spread quickly throughout Helena. When he first heard the report, John Xavier "X" Beidler, the celebrated Montana vigilante and lawman, did not believe it. Peel, he said, "was such a rattler that I didn't think he would be killed."[10] It was Beidler who took Bull into custody and jailed him. Later that night there were some tense moments when an angry crowd of Peel supporters closed in on the jail, but Beidler's deputies stood firm and averted the lynch threat. Indicted for murder, Bull stood trial. The jury, split nine to three for conviction, could not agree. Released, Bull lost no time getting out of Helena.[11]

He went to Cheyenne, Wyoming, at the time becoming notorious as the wildest of the wild end-of-track towns on the westward-building Union Pacific Railroad. Here was gathered the hell-on-wheels sporting crowd: the gamblers, con men, whiskey peddlers, madams, whores, pimps, pickpockets, footpads, and strong-arm robbers who had followed track construction all the way from Omaha. John Bull arrived on this scene like a conquering hero. All members of the frontier sporting gentry were familiar with the name and reputation of Langford Peel, and the man who had dispatched him was an instant celebrity. Men pumped his hand, women threw their arms around him, he could not pay for a drink, and suckers fought to lose their money in his rigged three-card monte games. It was just like the obsequiousness accorded Langford Peel in Virginia City so well described by Mark Twain: "The desperado stalked the streets with a swagger . . . and a nod of recognition from him was sufficient to make a humble admirer happy for the rest of the day. . . . When he moved along the sidewalk in his excessively long-tailed frock-coat, shiny stump-toed boots, and with dainty little slouch hat tipped over left eye, the small-fry roughs made room for his majesty; when he entered the restaurants, the waiters deserted bankers and merchants to overwhelm him with obsequious service; when he shouldered his way to a bar, the shouldered parties wheeled indignantly, recognized him, and—apologized."[12]

An aura of glamour had begun to form around the Western gunman. Certain of the Plains Indians believed that when a brave slew a man in battle he acquired from his vanquished enemy the personal credits of that warrior, and the victor's status was enhanced in direct proportion to the bloody distinction of his fallen foe. This concept was incorporated into the gunfighter mystique. When John Bull killed Langford Peel, reputed slayer of many men, he stepped into the higher echelons of frontier celebrity. As far as is known, after Peel, Bull never killed another man, but that brief moment of violence in Helena firmly established his reputation as a deadly gunman; it was a reputation that would remain with him throughout his long career.

When railroad construction resumed in the spring of 1868, Bull moved west with the hell-on-wheels gang and stayed with it to the historic linkup of the Union Pacific and Central Pacific at Promontory Point, Utah. About this time he married. His bride was apparently an estimable lady, ill suited to the half-world of the itinerant gambler. Bull took her to Chicago and rented rooms for her in the boarding house of Addison Snell, at 771 West Van Buren Street. She eventually bore him two children. Henry Hoyt, a young doctor who lived for a time in the same boarding house, described Mrs. Bull as a "beautiful young woman," who, in explanation of her husband's long absences, said that he was "a traveling man."[13] A few years later this woman died and Bull placed his children in foster homes.[14]

Bull was indeed "a traveling man." For years he crisscrossed the Northwest, working his crooked gambling games on trains, stagecoaches, and riverboats. From time to time he would settle in a lively town with a large transient population and tolerant law enforcement. During the early 1870s he operated in Omaha, working with a gang of sharpers led by William "Canada Bill" Jones, notorious in Western towns and rivers for a generation. Other sure-thing men in the Omaha crowd were George Devol, who would later write a book recounting his gambling experiences;[15] Charles "Doc" Baggs, a sartorially resplendent bunco steerer; Ben Marks, talented young sharper from Council Bluffs; W. E. Train, who claimed to be a nephew of George Francis Train, writer, eccentric, and onetime candidate for president; Sherman

Thurston, a former wrestler who acted as strong-arm man for the gang; Jim Bush, black sheep brother of wealthy Denver hotelman William H. Bush; and assorted lesser lights Bill Lawrence, George Mehaffy, Jim Shotwell, Jack Sullivan, John J. Doyle, and a scam artist remembered only as "Grasshopper Sam."[16]

This gang worked marks on trains running out of Omaha and within the city itself. Bull's role was usually that of steerer to a skin game. His polite manner, educated speech, austere good looks, well-trimmed black beard, and immaculate dress gave him the appearance of a successful professional man, one who could be trusted. Approaching a mark, he would flash a roll of greenbacks he had just won, he said, at the three-card monte game of Canada Bill or one of his understudies. Appealing to the mark's greed, Bull would then steer the sheep to his shearing. If tempers flared when victims realized they had been robbed, calm usually was restored when one of the gang dropped the word that the dark-bearded "professional man" was actually John Bull, the noted gunman and mankiller.

Shortly before midnight on July 12, 1873, Samuel Atwood, a railroad employee, was stabbed outside Harry Clayton's Crystal Saloon in Omaha. Witnesses charged John Bull and George Mehaffy with attacking Atwood because he was warning railroad passengers to avoid the gang's skin games. Six Omaha policemen led by City Marshal Gilbert Rustin conducted a search for the gamblers. At 4:30 in the morning they located Bull in Jack Sullivan's saloon. Posting his men at the doors, Marshal Rustin went in to make the arrest. Pulling what a newspaper report called "a large navy revolver a foot long," Bull covered the officer and refused to go with him. Knowing Bull "to be a desperate man when excited," Rustin "thought it better to work the matter gently," and withdrew.

Bull appeared to be very excited. Waving his pistol, he went into Sullivan's gambling room and declared he was "in a hell of a fix," but would not be taken until his gun was empty. The patrons scrambled for the exits and Bull soon had the place to himself. His excitement apparently abated quickly, for he sat down in a chair and promptly went to sleep. When awakened by a friend later, he quietly submitted to arrest.[17]

Sam Atwood's fellow railroad workers were enraged by the attack on him and, as he lay near death, organized a protest. Reported the *Omaha Bee* of July 16: "Last evening the employees of the Union

Pacific shops held a meeting for the purpose of forming a vigilance committee. There were several hundred men present. From a reliable party who was at the meeting we learn that in case young Atwood dies, they intend to have summary vengeance upon the men who are now confined in jail, and who are supposed to have stabbed him. Atwood's death was expected last night, and had he died, the vigilance committee . . . would have proceeded to the jail, and attempted to take Bull and Mehaffy out, to have punished them, as they thought best."

Atwood recovered, however, and the vigilantes never marched. At a preliminary examination held on July 28 Atwood said that several men had accosted him on the night of the stabbing. When he identified Mehaffy as one of the ruffians, but not Bull, the former was bound over for trial and the latter discharged. Mehaffy, released on bond, continued to work with Bull.[18]

Four months later Bull and the gang figured prominently in a wild affair billed as a pugilistic contest for the heavyweight championship of America. English-born Tom Allen was to defend the title in a bare-knuckle battle against Ben Hogan, a gambler from the oil fields of Pennsylvania. On November 18, while authorities threatened the use of militia to prevent the illegal prizefight, the promoters, gamblers, fighters, and their entourages convened across the Missouri River in Council Bluffs, Iowa. Boarding a special eight-car train, they went about ten miles to Pacific Junction where the battle was to be held. The fighters and their handlers, who had arrived secretly by carriage, were waiting for them there.[19]

An uproar developed immediately over referee selection. Members of the Canada Bill gang pushed for John Bull, but others shouted them down, as it was well known that Bull had bet heavily on the challenger, Hogan. The crowd also rejected two other proposed Omaha sports, George Mehaffy and Dan Allen, and finally agreed on Tom Riley of Kansas City as the third man in the ring. Bull acted as timekeeper. The fight was for an official prize of $2,000 and a $10,000 side bet, but backers of the fighters bet considerably more money at ringside.

In the second round, Hogan, who was taking a pretty good beating, suddenly doubled up, clutching his groin. Instantly Bull leaped into the ring and claimed victory for Hogan on a foul. The referee refused to allow the foul claim, and, when Hogan was able to come to scratch after the thirty-second rest period allowed under London Prize Ring rules, the fight continued. Hogan was badly hurt, however, and, after receiving another body blow his backers claimed to be low, sank to the ground and was finished. As Allen's adherents whooped and declared victory, Bull and other Hogan backers continued to shout "Foul!" The referee, fearing both camps, announced that the bout was "no contest" and ordered all bets off. The decision pleased no one, and pandemonium ensued as fights broke out among the spectators. Several were injured, and one man was reported killed.[20]

The following year officers hauled Bull and Mehaffy into court again. The charge was robbing a Missourian named Wilkinson of $440 in an Omaha gin mill. Union Pacific detective Jim Neligh, who worked up the case, named Doc Baggs and Ben Marks as codefendants. At separate trials, Bull, Baggs, and Marks got off, but a jury convicted Mehaffy. He jumped bail, skipped town, and in 1875 the case was dismissed.[21]

Depredations by the crooked gamblers operating out of Omaha steadily worsened. By the mid-1870s rail officials were receiving hundreds of complaints from swindled passengers. George Devol added the last straw. He and a partner were working suckers on the Cheyenne to Omaha run. "One evening I picked up a man on the sleeper and beat him out of $1200," Devol recalled sadly. "That game settled our hash, for he proved to be one of the directors of the road."[22]

The officials cracked down, and John Bull moved on to greener and safer fields. When Deadwood boomed in 1876, Bull was there. Returning from a trip east in May 1877, he chanced to be on the Bismarck to Deadwood stage with Dr. Henry Hoyt, the young doctor who roomed in the same boarding house in Chicago as Bull's wife. Hoyt had an opportunity to see how Mrs. Bull's "traveling man" husband worked his three-card monte gyp on gullible passengers. He also witnessed an exhibition of Bull's proficiency with a six-shooter. Recalled Hoyt: "We ran into a prairie-dog town, the driver pulled up for a few minutes, and everybody jumped out. Prairie dogs were in every direction, barking an invitation to us to try our marksmanship. Out came revolvers and several volleys were fired without result, as Mr. Prairie Dog is wary and very hard to hit. Bull watched the scene for a time. Suddenly his hand flew to his hip; a big six-shooter of the dragoon type with a short barrel was drawn. The gun barked, and a dead dog was the result. He apparently took no aim at all."[23]

By early 1879 Bull had settled in Denver. Over the next few years his name appeared frequently on the city's police blotters. Once he was arrested and fined $12 for public drunkenness.[24] On another occasion he made the mistake of tangling with one C. C. Joy, described by a paper as a "very large, powerful man." The undersized gambler, with one hand on the butt of a revolver in his pocket, took a swing at Joy, who dodged the blow, knocked Bull down with one punch, and was applying the shoe leather rather energetically to Bull's ribs when bystanders pulled him off. Both men were arrested and fined for disturbance of the peace.[25]

In Murphy's Exchange, known in the Denver Tenderloin as "The Slaughterhouse" because of the many killings committed there, Bull got into a dustup with the police. When a policeman attempted to arrest him, Bull struck the officer with his loaded walking stick and reinforcements had to be called to subdue him.[26]

During his long career, John Bull teamed up with some of the most colorful characters of the Western gambling circuit: Langford Peel, the dangerous gunfighting "chief" of the Comstock; George Devol, who claimed he made over two million dollars in a forty-year gambling career and ended up nearly destitute; Canada Bill Jones, premier three-card monte sharp who was such a sucker for poker that teams of experts followed him around the country relieving him of his ill-gotten gains; Frank Tarbeau, who retired from cardsharping to tour the world and number among his friends royalty and leading lights of the international set; and Doc Baggs, who once declared that his whole mission in life was "to trim suckers."

In Denver Bull formed a partnership with yet another extraordinary gambling figure, John E. Wilcoxon, who early in his career took the name "Jim Moon." A Civil War veteran, Moon was a powerfully built man of great physical strength whose violent temper often got him in trouble. Discharged from the Union army after almost killing another soldier in a brawl, he took up the life of a professional gambler. He was not known as a gunman, but wherever he went he was feared for his hair-trigger temper and great strength. At Denver in 1880 he partnered John Bull in the operation of a combination restaurant, saloon, and gambling house called the Oyster Ocean.

On the night of October 14, 1880, Moon, Bull, Moon's wife Emma, and another woman with whom Bull was living became involved in a farcical affair at their establishment. Two Denver policemen somehow provoked Moon. His notoriously low boiling point was quickly reached and fists flew. Bull entered the fray, and the two women began throwing chinaware. By the time the officers beat an undignified retreat and called for reserves, the place had been reduced to a mess of broken furniture and shattered crockery. A flying squad arrived in a paddy wagon to find Moon and Bull standing in the doorway with leveled revolvers. After a parley, the partners turned themselves in to accept the ritual fines.[27]

Less than a month later the violence-prone Moon killed a man named Sam Hall, crushing his skull with the barrel of a six-gun, but came clear on a plea of self-defense.

Brutal, cruel, and very dangerous, Moon's one redeeming quality was unflinching raw courage, which he demonstrated on October 31, 1880, when drunken mobs stormed through the Chinese section of Denver, beating and terrorizing the residents in a mindless display of racism. Moon, the only white man to defy the mob, stood in the doorway of a Chinese laundry with two six-shooters in his hands and defended those inside. He was reported to have also saved sixteen Chinese by hiding them in the cellar of the Arcade gambling hall.[28]

It was in this same gambling hall that Moon met his death seven months later. When he attacked gambler Clay Wilson for paying undue attention to Moon's wife, Wilson drew a pistol and fired twice. With two bullets in his chest, Moon locked his huge arms around the other man and almost managed to crush the life out of him. Wilson finally worked the muzzle of his pistol against his adversary's body and with two more shots closed out the career of big Jim Moon.[29]

A month prior to the sudden demise of his partner, John Bull opened a new enterprise on Larimer Street in the heart of Denver's sporting district. Described as a combination gambling hall and hotel, he called it the Turf Exchange. In January 1882 hotheaded Jim Bush, former member of the Canada Bill Jones gang in Omaha, shot Bull in the foot in an upstairs room of this place. Bull did not press charges, passing off the shooting as an accident, but one newspaper predicted that Bush, who was already under indictment for murder in Leadville, would "yet die with his boots on." However, Bull evidently let the matter drop.[30]

Soon after the Bush affair, Bull left Denver and resumed his travels. He worked his crooked games on the line of the Northern Pacific

Railroad from Minneapolis to Seattle for several years and was a familiar figure in gambling houses of towns all along the route. It was during this period that Bull, together with a swindler named Frank Pine, reportedly went to England and "cut a swath and dined with the Prince of Wales." Peddling stock in worthless mines, the partners are said to have cleared $25,000.[31]

One night in 1898 Bull emerged from the People's Theater in Spokane, accompanied by the manager, Fiskey Barnett.[32] Both men had been drinking and were laughing and joshing one another. Without warning Barnett suddenly jabbed the lighted end of his cigar into Bull's face. The fiery butt struck Bull squarely in the eye, and he roared with pain. Clapping one hand to his eye, he jerked his gun with the other. Barnett dodged behind a woman who chanced to be in front of the theater and pulled his own pistol. Bull, half-blinded, began shooting, and Barnett returned the fire. When both guns were empty, the woman lay on the sidewalk, one of Bull's bullets through her lung. Barnett clutched a bloody hand from which a finger had been neatly clipped by a slug; he was otherwise unhurt. Bull lay prostrate. Bullets had shattered his left arm and struck him in the groin, chin, and neck.

The woman teetered at death's door for several weeks but eventually recovered. Doctors amputated Bull's mangled arm and removed the bullets from his face and groin. But the slug in his neck rested against his windpipe, and the medical men decided not to touch it. For his part in the bloody affair Barnett lost a finger and a fine of ten dollars for firing a pistol within city limits. The magistrate waived Bull's fine, as he was expected to die.[33]

But he did not die. The tough old gambler and gunman lived on for more than thirty years. In 1921 the bullet he had carried in his neck for twenty-three of those years began to bother him. When doctors told him a sharp spur on the slug was puncturing his windpipe, he decided, at age eighty-five, to have it removed. Aided only by a local anesthetic, he underwent surgery at Excelsior Springs, Missouri, where a doctor took out the bullet. Bull lived eight more years, finally cashing in his chips at Vancouver, British Columbia, on September 9, 1929. He was ninety-three.[34]

— 2 —

PAT DESMOND
(1842–1890)

"Not exactly a desperado"

The Irish cop became a stereotype in Eastern seaboard cities of America in the late nineteenth and early twentieth centuries. He is remembered yet as a burly, florid-faced figure in blue with brass buttons and a star on his chest, a towering helmet atop his head, and a scarred nightstick in his meaty fist. Irish immigrants, pouring into the United States after the terrible famine years of 1845–46, often found employment as policemen in the tough underworld districts of the Eastern cities and were the progenitors of the image. Moving westward as pioneers in the latter half of the 1800s, many Irish-born carried the convention with them and became frontier lawmen and gunfighters of note.

Tom Cunningham, born in 1838 at Longford, Ireland, found his way to San Joaquin County, California, where he was sheriff for many years and gained renown as the "Thief Taker of San Joaquin."[1] Twin brothers John and Michael Meagher, born in County Cavan in 1843, enforced the law in several Kansas cow towns during the wild trail-drive days and were highly respected lawmen. Another pair of Irish-born twins, Pat and Mike Sughrue of County Kerry, also were outstanding peace officers in the early Kansas cattle towns.[2] But two men, Patrick J. Desmond and Martin J. Duggan, contemporaneous city marshals in raw Colorado towns little more than a hundred miles apart, best epitomized the popular image of the brawling, hard-drinking, hard-fighting, fear-no-man "son of the auld sod" law officer in the West. Duggan's tempestuous history will be chronicled in a later chapter; here we will deal with the life of Pat Desmond.

Born in County Cork in January 1842, Desmond was descended from the ancient kings of South Munster, Ireland. His father was imprisoned with his relative, the Earl of Desmond, and his property confiscated by the English. Emigrating to the United States in 1864, twenty-two-year-old Patrick spent two years in the copper and iron ore mining camps of Michigan's Upper Peninsula and the newly opened petroleum fields of northern Pennsylvania.[3]

Given his family's sad history in Ireland at the hands of the British, it is not surprising that in America he joined the Fenians, a revolutionary group committed to overthrowing English rule in Ireland and establishing an Irish republic. In May 1866 he was a member of a force led by Fenian general John O'Neill that invaded Canada from Buffalo, New York. Although the Fenians were victorious in the Battle of Ridgeway on June 1, their effort was doomed when the United States intervened. Pursued by American gunboats under the direction of General George G. Meade, O'Neill's men were taken into custody, but eventually released.[4]

Desmond went to Chicago, found employment with a bridge contractor for the Chicago & Northwestern Railroad, and was introduced to the frontier West where he would spend the rest of his days. His frontier apprenticeship was extensive and varied. As boss of government wagon trains hauling supplies between Council Bluffs, Iowa, and military posts in Nebraska and Wyoming, he engaged in several sharp battles with Indians. He hunted game to supply army commissaries, was a freight watchman for Wells, Fargo & Company, and worked as a detective for the Union Pacific during the construction of the transcontinental railroad. After the historic linkup with the Central Pacific at Promontory Point, Utah, on May 10, 1869, he went to Fort Hays, Kansas, and took employment as a construction foreman for the Kansas Pacific Railroad.[5]

With the completion of the great transcontinental road to the north, the rowdy hell-on-wheels crowd descended on Kit Carson, Colorado, end of track for the Kansas Pacific. The town that had been nothing but a sleepy trading post in the late fall of 1869 suddenly turned into a wild, raucous, border Babylon. Only ten days after the arrival of the first train on April 4, 1870, the population exploded to 1,500.[6] To maintain some semblance of order, the town leaders sent for Pat Desmond, who had gained considerable experience handling these same saloon roughnecks while working as a Union Pacific detective, and appointed him town constable and deputy sheriff of newly formed Greenwood County. To assist him in the dangerous work, Desmond selected another Irishman, Thomas J. Smith, a former professional boxer and New York City policeman who was known as "Bear River Tom" after playing a prominent role in putting down a bloody riot at Bear River City, Wyoming, in 1868.[7]

Few records remain of events in Kit Carson during its boom days, but evidently Desmond and Smith did their job. With the arrival of the railroad, the father of Miguel A. Otero, later governor of New Mexico, opened a commission house in the town, and when young Miguel reached there in the summer of 1871 he found the town "different . . . , somewhat more civilized . . . , comparatively clean and decent."[8]

By that time Desmond and Smith had moved on to their respective destinies. Tom Smith did not have long to live. In June he went to Abilene, Kansas, where, in a five-month period as city marshal, he achieved legendary status as the lawman who tamed that wild cow town. Following his murder there on November 2, 1870, he was succeeded by the even more celebrated James B. "Wild Bill" Hickok.

After leaving Kit Carson, Pat Desmond briefly ran a restaurant at Golden and a saloon at Georgetown. He then took work as a grading crew foreman again. The Denver & Rio Grande Railroad was building south from Denver, and Desmond worked for the line until it reached Pueblo in 1872. Married now, and with a growing family,[9] he decided it was time to settle down. He built a fine home on a mesa in the new railroad town called South Pueblo that had sprung up almost overnight across the Arkansas River from the older community. During the ensuing years he was involved in a number of enterprises, operating a hotel, a large livery stable, and several saloons, and invested in business real estate.[10]

The excitement of the chase and an inherent pugnacity constantly drew him back to law enforcement, however, and for many of those years he held at least one lawman's post. He served as a deputy under Pueblo County sheriffs Abe Ellis and Henly R. Price and as constable and city marshal of South Pueblo. He was the southern Colorado operative of the Rocky Mountain Detective Agency, established in Denver by renowned lawman David J. Cook, and for a time ran his own detective agency in South Pueblo.

Over the years Desmond developed a statewide reputation as a tough and dangerous fighting man, feared and respected by criminals and honest folk alike. One Denver paper described him as "a short man and thick-set . . . very muscular . . . afraid of nobody [who] did not know what danger was."[11] Another said he was "a tough customer . . . wholly unconscious of fear, [who] mixed brutality with his official duties, and . . . became a terror not only to the rough element . . . but also to the law abiding citizens."[12]

Desmond made a notable arrest on December 6, 1877, collaring a badly wanted man at West Las Animas. Two months before, Robert Schamle had murdered an inoffensive and respectable German butcher, father of three small children, for the eighty dollars he carried in his pocket. Coloradoans were outraged by the brutal crime, and Dave Cook alerted members of his detective agency to be on the watch for the murderer. Tipped off that a man matching the description of the fugitive had been seen in the boxcar of an eastbound freight train out of Pueblo, Desmond hurried to West Las Animas and made the arrest. Positively identified at Pueblo, Schamle was returned to Georgetown, where, a few days later, a mob dragged him from a cell and hanged him in a pigpen.[13]

Not all of Desmond's law enforcement work was exciting. As city marshal, he was responsible for ridding the streets of the town of public nuisances like dead animals and barking dogs. In March 1879 he announced in the pages of the local paper, the *Colorado Chieftain*, the start of a vigorous cleanup campaign: "Notice is hereby given to property owners in South Pueblo that all rubbish and disease breeding matter must be removed from their premises at once, or the work will be done by me at their expense. The town board, sitting as a board of health, have ordered all pig sty and other nuisances to be abated. This order will be rigidly enforced. All unlicensed dogs will be killed hereafter, without respect to owners. Let no one plead ignorance after this ample notice. (Signed) P. J. Desmond, Town Marshal, March 5, 1879."[14]

He went to work with a crew of jail inmates as laborers, and a few days later received the plaudits of the paper's editor: "Under the excellent supervision of our efficient town marshal, P. J. Desmond, Union

Avenue is undergoing a thorough renovation which adds very materially towards its service and appearance."[15]

Wearing his deputy sheriff's badge, Desmond that month assisted Sheriff Henly Price in the hanging of Victor Nunez, convicted murderer of Luis Rascone. It was the first judicial execution in Pueblo County.[16]

During this period Desmond was very popular in South Pueblo, as attested by the elections held in April in which he defeated his opponent for the city marshal job by a vote margin of three to one.[17]

Two months earlier Desmond had assisted Sheriff W. B. "Bat" Masterson of Ford County, Kansas, in the apprehension of an escapee from the jail at Dodge City,[18] but in June 1879 he and the legendary lawman found themselves on opposite sides in a bitter railroad battle that would become known as the Royal Gorge War. In a struggle for the right-of-way through the Royal Gorge to the rich silver mines at Leadville, the Denver & Rio Grande and the Santa Fe Railroads were locked in a legal battle that escalated into clashes between fighting men employed by both sides. While lawyers for the competing companies argued in the courts, armed Santa Fe mercenaries invaded and seized control of Rio Grande stations from Denver to Canon City. Bat Masterson, at the head of a force of about 150, including noted gunfighters Ben Thompson and John H. "Doc" Holliday, captured the roundhouse at Pueblo, a strategic point on the line.

Rio Grande officials obtained a writ from Judge T. M. Bowen of the Fourth Judicial District at Alamosa ordering the Santa Fe men to vacate the Rio Grande property and authorizing county lawmen to enforce the order. Armed with the writ, Sheriff Price at Pueblo directed Deputy Pat Desmond, his chief fighting man, to take action. On June 11 Desmond and a force of fifty, armed with rifles and fixed bayonets supplied by the Rio Grande, lay siege to the roundhouse. Desmond personally led an assault on the telegraph office and broke down the door with the butt of his rifle. In this and other skirmishes several partisans on both sides were wounded and one was killed, but the confrontation ended after Rio Grande officials met with Masterson and persuaded him to turn over the roundhouse without further bloodshed.[19]

Apparently as part of the agreement, Sheriff Price and Deputy Desmond were formally charged and arrested by a Pueblo constable following the incident, but they were quickly released on bond. No further action was taken against them, as the railroad officials decided to resolve their dispute in the courts.[20]

Following the excitement of the Royal Gorge War Desmond returned to his normal law enforcement work, including keeping the streets of South Pueblo free of noisy and noisome nuisances, as *Colorado Chieftain* editor R. M. Stevenson was quick to remind him. As city marshal he also rode herd on the boisterous saloon crowd. That he was able to do this for years without resorting to gun work is a testament to the power of his personality and the fear and respect in which he was held by the ruffian element.

As deputy sheriff he often traveled widely in search of criminal suspects, as in March 1881 when his work elicited high praise in the press. Following the loss of a "blooded horse and a fine mule stallion" to thieves, Pueblo businessman James McMillan published reward notices for the return of the animals and the arrest of the culprits. Other officers were reluctant to pursue the case without payment in advance, but Desmond, just back from another trip, set out on a trail now nine days old. With what McMillan admiringly called "the keenness of a tiger," he tracked down and captured the two thieves "at the mouth of a double barrel shot gun," and returned with his prisoners, the recovered stock, two saddles, and even McMillan's stolen dog. McMillan was effusive in his praise for Desmond in a letter to the *Chieftain:* No other manhunter, he said, was "so keen of scent, so intrepid in danger and so firm in his convictions as Capt. Desmond. . . . Let Desmond stand at the head of detectives and fearless officers. [He] has not only earned the reward but has earned the title of chief in his calling."[21]

Within a year, editor Stevenson of the *Chieftain* would be calling Desmond "the best thief catcher in the Pueblos."[22] Another local paper, the *South Pueblo News*, pointed out that the officer had been particularly tough on tinhorn gamblers and con artists: "Marshal Desmond is making it warm for the bunko men and has so far caused their displeasure, so he says, as to have them threaten to 'put him out of the way,' but he says they must leave this city . . . and he will never let up until the last one has disappeared from our midst. He has the hearty support of all the best citizens of the community."[23]

Desmond's celebrity had been enhanced in June 1881 when he collared one of the most wanted men in the West. Following the holdup of a stagecoach nine miles from Alamosa on June 28, Deputy U.S. Marshal M. W. Blain wired Desmond to watch for a suspect believed to be on a Pueblo-bound train. Desmond, waiting at the Union Depot in Pueblo, took a man answering the stage robber's description into custody, searched him, and found $478 in cash, a small bag of ore, and a silver watch believed to be part of the holdup loot. Desmond locked up the suspect and contacted an Arkansas officer who was in the city looking for a bandit who had pulled off the simultaneous robbery of two coaches near Fayetteville several weeks earlier. The officer identified Desmond's prisoner as Henry W. Burton, the man wanted for the double Arkansas robbery.

Since the stagecoach robberies involved interference with U.S. mail, the federal authorities were concerned in the case. Desmond wired L. Cass Carpenter, U.S. postal inspector at Denver for instructions and was directed to take the man known as Burton to Denver. With his handcuffed prisoner Desmond boarded the Denver train on July 1. En route, Burton tried to bribe Desmond to let him go. When that ploy failed, he made a desperate attempt to escape. Desmond was away from his seat getting a drink of water when the train slowed on a grade near Castle Rock. Seizing the opportunity, the prisoner ran to the end of the car, eluded the officer's lunging attempt to grab him, and leaped from the train. Desmond pulled the emergency cord and jumped after him as the train ground to a stop.

The man was several hundred yards away and scurrying off as fast as he could on legs badly battered from the fall. Desmond raced in pursuit, closed the gap, got within pistol range, and fired off several shots. One creased the head of his quarry, bringing him down. As Desmond marched him back to the train, the suspect, painfully bruised and bleeding, remarked that he wished the officer had killed him.

After delivering his prisoner to the postal authorities in Denver, Desmond learned that "Henry Burton" was in fact Hamilton "Ham" White, the most daring and successful stage robber in the country, and that rewards totaling $1,200 were outstanding for his apprehension.[24]

Almost a year later he had received only fifty dollars of the reward money, as he complained bitterly in a "card" he published in the *Chieftain*.[25] When his "card" produced no response from the federal authorities, he published a longer letter expressing indignation over the unfair treatment he had received. Audacity, belligerence, and defiance of authority were all becoming increasingly dominant in his behavior as evidenced by the letter, which clearly and unequivocally accused Postal Inspector Robert Cameron of keeping not only the reward money, but also the cash removed from the robber's person at the time of his capture. Desmond tried to ascribe a higher purpose to his concern rather than a personal craving for money. "Should I fail entirely in recovering this money," he said, "it will act as a bad precedent, and materially retard faithful work on the part of officers who risk their lives in the detection and capture of desperate criminals for the government."[26]

The loss of the reward money was only one of a series of financial setbacks and personal tragedies that afflicted Pat Desmond in the year 1882. As misfortunes mounted and he suffered blows that would have tested the fiber of a saint—and certainly Desmond was no saint—he increasingly sought solace in the bottle. Alcohol, however, only heightened his growing irascibility and belligerence.

His problems began on February 11 when he and a fellow lawman engaged in a shooting exchange that certainly ranks as one of the strangest gunfights in Western annals. Responding to a complaint by a party of black men and women that they had been abused by an officer near the Union Depot, Desmond returned with the group to the station. There the officer on duty, Patrolman John T. ("Jack") O'Connor, was pointed out as the offender. Desmond saw that his subordinate had been drinking and gave him an angry dressing-down. O'Connor, who also had a hair-trigger Irish temper, responded in kind. "Since I have been on the force," said Patrolman Rube Gutshall, who was in the station at the time and witnessed the scene, "I have never heard such language used between two officers of the police department."[27]

Desmond fired O'Connor on the spot. As he stepped forward to rip the badge from the officer's coat, O'Connor struck out with his left hand. Desmond reeled backward about six feet and fell to the ground. Before he could rise, O'Connor assumed a most peculiar fighting stance, according to eyewitness testimony: "He squatted, advanced his left leg, [and] dropped his right hand to his pocket."

Seeing O'Connor reaching for a gun, Desmond, still on the ground, reacted swiftly. "When he made a break for his [gun], I went for mine and happened to get it out first," he said. Firing twice, he struck

O'Connor in that extended left leg with both rounds. O'Connor triggered off three shots, hitting nothing, before Gutshall, Deputy Sheriff Dave Abrams, and Pinkerton detective William Richardson, who were also on hand, intervened and put an end to the shoot-out.

At a hearing Desmond stated quite frankly that he had every intention of killing O'Connor. "When I shot at him I meant to kill him," he said. "I wouldn't have fired if I did not think my life was in danger. . . . O'Connor had his revolver half out of his pocket before I fired and when I shot, I meant to have the balls from the gun take effect in his breast."[28]

O'Connor recovered and no charges were filed, but the incident set off a bitter battle within the police department and the city administration. In addition to firing O'Connor, Desmond suspended Patrolman Rube Gutshall, saying he failed to back him up in the affair. Gutshall objected strenuously, and Mayor Stephen Walley and city council members took sides in a controversy closely followed for days in the *Chieftain* under the continuing head: "The Police Muddle." At a special city council meeting held to resolve the issue, debate became so heated that Mayor Walley had to be ejected, but finally a majority of the council reached a decision. The *Chieftain* announced it in a simple two-word headline: "Desmond Deposed."[29]

In the next few days Gutshall and O'Connor were both reinstated on the police force, and a man named Henry Jameson was appointed as the new city marshal. Desmond, of course, was outraged and fumed to a reporter: "I have been a resident of this city for some time and have been elected city marshal three times and appointed five times. I was also elected four times constable of the thirteenth precinct and have always attended to my duties in a faithful, independent, honest and honorable manner." He added that he intended to bring suit against the city for damages in the amount of $25,000.[30]

Supporters and friends spoke up in his defense. F. Otto and Michael Canning, identifying themselves as "Independents of South Pueblo," wrote a joint letter to the *Chieftain*, recommending him for higher office: "Mr. Desmond has been wronged. We call upon all good independents to unite and nominate Mr. Desmond for mayor of South Pueblo. We need a change. We believe a good independent democratic ticket with Mr. Desmond at the head would give satisfaction to all liberal democrats as well as republicans. So unite independent democrats, republicans and all others in favor of a Desmond ticket and let us nominate and elect him."[31]

Desmond never ran for mayor, nor did his bruised ego ever quite heal after his abrupt dismissal as city marshal. His drinking increased markedly, and he engaged in a number of saloon brawls. On April 18, a month after his firing, he and some of his supporters, being "inclined to pugnacity," as the *Chieftain* put it rather gently, set out to "make things disagreeable for the powers that be. The principal among the 'kickers' [was] Ex-Marshal Desmond [who] collided with City Attorney Wescott and several hard names were exchanged, but quiet was restored before any harm could be done. Last evening Desmond, accompanied by several others, visited the *Republican* sanctum for the purpose of chastising the managing editor, Mr. George Kent. However, with the exception of pouring out abuse on the innocent head of the complacent foreman, nothing was done. Alderman Slitt was also captured by the party and abused. All of the party was under the influence of liquor when the breaks were made."[32]

George Kent of the *Pueblo Republican*, a political opponent of Democrat Desmond, had given prominence to stories of the former marshal's erratic and violent behavior. (Desmond's name appeared regularly as a defendant on the district court dockets. In the month of April, there were no less than three cases in which he was charged with assault with intent to inflict bodily harm.)[33] The former marshal published a "card" in R. M. Stevenson's more sympathetic *Chieftain* denying he and others had mounted a threatening or intimidating attack on the *Republican* offices. He had gone there, he said, to cancel his subscription, to inform them "in plain language [he] didn't want the sheet." The two friends accompanying him, he said, weighed less than 120 pound each. "If a republican newspaper outfit can be 'bulldozed' by such . . . diminutive citizens, what is the republican press of the country coming to?" he asked.[34]

More than anger at his dismissal set the former marshal off on his drunken binges. At home he had been struck with blows more painful than any suffered in his saloon battles. His children all had been stricken with diphtheria, then sweeping the town. Early in April his eight-year-old daughter, Mamie, died, and two weeks later Johnnie, age two, also succumbed to the dread disease. Two other boys hovered near death but survived.[35]

The bad year of 1882 continued. "Pat Desmond is having a run of hard luck," the *Chieftain* noted in July. At the Independence Day celebrations he was carrying his "off arm" in a sling after being kicked by a mule when an errant Roman candle "took him just under the eye, peeling the bark off."[36]

The calamities mounted. Having lost his job and two of his children, Desmond now lost his wife, Annie. Depressed by the death of her children and her husband's alcoholism, Annie took her boys and left for Peoria, Illinois, to stay with relatives. Desmond followed her, brought his family back, and tried to salvage the marriage, but it was a lost cause. In November Annie was granted a divorce.[37]

In addition to his other troubles, Desmond also had cash problems. Fines and attorneys' fees had depleted his savings, but, fortunately, with the city's rapid growth his real estate holdings had appreciated. In March he sold lots opposite the South Pueblo National Bank for $12,000.[38] Then in November he put his livery business up for sale. The property, at the corner of Third and C Streets, included a large barn, seventeen head of livery horses, fourteen rigs, and necessary harness. In his sales ad Desmond announced that the "outfit must be sold as the proprietor has other business to attend to."[39]

The other business was an investigative and merchants' security company he established in May as the Southern Colorado Detective Agency. Affiliated with Dave Cook's Denver-based Rocky Mountain Detective Agency, the new organization was headed by Pat Desmond as superintendent and staffed by former Pueblo policemen who had remained loyal to him during the "Police Muddle." William Richardson, the former Pinkerton detective, also joined up, presumably bringing with him some professional expertise. The company was controversial from the outset. City Marshal Henry Jameson, most of his officers, and some city council members were outspoken in their opposition to a private police organization operating within the city, in competition, as they saw it, with the regularly constituted constabulary. Despite the objections of the police, Desmond forged ahead with his new company and over the next few months managed to make some notable arrests, including one of a murderer.[40] "Detective Desmond has his hands full just now looking after crooks and thieves," commented the *Chieftain* on August 3.

Union Avenue in South Pueblo, Colorado. Site of a Desmond
gunfight. Courtesy of the Colorado Historical Society.

In May 1883 he nabbed a "Mexican half-breed" named Joe Ward,
charged with horse theft. Tom Tobin, legendary Colorado mountain
man then living in the southern part of Pueblo County, assisted him in
running down the culprit. Desmond, according to the papers, located
and arrested Ward, but "had considerable difficulty in getting away
with him from the angered Mexicans.[41]

On February 9, 1883, almost a year to the day after his gunfight
with O'Connor, Desmond again had a six-gun set-to with a South
Pueblo policeman. There were rumors that a woman was at the
bottom of the trouble, but the dispute over Desmond's private security
agency probably was also a factor. As reported in the press, the affair
started when Desmond and Policeman R. A. Caldwell exchanged
some hard words in the Big Tree Saloon on Union Avenue. Desmond
was unarmed and tried to end the argument by walking out of the
place. But Caldwell followed and continued to berate Desmond in the
street. Suddenly the officer pulled his pistol, struck Desmond over the
head, and the weapon discharged. Dazed by the blow, Desmond
staggered down the street.

Regaining his wits and his Irish temper afire, Desmond obtained a
pistol from a friend and went back in search of Caldwell. He wasn't

hard to find. As soon as the two saw each other, the guns began to roar and continued until empty. The gunfight was not an exhibition of great marksmanship. Both men were still standing when Marshal Jameson arrived on the scene. Desmond was unscathed except for a bullet that had grazed his head, "cutting a swath through his raven locks."[42] One of his shots had struck Caldwell in the right shoulder, but that officer, still enraged, ran up to Desmond and struck him over the head again with his empty revolver. This last injury to Desmond's battered cranium sent him to the sidewalk, unconscious.

Also wounded in the affray by stray bullets were two others, George Wilson and Frank Howard, the proverbial innocent bystanders. Wilson, with a shattered ankle, had the most serious injury. One of the combatants had fought from behind a telephone pole, and the *Chieftain* wondered if the telephone company would sue to recover damage to the pole, "which was filled so full of lead that it has sunk into the ground four feet."[43]

Charges of assault with intent to kill were brought against Desmond, but Henry Jameson and J. C. Lilly were also named as codefendants, which leads to a suspicion that there was more to the story than appeared in the press. A preliminary hearing held on February 28 before Justice F. H. Schrock took all day to complete. But after hearing testimony from eight witnesses for the prosecution and six for the defense, the judge ruled there was insufficient evidence to bind the defendants over and they were released.[44]

Misfortune struck Pat Desmond again as the year 1884 was just beginning. In the early hours of January 2 fire broke out in the livery stable that he had been unable to sell and still operated on C Street. High winds quickly spread the flames throughout the structure and to adjoining buildings. Almost the entire block was destroyed before the fire was at last contained. Thirteen horses died in Desmond's stable, including a fine-blooded stallion he prized highly. Total estimated losses in the fire were $25,000. Desmond claimed losses of $10,000, most of which was covered by insurance.[45]

He never returned to the livery business, but soon opened the Star Saloon on Union Avenue. His private detective business languished and finally died a quiet death, but Desmond remained in the law enforcement field, serving both as a deputy sheriff for the county and constable for South Pueblo.

His continued heavy drinking led to frequent appearances in police court. In 1883 he had remarried, and Eva, the new Mrs. Desmond, evidently condoned his rowdy behavior and even participated in some of his escapades herself. His notoriety as a saloon brawler made him an easy target for unfounded accusations. In early 1885 a man named Thomas Mulready charged him with an assault in which Mulready "lost his left eye-ball and had his shoulder dislocated by blows." But at a June hearing several witnesses testified that on the night of the incident Mulready, very drunk, had fallen over a beer keg, injuring himself, and Desmond had merely picked him up and told him to go home. When a doctor testified that Mulready had lost his eye more than a year before, the judge dismissed the charges and assessed court costs to the plaintiff.[46]

More typical of news items concerning Desmond's rowdiness was this police court report in the March 3, 1887, *Chieftain*: "Pat J. Desmond had his two trials for assault yesterday. The first before Justice [George T.] Breed, he resisted and it was taken under advisement until Monday. In the other case . . . he was fined $5 and costs."

Desmond's next shooting scrape grew out of an altercation with Frank Owenby, an emigration agent from La Veta, Colorado, who, during an earlier residence in Pueblo, had been charged with numerous offenses and had acquired an unsavory reputation. After borrowing five dollars from Desmond, Owenby repaid the loan with a check that bounced. On December 19, 1888, an infuriated Desmond confronted Owenby in A. C. Daniel's drugstore and, wielding his cane like a shillelagh, slammed it down on his head. "If I had a gun I'd kill you," he roared. The frightened druggist blew a police whistle, and Jack O'Connor, the officer who had exchanged bullets with Desmond six years before, and two other Irish policemen, O'Kelly and Burke, came running. They escorted Desmond out, calmed the situation, and made no arrests.

But fifteen minutes later Desmond was back. He evidently did not expect to find Owenby still there, as he was accompanied by his wife and still armed only with his walking stick. But Frank Owenby was still there. When Desmond saw him, he advanced, his cane uplifted, and ignored Owenby's shouted warnings to back off. Owenby drew a .38-caliber pistol and pumped two bullets into his attacker before Eva Desmond jumped between the men. Patrons and employees in the store scurried for the exits as Desmond sank to the floor with wounds in the left shoulder and just below the breastbone. Officers O'Connor and O'Kelly returned, placed Owenby under arrest, and called for a hack to transport Desmond to his home. There doctors probed unsuccessfully for two bullets. The one in the shoulder was not considered dangerous, but the other was life threatening.[47]

Desmond recovered, charges against Owenby were dropped, and most folks quickly forgot the affair. But Owenby, proud of having gunned down one of the most dangerous fighting men in Colorado, reminded everyone of that fact at every opportunity and eventually claimed he had killed Desmond. Back in La Veta he did a little moonshining and detective work and kept a curio shop where he bragged to visitors about dispatching the redoubtable Pueblo gunfighter and displayed in a glass case the pistol with which he had accomplished the feat.[48]

But Pat Desmond was not dead yet. He had soured on Pueblo and Colorado, however, and for several months he traveled across Wyoming and Utah looking for a likely spot to settle and pursue his business interests. He finally chose Ogden, a thriving, growing community, and invested in several saloons there. One of his places was the Ogden River Resort, described in a newspaper as "one of the toughest dives in the city."[49]

In this establishment in the summer of 1889 he became involved in another of the sordid brawls that had marked his career, an affair described by the *Ogden Daily Commercial* as "a regular knock down and drag out."[50] Desmond was forty-seven years old when he tangled with Jack Williams, a much younger man, and he paid dearly for rashly ignoring the age discrepancy. The fight, triggered by some minor disagreement, quickly escalated on the night of July 18 from epithet to assault. Desmond and Williams broke beer bottles over each other's heads as onlookers urged them on and placed bets on the outcome. Eva Desmond was present, and when she saw her husband getting the worst of the battle, she rushed forward and thrust a pistol into his hand. Desmond shoved the muzzle against his adversary's chest and thumbed back the hammer, but, just as he fired, someone jerked his arm upward and the bullet only creased Williams's scalp. At this point bystanders intervened and took the revolver from Desmond, but the enraged combatants continued to fight until Desmond, his head "cut and bleeding till he presented a dilapidated appearance," collapsed, unconscious.[51]

Desmond closed the Ogden River Resort shortly after the fracas with Williams and returned with his wife to Pueblo. When a story reached Ogden in February 1890 that he had been shot and killed in Colorado, the editor of the *Daily Commercial* observed that death by gunshot was a fitting death for a man of his type, and it had long been expected that he would die with his boots on. Desmond, easily offended by critical press, rushed back to Ogden, hired lawyer L. R. Rogers, and filed a $10,000 lawsuit against the newspaper for libel.[52]

He also seemed determined to settle a long smoldering account with a former employee named Thomas S. Todd. A Missourian in his late thirties, Todd had worked as a telephone lineman in Pueblo, but since "work and he did not agree," as one paper noted,[53] he spent most of his time in saloons tending bar or dealing at the gambling tables. He got in trouble in Pueblo when he took a shot at Bert Reynolds, proprietor of a variety theater, and spent some time in jail. It was rumored that he had been arrested and charged in the October 8, 1879, robbery of the Chicago & Alton train at Blue Cut, Missouri, but had jumped $1,000 bail put up by his mother and fled west. The *Chieftain* noted that he had been "credited with a good many shady transactions while in Pueblo, and his reputation is not of the best even among his class."[54]

As a saloon owner and notorious brawler Pat Desmond was of Todd's class. Despite the man's unsavory reputation Desmond hired him to tend bar in his Ogden River Resort. Todd worked there for three months in 1889, but when the business folded, employer and employee parted rancorously.

Animosity between them flared up again when Desmond returned to Ogden. They got into a shouting match in the Bear Saloon and Desmond pulled a gun. But Todd was unarmed, and Bear proprietor Gus Vogus, an old friend of Desmond's, interceded in the dispute. He calmed Desmond down, took his pistol away, and put it in the cash drawer for safekeeping. "I was afraid of Desmond," Todd later admitted. He said that after seeing him "in lots of rows" and seeing him "pull his gun several times," he decided it would be prudent to arm himself. He began carrying a double-action, .44-caliber "American Bulldog."[55]

About midnight on February 28 Desmond met Todd and a man named Tom O'Neil in the Little King Saloon. They had a drink together and engaged in what appeared to be a quiet, friendly conversation. At Desmond's suggestion they then moved on to the Capital Saloon, where they downed a few more libations. As Desmond's voice grew louder and more menacing, O'Neil decided it was time to depart, leaving Todd alone with the increasingly belligerent Desmond. Todd watched warily as Desmond and bartender W. P. Collier conversed briefly and saw Collier remove something from the cash drawer and pass it to Desmond, who slipped it in his pocket.

In an obvious effort to goad Todd into making a hostile move, Desmond reached out and pulled a white silk handkerchief and a pair of leather gloves from the other man's pocket. Reports conflict as to what occurred when Todd demanded the return of his property. Todd claimed that Desmond responded, "I will give you this!" and started to pull a pistol from his pocket. Others present saw no such move.

But suddenly shots rang out and smoke filled the room. A Saint Joseph, Missouri, drummer named E. T. Roach was so close when the shooting started, he said, that Desmond's hand was resting on his shoulder. After several shots, he saw Desmond reel backward against the bar, slide along it to the end, and collapse on the floor. Todd then strode over, said Roach, and deliberately fired into the prone figure.

Quickly arriving on the scene, night watchman Thomas Luty relieved Todd of his weapon and arrested him. A physician named Dr. J. G. Bryant, who had left the saloon only moments earlier, rushed back to examine Desmond. He found him very dead with five bullets holes in his body. One slug had torn through his scrotum into his abdomen; another passed through his arm; a third struck him in the mouth, knocking out a tooth in its trajectory to his brain; a fourth hit him right between the eyes. It was clear these shots had all been fired from the front. A fifth bullet, fired after Desmond had fallen, entered the brain through the back of the head. The doctor concluded that any of the shots to the head would have been instantly fatal.

Murder charges were filed against Todd. He offered the classic plea of self-defense, saying that when he saw the gun in Desmond's hand he said to himself, "Old boy, you've got to do something awful quick," so he pulled his gun "and let him have it."

Skeptics scoffed at Todd's account back in Pueblo. The *Chieftain* found it "improbable and altogether unlikely to those who know Desmond and his ability to handle a gun. No one will believe that Pat Desmond got the drop on an enemy and then permitted that enemy to shoot him five times without even returning the fire."[56] Evidence presented at the preliminary hearing seemed to substantiate this view. Desmond's pistol was still in his pocket when the body was examined. A freshly lit cigar lay near his right hand and appeared to be the only weapon he was holding when bullets cut him down.

Eva Desmond returned to Pueblo with the body of her husband and arranged for interment in the Northside Cemetery. Whatever problems Pat Desmond may have given his family during his lifetime, he left his wife and two children well off financially when he departed; his estate was estimated at between $65,000 and $75,000, a large fortune in 1890.[57]

While acknowledging Desmond's success as a businessman and his achievements as an officer of the law, Colorado and Utah newspapers emphasized his unsavory reputation as a violent bully. He "was regarded as a desperado, and although he had some redeeming traits in his character, he was generally feared and hated," said the *Rocky Mountain News*. "He was not exactly a desperado, but was known to be a man who would take a hand in any scuffle regardless of the consequences. . . . He was a good man with his fists and could knock out almost any one, [but] when drunk he was liable to pull his revolver needlessly. . . . A common saying was that Desmond was afraid of nobody, and did not know what danger was. [He] was really a brave man."[58]

To the *Denver Republican* he was "a thoroughly bad man and at the same time very smooth and pliant. . . . Brutal by instinct, he was one of those peculiar characters which all right minded people abhor, while at the same time they admire."[59]

"Those who knew Pat best," said the *Colorado Chieftain*, "had long predicted that some day the brave and reckless fellow would die with his boots on."[60]

Perhaps the complex character of Pat Desmond was summed up best in the *Ogden Standard*: "He had hundreds of friends in business circles and he had a great many enemies. He had a faculty for creating both. It appeared to be an ambition with him to reward the former and punish the latter. All men who knew him admired him for his ability to make money and his generous spending of it. They disliked his vindictiveness."[61]

The first-degree murder trial of Thomas Todd opened in Ogden on June 24, 1890, and lasted three days. After eleven hours of deliberation the jury found the defendant guilty of voluntary manslaughter, an obvious compromise verdict. In imposing a five-year sentence on June 30, the judge noted that Todd was fortunate in not having committed his crime two weeks later, for the Utah legislature had at that time extended the maximum sentence for voluntary manslaughter from five to ten years.[62]

Shortly after his early release from the Utah penitentiary, Todd shot another man at Denver. On March 31, 1894, he was convicted in Arapahoe County, Colorado, of "assault to murder" and given an eight-year sentence. On March 5, 1895, he escaped from the Colorado State Penitentiary at Canon City and disappeared from the pages of history.[63]

— 3 —

MART DUGGAN
(1848–1888)

"They understood that I would not do to fool with."

Matt Dillon, fearless Dodge City marshal hero of the long-running *Gunsmoke* series on radio and television, was a fictional character, but a real-life lawman with a similar name wielded a six-shooter during the same period to effect a semblance of order in another camp every bit as wild as Dodge. Mart Duggan was the law in booming Leadville, Colorado, when that mining town, perched two miles high in the Rockies, was considered by many to be the toughest town in the West.

Martin J. Duggan, like his contemporary Pat Desmond, was an Irish immigrant, born in County Limerick on November 10, 1848. Brought to America by his parents, he grew up in the Irish slums of New York City. Following the July 1863 antidraft riots in the city, fomented primarily by Irish immigrants, in which more than a hundred were killed and injured, he left for the West. While still a teenager, he drifted through the mining camps of Colorado, working as a miner or mule skinner.[1]

By his mid-twenties he had grown into a wide-shouldered, barrel-chested man with that look of determination and fearlessness that marked him as one who would be dangerous to cross. A contemporary described him as of "medium height, but of compact, massive build. He had sinews of steel. His features were good. He had a square face, with broad forehead and pleasing expression. His hair and complexion were light and his eyes blue. He was a man you would look at twice as you first met him."[2] It was during this period that he acquired a local reputation as a notable Indian fighter, but details of experiences that earned him this fame have been lost to history.

Duggan spent the summer of his twenty-eighth year prospecting the creeks near the mining camp of Georgetown, but met with little success. The following winter he moved into town and obtained a job as a bouncer in the Occidental Dance Hall and Saloon. According to an account that later appeared in a newspaper in far-off Chicago, one night an inebriated patron, deciding to shoot the lights out of the place, pulled out a pistol for that purpose. Duggan descended on him at once, took his revolver from him, and beat him over the head with it. Battered and bleeding, the drunk still showed fight, muttering through mangled lips that Duggan would not fare so well if he had the nerve to face him in a standup gun battle. His Irish temper fully aroused, Duggan accepted the challenge. Pointing to the man's weapon in the corner where he'd thrown it, he strode out of the saloon and waited across the street for his adversary to appear. When that worthy emerged, the two began advancing, shooting at each other across thirty feet of snow-covered roadway. Duggan's third shot struck his opponent in the chest, killing him instantly. A miners' court found the killing an open-and-shut case of self-defense.[3]

When Duggan arrived in the burgeoning new mining camp of Leadville in the spring of 1878 he brought with him a reputation as a formidable fighting man, equally dangerous with his fists or his guns. There were reports that in his frontier wanderings he had already dispatched seven men in gunfights and bragged of the notches on his gun.[4] Other than the reported shootout at Georgetown, however, no evidence supports this claim. Some may have confused Martin Duggan with a desperado named Sanford "Sam" Duggan, who had terrorized Colorado mining camps a decade earlier, murdering several men before a Denver lynch mob disposed of him in 1868.

Leadville, the great mining camp 10,000 feet high in the Rockies, soon to be known as "Colorado's Magic City," was established in early 1877 when eighteen early arrivals met and chose the name "Leadville" in reference to the lead-silver carbonate deposits that were the reason for the camp's existence. At a special election held on February 12, 1878, H. A. W. Tabor, destined to become one of the wealthiest men in America, was elected mayor. A man named T. H. Harrison was appointed city marshal. There were perhaps 300 residents of the new town when it was founded, but its growth would be extraordinary. By the next year the population would reach 15,000, and by the 1880s Leadville would become the second largest city in Colorado, with 30,000 residents.[5]

A certain number of criminals and troublemakers were a normal part of every new mining town in the West, but from its earliest days Leadville seemed to attract more than its quota of violent ruffians and gunmen. The criminal element soon threatened to take over the town, running T. H. Harrison, the first city marshal, out of town only two days after his appointment.[6] Mayor Tabor named George O'Connor as his replacement. O'Connor had plenty of grit, but he did not last very long. Within a month of his appointment he was shot dead by one of his own deputies, James M. "Tex" Bloodsworth, an associate of the rough crowd. When the new marshal reprimanded his subordinate for spending too much time carousing in the saloons and dance halls with his pals during his tour of duty, Bloodsworth was infuriated. The two officers met on the evening of April 25 in Billy Nye's Saloon, and the disagreement quickly escalated into violence. Bloodsworth pulled a pistol and pumped five bullets into his boss. As O'Connor fell to the floor, mortally wounded, Bloodsworth ran from the saloon and galloped out of town on a stolen horse, never to be seen in Leadville again.[7]

O'Connor survived for several hours only, but even before he breathed his last, Mayor Tabor had called an emergency meeting of the city council and appointed Mart Duggan to replace him. The rough-neck crowd who had so quickly disposed of the first two Leadville marshals wasted little time warning the new officer that he was next. "Immediately after I was appointed," Duggan told an interviewer several years later, "I received a written notice from the roughs to leave town and if I stayed 24 hours I would follow George O'Connor. Paid no attention to notice but took every precaution to always be on guard." He explained that "the town was not only full of thieves, thugs and desperate characters, but there was some quarrelsome, shooting miners . . . who had been here a number of years and were determined that no newcomer should have any authority over them."[8]

But City Marshal Duggan, they were to learn, feared no man or group of men. Soon after he pinned on his star he demonstrated how he would impose his authority. Notified that a crowd of rowdies were hurrahing the Tontine Restaurant, he entered the establishment, sized up the situation, and picked out the leader of the troublemakers. Stepping up close, he ordered the man outside.

"What if I don't go?" sneered the ruffian.

"Then say a 'Hail Mary,'" Duggan growled, "because you're dead where you stand."

Staring into Duggan's cold blue eyes and seeing absolute determination there, the roughneck blinked and headed for the door.[9]

Twentieth-century civil rights advocates would have been shocked at Duggan's bullying brand of law enforcement. He ignored the law when it suited him and respected no authority but his own, which he enforced with fists, club, or revolver. He summarily fired any policemen he suspected of being friendly with the criminal element. Finding the rulings of a municipal magistrate too lenient for his taste, he announced that he was kicking him off the bench. When the indignant official demanded to know by what authority a city marshal could oust a judge, Duggan stuck the muzzle of his six-shooter under the magistrate's nose and marched him into the street. A handpicked Duggan replacement held court for six days with the marshal constantly at his side to see that punishment to malefactors was meted out to his satisfaction. The deposed judge finally regained his seat after apologizing to Duggan and promising to do better in the future.[10]

On another occasion Duggan, called to a disturbance, found mining magnate August Rische drunk and disorderly and promptly placed him under arrest. When the man, one of the original Leadville silver kings, resisted, the marshal whacked him over the head with his nightstick and dragged him off to the jail. Mayor Tabor heard of the affair and remonstrated with his officer, pointing out that Rische was his partner in the fabulous Little Pittsburg mine and, as a man of distinction, deserved special consideration. Duggan replied that in this matter Rische was nothing but a common drunk and would be treated as such. If Tabor continued his objections, Duggan added, he would be charged with obstruction of justice and join his partner in the lockup. H. A. W. Tabor, one of the wealthiest and most influential men in Colorado, backed down, and August Rische remained in jail until Leadville's marshal chose to release him.[11]

Mart Duggan's dauntless courage was clearly demonstrated one night after a barroom fight led to mob action. The trouble began over a poker game in the Pioneer Saloon when John Elkins, a black man, and a white man named Charlie Hines quarreled over a pot. Fists flew and Elkins pulled a knife, stabbed the other man, and fled the scene. He was quickly found and arrested by city officers, but as word spread through the streets that Hines was dying, race hatred flared, and a lynch mob gathered. As Duggan later related the tale:

> One of my policemen woke me up in the middle of the night to tell me that a Negro had cut a man to death in the Pioneer Saloon and the officers had put the Negro in jail, but a mob was forming to take him out and hang him. I got my clothes on as soon as possible and, sending the officer to assist in guarding the jail, I started out alone to get ahead of the mob, who by this time I could hear coming down the street. By running, I managed to get ahead of them and halted them on a street corner under a dance hall lamp. I stood in the middle of the street with a cocked revolver in each hand and told them I would kill the first man who attempted to pass the lamppost. There was about two hundred men in the mob and I managed to make them understand that some of them were sure to be killed if they persisted in interfering with the law, and from that time on they understood that I would not do to fool with.[12]

Charlie Hines recovered from his wound and later served under Duggan on the city's police force. Elkins wasted no time shaking the dust of Leadville from his shoes after his release.[13]

Duggan again displayed his ability to control a lynch mob in March 1879. William H. Bush, business associate of H. A. W. Tabor and owner of the imposing Clarendon Hotel, nearing completion at that time, had arrived a few months before from Central City with his ne'er-do-well brother Jim,[14] and the two quickly made a great deal of money dealing in town lots. When Mortimer Arbuckle[15] jumped one of the lots, throwing up a slab shanty and a fence "before breakfast" on the morning of March 10, the Bush brothers attempted to remove him. There was a scuffle and the ever-impetuous Jim Bush pulled a pistol and shot Arbuckle dead. When word spread that the dead man had been unarmed, an angry mob, bent on lynching Jim and burning down William's hotel, began to form. Marshal Duggan quickly organized a force of one hundred special deputies to protect the brothers and their property. At a hearing held that afternoon, Jim Bush was bound over on a charge of murder. Just before dawn, following a tense and anxious night, Duggan spirited Bush out of town and conveyed him to Denver under heavy guard.[16]

Mart Duggan had certainly shown that he was a man it "would not do to fool with." Everyone in Leadville, businessmen and saloon loafers alike, respected him for his raw courage and direct, no-nonsense way of keeping a lid on the town. Normally well mannered and soft spoken, Duggan, like many fighting men of his type, could turn viciously violent when drinking. "Sober, there was no more courteous, obliging person," said the *Leadville Evening Chronicle*, but "under the influence of liquor, he was the incarnation of deviltry, and had as little regard for human life as a wild beast."[17] Early Leadville resident G. W. Bartlett, while acknowledging that "there was no braver man in camp" than Mart Duggan, remembered watching disgustedly as a rowdy named "Texas Jack" and Duggan "both mad with drink, with drawn revolvers . . . , rolling and fighting on the sidewalk."[18]

Duggan, according to one historian of Leadville, "swaggered about town eager for challenge. Quick with both fist and gun, he terrorized innocent and guilty alike, boldly hunting out the most bloodthirsty desperados to force a duel, just as boldly assaulting innocent citizens on any or no provocation. . . . But for all his brutality and lawlessness . . . , it must be said of him that, being absolutely fearless, he was the one man in camp to intimidate roughs and cutthroats."[19]

A drunken binge in February 1879 resulted in the marshal's suspension from duty. At the bar of the Tontine he paid for a drink with a silver coin called a "trade dollar." Following accepted practice, the bartender, L. H. Beasy, deducted a 25 percent charge from Duggan's change. This triggered a furious outburst from the marshal, who, according to Beasy's formal complaint, "became violent and abusive, drew his revolver and, threatening my life, came behind the bar, knocked me down, called me all kinds of bad and dirty names, and denounced the owners of the Tontine as thieves and robbers."[20] The city fathers suspended the marshal, but when Beasy, on reflection, decided that incurring the continuing wrath of Mart Duggan might be unhealthy and dropped his charges, Duggan was soon reinstated.

Despite Duggan's periodic displays of rowdyism, the city officials, still impressed by his ability to control the criminal element, offered him reappointment as marshal when his term expired in April 1879.

He declined, however, saying that he intended to accompany his wife on a visit to her former home in Flint, Michigan.

P. A. "Pat" Kelly succeeded Duggan as Leadville city marshal, but it soon became evident that this Irish lawman lacked the toughness to control the town as had his predecessor. Under Kelly's lax law enforcement, the hoodlums, claim jumpers, and strong-arm robbers grew increasingly bold, and local newspapers began referring to the summer of 1879 as the "Reign of the Footpads."[21] *Chronicle* excerpts reveal the escalating levels of crime:

> It is getting to be a nuisance, this indiscriminate pistol practice from ten p.m. to midnight.[22]

> Not one-twentieth part of the depredations committed by the several scores of well-known bunco thieves and highway robbers in the city ever find their way into print. None of the local papers desires to deter capital and enterprise from seeking this camp. They report only the most glaring crimes that are publicly known.[23]

> There is a general feeling that every man must be his own bodyguard and be prepared to shoot down anyone who attempts to invade his personal or property rights.[24]

> The buncos positively, unequivocally, and without the least reservation of mind or matter, have things all their own way in Leadville. Footpads may rob a man in broad daylight on the most public streets, and there is no civil power in Colorado that can give the robbed redress.[25]

Gangs of hoodlums brazenly took over city property at gunpoint and threw the owners into the street. Pitched battles were waged at the mines between employees of the operators and organized bands of claim jumpers. The recognized leader of these property thieves was a notorious character named Edward Frodsham. An Englishman by birth, thirty-seven-year-old Frodsham was raised in Brigham, Utah. Married, with three children, he first got crossways with the law in 1876 at Evanston, Wyoming, where he shot and killed a gambler named Peasley, whom he accused of seducing Mrs. Frodsham. Sentenced on May 6 of that year to ten years in the Wyoming Territorial Prison at Laramie for manslaughter, he served less than two; Governor John M.

DEADLY DOZEN

Thayer granted him a pardon on December 29, 1877. A jeweler by trade, Frodsham opened a shop in Laramie, but in less than a year he was in gun trouble again. On August 8, 1878, he and a pal, escaped convict Lee Landers, alias Eli Lee, had a shootout with two other men in front of Susie Parker's parlor house. A cattle dealer named Taylor was killed. Arrested and charged with murder, Frodsham, despite two gunshot wounds, managed to post bail, steal a horse, and flee Laramie and Wyoming Territory.

Frodsham next turned up in Leadville, where on December 29, 1878, he reportedly shot to death another former Laramie resident named Peter Thams.[26] By the following summer during the "Reign of the Footpads," he was in command of Leadville's lawless. Perhaps out of fear of the desperado, City Marshal Kelly refused to arrest him. Many suspected the city officers were in league with the criminals. Finally a Lake County officer moved against the ringleader. Undersheriff Edmund H. Watson, on November 17, 1879, took Frodsham into custody on a charge of "Riot," or disturbing the peace. Denied bail, he was still incarcerated two days later when vigilantes stormed the jail, removed Frodsham and a notorious footpad named Patrick Stewart, and hanged them from the rafters of a nearby building. Pinned to Frodsham's back was a placard: "Notice to all lot thieves, bunko steerers, footpads, thieves and chronic bondsmen for the same, and sympathizers for the above class of criminals: This is our commencement, and this shall be your fates. We mean business, and let this be your last warning. . . ." It was signed "Vigilantes' Committee. We are 700 strong."[27]

Undaunted by this threat, the criminals mobilized for war. According to a story in the *Denver Republican*, reprinted in the *Leadville Chronicle*, they met the day after the hangings and raised the membership ante, boasting they were 756 strong. "Armed to the teeth . . . , they claim to know every one of the vigilantes, and that as soon as the excitement subsides they will hang every one of them and burn the town."[28]

The town was like a bomb with a burning fuse. "You see firearms on all sides, every third man carries a Sharps, Spencer, or Winchester rifle and every man has one or two revolvers in a condition for immediate use," wrote a resident to his parents.[29]

Mine owners and businessmen, fearing anarchy that could destroy the money-pot that was Leadville, demanded action. City officials fired Kelly and sent for Mart Duggan. "The city council telegraphed me at Flint, Michigan . . . , asking me to come back at once and take the marshalship as they did not believe that anyone else could prevent the roughs from running the town," Duggan said, without a hint of modesty. "I came back at once."[30]

In December 1879 Duggan pinned on the badge of Leadville city marshal for the second time. He dismissed Kelly's cronies on the police force, hired all new officers, and set about cracking heads and arresting thugs. Soon "Big Ed" Burns, "Slim Jim" Bruce, J. J. "Off-Wheeler" Harlan, "Nut Shell Bill" Billy Thompson (brother of the celebrated Texas gunfighter Ben Thompson), and a host of lesser lights sought more salubrious climes. By year's end newspaper editors at Buena Vista and other towns down the valley of the Arkansas were bemoaning an influx of unwelcome newcomers "lately of Leadville."[31]

Duggan completed Kelly's term, remaining in the office of city marshal until April 1880 when again he refused reappointment. Ed Watson, the doughty county officer whose arrest of Frodsham began the process of ending the footpad reign, a process completed by Duggan, succeeded him.

Opening a livery stable next to his home at the corner of West Fourth and Pine Streets, Duggan appeared to have settled into a life of tranquil domesticity. He was never far from scenes of action, however.

A wage dispute at the mines in May 1880 resulted in a bitter strike in which the operators rejected the miners' demands and enlisted toughs to defend their interests. Conditions grew increasingly ominous in June, and Colorado governor Frederick R. Pitkin ordered General David J. Cook, commander of the state militia, to Leadville to take charge. Cook was aware that many members of his own militia companies, miners themselves, were in sympathy with the strikers. When he learned that the miners and their militia supporters, meeting in secret, had hatched plans to attack their opponents and conduct a general lynching, he called in the officers of the Tabor Tigers. This was a company composed of Leadville sporting men, gamblers, and saloonmen who made their living by their own wits and had little sympathy for the problems of hard-rock miners. Cook knew they had even less love for lynching parties, as their own class had often suffered at the hands of such "stranglers." The officers of the Tabor Tigers were Captain James Murphy and Lieutenant Mart Duggan. Cook directed them to hunt down and arrest the conspirators, militiamen and miners alike. This they did, reportedly rounding up more than two hundred. The action cooled the situation and helped lead to a nonviolent resolution of the strike.[32]

A few months later Duggan's penchant for violence was again exhibited. On the afternoon of November 22, 1880, he left his livery stable and set off down snow-covered Pine Street in a sleigh drawn by an elegant pair of matched black horses. He intended to deliver sleigh and team to Winnie Purdy, madam of a high-toned parlor house on West Fifth, only a block away. Near the corner a mining man named Louis Lamb, with whom Duggan had quarreled previously, stepped out into the street in front of the blacks and was almost run down. The incident triggered a new exchange of bitter words, and Duggan excoriated Lamb in fighting language. Lamb turned and walked away in silence.

The matter should have ended there, but Duggan's Irish temper was now fully aroused and he followed in his sleigh, blistering the other man in loud and profane terms. By the time he reached a point directly in front of the Purdy brothel, Lamb, having taken all the verbal abuse he could handle, whirled and demanded an apology. When Duggan refused, Lamb reached for his pistol. He got it out and cocked, but before he could fire, Duggan leaped from the sleigh, pulled his own weapon, and triggered off a round that struck Lamb in the mouth, killing him instantly. Duggan turned himself in to Police Captain Charles Perkins and at a hearing was cleared on a claim of self-defense.[33]

Lamb's widow considered the shooting of her husband plain, unmitigated murder, however. She swore undying hatred of the former marshal and vowed that she would wear her widow's weeds until Duggan was dead and she could deliver them to his wife. She said she would never rest until she could dance on Duggan's grave.[34]

Although Mart Duggan never received official punishment for the killing of Louis Lamb, the affair affected his life negatively. He lost much of his popularity following the shooting, and his livery business suffered, failing altogether in 1882. To pay his debts he sold his house in Leadville and moved to Douglass City, a railroad construction town at the east end of the Hagerman Tunnel, where the Colorado Midland line pierced the mountains on its way to Aspen. There he tended bar and wore a deputy sheriff's badge.

In 1887 several Douglass City dance hall girls were conned by a traveling salesman into buying some fake jewelry. Duggan hunted the drummer down and, when the man resisted arrest, worked him over a little with his big fists. Marching the bloody and thoroughly chastened fellow back to the dance hall, he made him return all the money he had taken from the girls and buy a round of drinks for the house before booting him out of town.

The incident enhanced Duggan's popularity in Douglass City, but resulted in a legal problem in Leadville. The salesman had gone immediately to the "Magic City," found a magistrate, and filed charges against Duggan for robbery and assault. The justice ordered Duggan's appearance to answer the charges, and he complied, bringing with him a covey of dance hall girls. After hearing the evidence, the magistrate acquitted Duggan on the robbery charge, but found him guilty of assault and fined him ten dollars and court costs. Flying into one of his famous rages, Duggan demanded that the salesman pay the fine and suggested an orifice for the deposit of the judge's court costs. The performance so completely shocked and frightened the salesman that he dropped the charges and fled the scene. Exultant in what he considered a complete victory, Duggan returned to Douglass City, his gaggle of girls in tow.[35]

Late that year Duggan returned to Leadville to take a job as a police patrolman. In the decade since he had first come to Leadville, the town had advanced well beyond the wild frontier mining camp he had first known, and was now a bustling community challenging Denver for state capital honors and boasting a police force seventeen men strong. If Leadville had discarded much of its wild frontier roughness, Mart Duggan had not. He was constantly in trouble because of the heavy-handed approach to law enforcement that had served him well in earlier times and had brought him local fame and respect.

After his difficulty with the jewelry peddler at Douglass City, he seemed to have a particular antipathy for gem salesmen. In March 1888 he mauled a local jeweler named S. W. Rice, who filed a complaint against him. Duggan contemptuously refused to defend his actions at a hearing before Police Judge Lorenzo F. Long and was fined twenty-five dollars.

In high dudgeon, Duggan resigned from the police force and went off on a monumental drinking binge. He was still carousing and

Harrison Street, Leadville, Colorado. The building with the large awning is the Texas House, a gambling hall managed by Bailey Youngson, Tom Dennison, and Jim Harrington. Mart Duggan was shot in front of this building at 4 A.M. on April 9, 1888. He later died in the Bradford Drug Store two doors farther down. From the author's collection.

quarrelsome some two weeks later when he got into a heated argument with William Gordon, a dealer in the Texas House, a popular Harrison Street gambling establishment. Bailey Youngson,[36] one of the owners of the place, intervened, defending his employee. Duggan invited them both outside to settle the dispute with six-shooters. The gamblers declined.

Friends tried to calm Duggan down, and about four in the morning convinced him he should go home. Leaving the Texas House, he had gone only a few steps when someone approached him from behind, leveled a pistol at his head, and fired. Night patrolmen, responding to the sound of the shot, found him lying in a pool of blood on the sidewalk, unconscious but still alive. Doctors summoned to the scene moved him to a room in the Bradford Drug Store, two doors away, but could do little for him.

His wife was called and sat with him through the long hours of the morning. About dawn he opened his eyes and asked for a drink of water. Asked if he knew who shot him, Duggan replied "Bailey Youngson" in a strong clear voice, before lapsing into unconsciousness. Later he revived again and told officers that he only knew he had been struck down by "one of the gang." "Was it Bailey Youngson?" they pressed.

"No," Duggan said, "and I'll die before I ever tell you."

These were his last words. Martin Duggan died shortly after eleven o'clock on the morning of April 9, 1888. His body was taken to Denver and interred in Riverside Cemetery near the graves of his parents.[37]

Despite his inelegant behavior and rough ways, Duggan still had many friends and admirers in Leadville who remembered the courage and audacity he demonstrated in taming the town's lawless element in its earliest days. Only the wife of Louis Lamb rejoiced in his passing. As promised, she danced on the bloodstained sidewalk where he had been shot down and presented Mrs. Duggan with her widow's weeds.

Bailey Youngson and Jim Harrington, partners in the operation of the Texas House, together with George Evans, one of their employees, were arrested as suspects in Duggan's murder. Prosecutors later dropped charges against Harrington and Evans, but Youngson stood trial and was acquitted.

No one was ever convicted in the slaying, but years later the generally accepted story in the sporting communities of Denver and Leadville was that Duggan's killer was faro dealer George Evans. Those professing to be "in the know" claimed Evans was paid to murder the former marshal by a group who held "old grudges" against him. Evans left Colorado soon after his release and went on an extended tour of Mexico and Central America, reportedly funded by these unnamed enemies of Duggan. It was only after news of the death of Evans in a gunfight in Nicaragua in 1902 reached Colorado that

Leadville residents with "inside" knowledge agreed to talk of the affair.[38]

Mart Duggan was a quick-shooting, hard-drinking, brawling, tough Irishman, but he was exactly the kind of man a tough, brawling, hard-drinking, quick-shooting camp like Leadville needed in its earliest days. His name is all but forgotten today, while the name "Matt Dillon" is recognized around the world. Such are the vagaries of life.

— 4 —

MILT YARBERRY
(1849–1888)

"An illustrious brave of the West"

"Young man, lay away your gun. Remember poor Yarberry," ran the admonition in the *Santa Fe Daily New Mexican* of February 10, 1883.

The day before, Milton J. Yarberry, gunfighter and erstwhile peace officer, had stood in the Albuquerque jail yard, a noose around his neck, and proclaimed his innocence of the murder charge for which he was being hanged. Precisely at three o'clock Bernalillo County sheriff Perfecto Armijo had snapped shut the cover of his watch, the great weight dropped, and Yarberry's long body had jerked into the air.

The Santa Fe paper editorialized that the hanging marked the end of the gunfighter era that had brought such notoriety to the West in general and New Mexico Territory in particular: "The day has passed when the illustrious braves of the west, such as Yarberry was, shall walk about in the bright sunlight, the envy and the admiration of the lesser lights in the criminal crowds who assemble to burn incense before them."

The "illustrious braves of the west," of course, ignored the newspaper's warning and continued to pack and use their guns. They soon forgot "poor Yarberry" and forgotten he has been for more than a century. But for one brief moment he held center stage as hundreds of Albuquerque citizens listened to the final speech of their former law officer and then watched his death dance.

Milton J. Yarberry, thirty-three years old in 1883, was not a handsome man according to all contemporary reports. Long, lanky, and slightly stooped, he stood six feet, three inches tall without his boots and walked with a peculiar loose-jointed, shambling gait. A "long, crane-like neck" supported his "small, poorly developed head" with its dark hair and mustache, restless, cold gray eyes, straight thin nose, and mouth "expressing chiefly cunning and cruelty." He could neither read nor write. "Brute dominated over the intellectual in his countenance, and his conversation showed plainly an entire lack of education and culture." After interviewing him, one reporter concluded that he lacked the mentality to distinguish between a legal and an unlawful act.[1]

Little is known of Yarberry's early life. Shortly before his hanging he confided to a friend, Elwood Maden, that he was born in 1849 at Walnut Ridge, Arkansas, of respectable parents whose name was not Yarberry. To keep the news of his inglorious end from his family, he had refused to divulge his true name to law authorities or the press. He told Maden but swore him to secrecy. He admitted to hurriedly leaving Arkansas after a man was killed in a land dispute with members of his family, but denied involvement in the murder. In fact, he said, he had never killed a man before coming to Albuquerque.[2]

Contemporary newspapers, however, reported that the man had traveled a long, tortuous, often blood-spattered trail to his destiny on the Albuquerque gallows.[3]

According to these accounts, he was known as John Armstrong, possibly his true name, when he fled Sharp County, Arkansas, with a $200 reward on his head for murder. Implicated in another killing at Helena, Arkansas, he scurried across the state and in 1873 joined a rustling gang operating near Fort Smith that included Dave Rudabaugh and "Mysterious Dave" Mather, two colorful characters who later attained wide-ranging frontier notoriety. During a robbery the gang members killed a popular cattleman and were forced to scatter ahead of an aroused citizenry.[4]

Yarberry is said to have gone to Texarkana, at the time "the rendezvous of more criminals than any spot in the West." There he killed a man he suspected of being a detective on his trail, but was in reality only an inoffensive traveler. Still on the dodge, he joined Company B of the Texas Ranger Frontier Battalion, stationed in Jack County.

Jim McIntire, another gunman of note, was a member of the same company and later recalled a "duel" in which Yarberry and another Arkansas recruit faced off. Yarberry had embarrassed the young fellow with a practical joke and was challenged to a duel. Lieutenant G. R. Hamilton, the company commander, secretly loaded two six-shooters with blank rounds, handed the weapons to the combatants, and told them to go to it. The unsuspecting duelists stood back to back, marched off the required number of steps, and whirled. Yarberry fired, but his white-faced adversary dropped his pistol and "hit the prairie with the speed of a jack-rabbit." As McIntire told it, "he never stopped until he reached Arkansas. He left a good horse and eighty dollars pay coming."[5]

Yarberry remained with the Rangers only a short time. According to the newspaper stories, about 1876 he next turned up in Decatur, Texas. Now calling himself "John Johnson," he opened a saloon and billiard parlor in partnership with a man named Jones. When a reward-seeking detective appeared one day and began asking questions about that old Arkansas murder case, Yarberry hurriedly sold out to his partner and left town. Rumor had it that the bullet-punctured body of the bounty hunter was discovered shortly thereafter.

Yarberry spent some time in Dodge City, Kansas, and then in late 1878 appeared in Canon City, Colorado, where he partnered a man named Tony Preston in the operation of a combination saloon and variety theater. He was now using the name Milton J. Yarberry. Eddie Foy, the great vaudeville performer, and his partner, Jim Thompson, played the theater in the spring of 1879. In his memoirs Foy recalled that Yarberry "rather fancied himself as a violinist." He described his employer as "citified" and prosperous-appearing in "a broadcloth suit, velvet vest, frilled shirt front and white collar . . . , expensive Eastern-made boots, and a long black mustache, [but] none too sweet a character."[6]

Yarberry, it seems, was slow in his payments to suppliers and performers. When Foy and Thompson concluded their engagement, he still owed them several weeks back pay. In an attempt to recover some of their loss, Jim Thompson stole a barrel of whiskey from the saloon storeroom and sold it. Aware of Yarberry's reputation as a dangerous bad man, Foy said he was amazed at Thompson's courage "in daring to pull such a trick on a man of this type. He had killed one or two men already, and he was not the sort that would hesitate to take direct and violent action whenever it suited his mood to do so."[7]

On March 6, 1879, the bartender of the Gem Saloon in Canon City shot Tony Preston. The bullet struck Yarberry's partner near the right nipple and came out near the spine. Yarberry fired three ineffectual shots at the gunman and joined a posse in pursuit of the man, who later gave himself up to the city marshal.[8] Preston hovered near death for several days but eventually recovered.

Soon thereafter, Yarberry left Canon City to join the hell-on-wheels crowd following the construction gangs of the Santa Fe Railroad, then building south through New Mexico. With a Mexican female partner remembered only as "Steamboat," he operated brothels in a succession of railroad boom camps.[9] He departed Las Vegas suddenly after a freighter was found robbed and murdered some twenty miles from town. Yarberry was suspected but never arrested or charged.[10]

He reportedly shot and killed a man named Morgan in the dining room of a Rincon hotel.[11] Later he showed up in San Marcial, where Tony Preston had settled to recover from the effects of his severe gunshot wound. At San Marcial Yarberry began an affair with the wife of his former partner. When he left town, Sadie Preston and her four-year-old daughter went with him.

During his New Mexico travels Yarberry had developed a friendship with Perfecto Armijo, resident of Albuquerque, sheriff of Bernalillo County, and scion of an old, well-respected and prosperous New Mexican family. They made an odd pair, the well-to-do college-educated Mexican American and the illiterate whoremonger and desperado from Texas. Perhaps Armijo recognized something of value in Yarberry's character, for he hired him as a deputy and used his influence to get him appointed constable at Albuquerque. Throughout Yarberry's short, tumultuous career as a lawman, Sheriff Armijo remained staunchly loyal to his friend, right up to the moment when they stood together in the jail yard and Armijo gave the signal that ended Yarberry's life.

Trouble dogged Yarberry's trail and soon appeared again, this time in the person of Harry A. Brown, a twenty-four-year-old member of a distinguished Tennessee family. Brown's father, Neill Smith Brown, and his uncle, John Calvin Brown, had both served as governor of Tennessee. Seeking adventure, Harry Brown in 1876 went west and took a job guarding valuable shipments for the Adams Express

Company. He was aboard a Santa Fe express car in January 1878 when an outlaw band led by Dave Rudabaugh attempted a train robbery at Kinsley, Kansas. Brown played a minor role in thwarting the holdup, but later magnified that part, bragging in saloons along the line how he had single-handedly saved the treasure and killed three bandits in the process. At Albuquerque he had a reputation as a hard drinker, a quarrelsome sort who was quick to pull a gun.[12]

Young Brown caught the eye of Sadie Preston, who had left her husband to accompany Yarberry to Albuquerque, and soon Yarberry joined Tony Preston on the list of Sadie's former lovers. Brown and Yarberry exchanged angry words over the matter and threats were made.

On the evening of March 27, 1881, Brown and Sadie went to dinner at Girard's Restaurant. As later events would indicate, the brazen Mrs. Preston had left her little daughter with Yarberry, using his services as a baby-sitter while she enjoyed the company of Brown. The couple arrived at Girard's in a hack driven by a man named John Clark. Waiting in his hack, Clark was the only witness to what happened next. The couple entered the restaurant, but Brown quickly reappeared and stood outside the door. Yarberry, holding the hand of Sadie's little girl, walked up the street a few minutes later. He took the child in the restaurant and then came out to where Brown was standing. The two men engaged in an increasingly heated discussion as they walked slowly toward a nearby vacant lot. Apparently Yarberry threatened to use the power of his office as constable against Brown, for hack driver Clark, who caught only part of the conversation, heard Brown say: "Milt, I want you to understand I am not afraid of you and would not be even if you were marshal of the United States."

Yarberry testified later that when they reached the empty lot the other man cut loose with "the vilest language he could lay his tongue to." He did not reply in kind, Yarberry said, but watched Brown closely. "He was, I could see, trying hard to get the drop on me."

At this moment Sadie came out of the restaurant and called out to Brown. Yarberry, who had his back to the building, thought her action was a planned ploy designed to distract him long enough for Brown to beat him to the draw. "I did not look round," he said, "and a moment later Brown struck me a blow in the face with his left hand, at the same time drawing his six-shooter with his right, and immediately firing his first shot, grazing my right hand and inflicting a trifling scratch on the thumb. In an instant I realized that I must either kill him or die, and quicker than it takes to tell, I whipped out my gun and began firing." Clark said he saw Yarberry pump two bullets into Brown's chest and two more into his body after he fell to the ground.

Sheriff Armijo soon arrived at the scene and took Yarberry into custody. After several witnesses testified at a preliminary hearing that Brown had publicly announced his intention to kill his rival for Sadie's affections on sight, Yarberry was cleared.[13]

Many in Albuquerque expressed dissatisfaction with the verdict. A newspaper editor in Santa Fe complained: "Yarberry, who killed Brown in Albuquerque not long since, has been acquitted on the ground of self-defense. From what we can learn of the affair, it seems to be murder in the first degree and called for hanging. There was some talk of lynching, but better counsel prevailed and the felon escaped. Crime is sometimes punished in Albuquerque, but it is generally done by parties unknown to the coroner's jury."[14]

A grand jury meeting in Albuquerque in May 1881 took heed of the mounting protests and brought in a murder indictment against Yarberry. But at a trial that month his attorney, S. M. Barnes, again produced the parade of witnesses who testified to hearing Brown's threats, and the jury acquitted Yarberry on May 19.[15]

Less than a month later Yarberry killed again. On the sultry summer evening of Saturday, June 18, 1881, he was sitting on a bench in front of the house of his friend Elwood Maden, conversing with a gambler named "Monte Frank" Boyd, when a shot rang out. The sound seemed to come from the crowded restaurant of R. H. Greenleaf around the corner. Constable Yarberry, accompanied by Boyd, headed in that direction. "Who fired that shot?" Yarberry asked a bystander. The man pointed to a figure rapidly walking away. The constable and the gambler followed.

"Stop there, I want you!" Yarberry called out.

Testimony conflicts as to what happened next, but seconds later a man named Charles D. Campbell lay dead on Front Street with three bullet holes in his body.

Campbell, like Harry Brown, was a native of Tennessee. Coming west in 1875 he was something of a jack-of-all-trades. He had hunted buffalo, worked in the mines, and operated a restaurant at Deming.

More recently he had worked as a carpenter for bridge-building contractors in New Mexico. Acquaintances described him as a quiet, inoffensive man, whose only vice was a taste for whiskey.

Sheriff Armijo arrested Yarberry and Boyd and locked them up in the jail. "Great excitement prevails in Albuquerque," a Santa Fe newspaper reported, "and the feeling against the men, who were certainly not justified in shooting poor Campbell down like a dog, is very strong. The air is filled with threats of lynching so an unusually heavy guard has been placed over the prisoners."[16]

At the coroner's hearing Constable Yarberry advanced the time-honored claim of self-defense. He said that Campbell had refused to comply with his order to halt and had turned and shot at him. He had returned the fire only to protect his own life. Physicians who attended the deceased, however, testified that Campbell died from the effects of three bullets, all of which struck him in the back. Others said they saw the constable continue to fire at the man after he fell to the ground. The coroner's jury found that Campbell had died at the hands of Yarberry and Boyd, but the question of possible criminality went unanswered, pending a preliminary hearing.

The town buzzed with talk of the killing all day Sunday. Rumors that Yarberry had been lynched were telegraphed to newspapers across the territory.[17] A newspaper described Campbell's burial on Monday morning as "the largest and most impressive funeral ever known in Albuquerque. A very large number of railroad hands were present and almost the entire male population of the town was in attendance."[18] After the procession to the cemetery, the mourners held an indignation meeting where many called for an immediate lynching. Calmer leaders succeeded in getting an adjournment until the afternoon in the hope that tempers would cool. An even larger crowd gathered at one o'clock, and again the lynch cry went up. After lengthy debate the throng adopted a series of resolutions. Following a statement condemning law enforcement practices in Albuquerque, the attendees demanded that Yarberry resign as constable and be dismissed as deputy sheriff. They directed Sheriff Armijo to arrest and jail both Yarberry and Boyd immediately. An appointed committee went with Armijo to see that the directives were carried out.[19]

Sheriff Armijo locked up Yarberry, but Boyd had skipped. Frightened by the intense excitement throughout the town over the killing, he had boarded a westbound train on Sunday. Officials distributed broadsides for him, but Albuquerque never saw him again. Sixteen months later he reportedly met the end of the trail in Arizona. After he murdered an unarmed Navajo near Holbrook on October 5, 1882, forty armed and angry tribesmen hunted him down and riddled him with rifle fire.[20]

At a preliminary hearing into the death of Charles Campbell on July 5, 1881, Alcalde (Mayor) Martin bound Milt Yarberry over for the grand jury, not scheduled to meet until May 1882. In a move as much designed to forestall a lynching as to prevent an escape, Sheriff Armijo transferred the prisoner to the jail at Santa Fe for his ten-month wait.

The grand jury on May 11, 1882, indicted Yarberry for the Campbell slaying, and his trial before Judge Bell began a week later. New Mexico governor Lionel A. Sheldon, the recipient of a great deal of recent criticism because of the nationally publicized activity of outlaw gangs led by Billy the Kid, John Kinney, and Ike Stockton in the territory, decided to make an example of Milt Yarberry. To show that desperadoes and killers would be dealt with severely in New Mexico, he directed his attorney general, William Breedon, to take personal charge of the Yarberry case, with District Attorney Arnet R. Owen assisting. Jose Francisco Chaves, I. S. Trimble, and John H. Knaebel represented Yarberry.

At the three-day trial, the prosecution presented a straightforward case refuting the defendant's claim of self-defense. No one other than Yarberry could be found who saw Campbell fire at the defendant. Witnesses testified that no gun was found near the body. The victim had died from three bullets in the back. The conclusion seemed clear: Yarberry murdered Campbell in cold blood. Perhaps the testimony of Thomas W. Parks, an attorney from Platt City, Nebraska, who said he saw the whole affair, provided the most damaging evidence against Yarberry. Parks testified that the constable advanced on Campbell, ordered him to hold up his hands, and immediately began firing. He insisted there was no weapon in Campbell's hands.

Other than a few witnesses who attempted to blacken the victim's character, depicting him as a desperate character—one claimed Campbell killed a Chinese at Deming and another that he bit off a man's nose in a Silver City brawl—the defense relied on Yarberry's testimony on the stand. He swore that when ordered to stop, Campbell turned, drew a revolver, and yelled "Go back!" Yarberry said he then ordered the man to raise his hands: "As soon as I said this he began firing at me and I returned it without much delay. I only hit him once. . . . The other shots were fired by Boyd who was some yards to my left and the bullets from his six-shooter struck Campbell in the back. My shot struck him in the right side. . . . I killed him, or shot at him—for no one knows whether my shot or Boyd's killed him—because I know he meant to kill me."

Members of the jury did not believe him. After only ten minutes of deliberation, they brought in a verdict of murder in the first degree. On May 23 Judge Bell sentenced Yarberry to death by hanging and set June 16 as the execution date. The next day defense lawyers filed an appeal, and the judge granted a stay of execution pending a New Mexico Supreme Court review of the case.[21]

The return of Yarberry to the confines of the Santa Fe jail elicited this grumbling comment from a local paper: "Bernalillo County has a very interesting way of unloading the burden of supporting its criminals upon the shoulders of Santa Fe County, giving as an excuse the lack of a secure jail at Albuquerque. Yesterday Milt Yarberry was unloaded at the door of this jail and had to be admitted. . . . He does not evince great uneasiness [and] has taken an appeal to the Supreme Court. There will be no June term of the court and he will have until next January or longer on this terrestrial orb."[22]

On the night of September 9, 1882, Milt Yarberry and three other prisoners escaped from the supposedly "secure" jail at Santa Fe. Together with a holdup man named Harris, George Pease, a wife murderer, and Billy Wilson, a counterfeiter and compadre of Billy the Kid, Yarberry used a smuggled file to cut through his shackles. The four men then surprised the guard, Juan Pablo Domingues, threw a blanket over his head, and tied him up. Making their way to the roof of the building, they escaped into the darkness as other guards fired several ineffectual shots in their direction. Officers nabbed Pease within hours, but the others managed to get out of town.[23]

Santa Fe County sheriff Romulo Martinez, Chief of Police Frank Chavez, and Deputy U.S. Marshal Tony Neis organized posses to scour the countryside for the escapees. Governor Sheldon posted a $500 reward for the capture of Yarberry, considered to be the most important of the fugitives. Yarberry enjoyed only three days of freedom.

On September 12 a posse led by Frank Chavez captured him in an arroyo twenty-eight miles from town and returned him to jail. "Yarberry Yanked," proclaimed a headline. A reporter who visited the prisoner in his cell found him despondent, his spirits crushed by "having all the world against him and being hunted like a wild animal."[24]

Yarberry spent the next five uneventful months in the Santa Fe jail awaiting a decision on his appeal. On January 25, 1883, the New Mexico Supreme Court ruled, denying his claim. That same day Governor Sheldon issued a death warrant, directing Sheriff Armijo to take Yarberry "to some safe and convenient place" between the hours of 11:00 A.M. and 3:00 P.M. on Friday, February 9, 1883, and "there hang the said Milton J. Yarberry, or cause him to be hung by the neck until he is dead."[25]

As attorney John Knaebel dispatched wires to high government officials in Washington in a desperate effort to save his client, Sheriff Armijo prepared for the hanging. He obtained a rope one and a half inches thick and soaked and stretched it to half that diameter. Announcing that he would hang Yarberry by the "jerk plan," rather than the traditional trapdoor method, he enclosed the jail yard with a six-foot fence and began construction of a gallows. Flanking a low platform he erected two fifteen-foot uprights connected to a cross-beam. The rope ran from its noosed end upward to a pulley midway on the beam, thence along the beam to another pulley, and down to an enclosure where it was tied to a 400-pound weight. A smaller cord held the weight suspended six feet above the ground. When the executioner cut the cord the weight would plunge to the ground and the condemned man at the other end of the rope would be snapped suddenly upward. A newspaper called the "scaffold for jerking Yarberry into eternity a model of scientific skill, being of the improved pattern used in all well regulated hanging bees." His preparations completed, Armijo sent out a hundred invitations to witness the bizarre event.[26]

Interviewed in his cell at Santa Fe two days before the execution, Yarberry put on a bold front, saying he had confidence in lawyer Knaebel's ability to obtain a last-minute stay.

"How is your health?" the reporter asked. "The Albuquerque papers say you are too weak to escape if you were turned loose."

"Oh, I'm feeling first rate," Yarberry replied. "Take my meals regular. Do I look like a man who is sick or scared?"

"You look pale."

"That may be, but I ain't sick and I ain't scared either. Hell, I wouldn't get scared if they walked me out on the scaffold right now."

To demonstrate his steely nerves, he picked up his fiddle and tore through several choruses of "Old Zip Coon."[27]

Despite Yarberry's bravado, his jailers said he was noticeably depressed and asked repeatedly for liquor. They were giving him a bottle a day. "Whiskey is all that keeps me up. I would break down without it," he confessed to Sheriff Martinez.[28]

As dawn broke over Santa Fe on February 9, a detachment of New Mexico militia, the Governor's Rifles, under the command of Colonel Max Frost, marched to the jail. They placed Yarberry in an omnibus, conducted him to the depot, and put him on a special one-coach train bound for Albuquerque. Four reporters, Sheriff Mason T. Bowman of Colfax County, a Dr. Symington, and Colonel Frost and his militiamen accompanied the condemned man on his final journey. Several times during the three hour and twenty minute trip Bowman granted Yarberry's request for whiskey. However, when Yarberry asked the Colfax County sheriff to take Perfecto Armijo's place on the gallows so that his good friend would not have to hang him, Bowman politely declined.[29]

A crowd of 1,500 was on hand when the train arrived at Albuquerque. Sheriff Armijo and the Albuquerque Guards, another militia company, took formal custody of the prisoner and conveyed him by horsecar to the jail. At Yarberry's request, Father S. J. Personne came to his cell and performed a baptismal ceremony, accepting him into the Catholic faith. The prisoner had arrived wearing a worn and wrinkled brown suit and a frayed shirt with no collar. Friends coming to say their good-byes brought him a new suit of black broadcloth, a white shirt with turndown collar, a black cravat, and a black slouch hat. For his last meal Yarberry placed an extraordinary order: cranberry pie, a pint of whiskey, and a bottle of ale.

The governor's death warrant had specified that Yarberry must hang by three o'clock; Sheriff Armijo allowed his friend every possible minute. At a quarter to three the militia formed a double line from the jailhouse door to the waiting gallows. Yarberry, wearing his new suit, with his arms tied to his sides, emerged and in his distinctive shuffling gait passed between the ranks. Sheriff Armijo, two deputies, four doctors, and Father Personne followed in the somber procession. On the platform the deputies bound Yarberry's legs and placed the noose around his neck. After Deputy Howe read the death warrant, Armijo asked Yarberry if he had anything to say.[30]

Yarberry looked out over the crowd, twisted his head to view the hundreds more that covered the roofs of nearby buildings, and began a rambling harangue about the men he had gunned down in Albuquerque. He started with the Harry Brown killing. "Well, Milt, they are going to hang you," he began. "Yes, they are going to hang you because you killed a son of Governor Brown of Tennessee. . . . Several of my friends told me he had made threats on my life and wanted to kill me and told me to keep out of his way. I told them I didn't want no row with Brown but I wasn't going to hide from him or keep in any back rooms out of his sight. When I did kill him I did it in defense of my life and I was tried and acquitted, but they are determined to hang Milt and they are going to do it."

He then plunged into a recitation of the details of the Campbell shooting, repeating his claim: "He shot at me and I shot back."

At that point, Sheriff Armijo, who had stared intently at his pocket watch throughout the oration, motioned for a deputy to draw the black cap over Yarberry's head. His voice muffled, but clearly audible to the assembly, Yarberry called out: "Gentlemen, you are hanging an innocent man!"

Waiting in the enclosure with raised axe was Count Epur, a Polish nobleman who had volunteered to perform the execution. The hands on Armijo's watch pointed to three o'clock. He snapped shut the cover, a signal to Count Epur. The axe fell, the weight dropped, and the body of Milton J. Yarberry shot high in the air. Spectators distinctly head the crack as his neck broke. His head struck the crossbeam and then his body dropped back and swung slowly without a perceptible shudder. The doctors cut him down and examined the body. For a short time his pulse accelerated from 100 to 184 beats per minute, but at nine minutes past three there was no pulse and the doctors pronounced Yarberry dead.

Father Personne and some of Yarberry's friends placed the body, the noose still around the neck, in a plain wooden coffin and removed

Nothing seemed to turn out right for Yarberry. Even his gravestone had his name spelled incorrectly. From the author's collection.

it to the Catholic cemetery for burial. The man's earthly possessions consisted only of the threadbare clothes he wore when he arrived from Santa Fe that day.[31]

Even in death Yarberry remained a controversial figure. He still had his supporters in Albuquerque. Perfecto Armijo never wavered in his defense of the man. After the hanging he told a reporter, "Yarberry should have been rewarded instead of punished for killing [Brown and Campbell]." They were, he said, "desperadoes of the worst type and their deaths a blessing to the people of Albuquerque. Yarberry acted exactly right in both instances and should not have been hung." Elwood Maden said sadly, "Well, he is gone. I tried hard to save him, but without avail." When asked about their friend, Charles Zeigler argued heatedly that Yarberry killed both Brown and Campbell in discharge of his duty as an officer, and Al Conners admitted breaking down completely when he said goodbye to Yarberry in his cell.

However, most influential men in Albuquerque were convinced Yarberry got his just desserts. Wholesale liquor dealer W. E. Talbot did not for a moment believe Yarberry's self-defense claim, but thought a sentence of life imprisonment would have been better than hanging. Attorney William B. Childers thought Yarberry was a desperado who deserved his fate. Colonel Bell, president of the streetcar company, and F. W. Smith, superintendent of the A&P Railroad, agreed.[32]

The editors of the *Santa Fe Daily New Mexican* left no doubt as to where they stood on the question of Yarberry. Their editorial asserted that he lacked "the virtue even of physical courage. His murders were base and cowardly, wanton, cruel and useless." Even compared to his "illustrious prototype," Billy the Kid, he came out looking bad. "But he is dead. Let us wipe out from memory his entire history. Would that we could erase it entirely from the records of the courts and forget that any such man ever lived or ever so polluted the fair history of New Mexico by the commission of a crime so cruel, so cowardly, and so entirely useless. We trust the great Father in the plenitude of his mercy can forgive him. We, the patriotic citizens of New Mexico, never can."[33]

— 5 —

DAN TUCKER
(1849–?)

"Of a shy and retiring disposition"

New Mexico was a violent and dangerous place during the 1870s and 1880s, infested with outlaws and gunmen. Large-caliber lawmen were required to maintain a semblance of order in the territory. Of these, Lincoln County sheriff Pat Garrett would become nationally famous for his destruction of the Billy the Kid Gang, but in New Mexico at the time no officer was held in higher regard than Sheriff Harvey Whitehill of Silver City, Grant County. "Whitehill arrested more culprits than any man in the territory," said no less an authority than New Mexico governor Miguel Otero.[1] An imposing figure, well over six feet tall and 240 pounds, Whitehill served six terms as Grant County sheriff as well as a term in the upper house of the territorial legislature.[2] He was no gunman—he never killed a man and normally did not even carry a weapon—but Whitehill prudently appointed deputies of demonstrated leather-slapping ability to handle the necessary gun work.

Foremost of these fighting men was a young fellow who rode into Silver City in 1875, a few months after Whitehill first took office as sheriff. At first glance the new arrival was as ordinary in appearance as Whitehill was striking. Twenty-six years old, he was described by an early resident as "slim built," fair-haired and blue-eyed, and "of a shy and retiring disposition."[3] Another remembered him as a "rather tall, slender young man [with] blue eyes, light brown hair and mustache." Dressed in "dark sombrero, blue flannel shirt, overalls, and light calf-skin boots,"[4] he was indistinguishable from hundreds of other young men drawn to Silver City by the district's new mining excitement. In a peculiar slow drawl, he said his name was David Tucker, but everybody called him "Dan." A machinist by trade, he was born in Canada, raised in Indiana. He went west and spent some time in Colorado before locating in New Mexico, where he managed a stage station near Fort Selden on the Jornado del Muerto (Journey of Death), a desolate and dangerous stretch of road between El Paso and Santa Fe.[5]

A few eyebrows may have been raised when Sheriff Whitehill pinned a deputy's badge on the soft-spoken newcomer, but already rumors were spreading that Tucker was a dangerous man with a violent past. It was said that he had been forced to leave Colorado after stabbing a black man to death.[6] Others were sure Whitehill had sent for Tucker after hearing of his displays of gun-handling skill in Colorado.

Whatever deeds lay on Dan Tucker's back trail, during his thirteen-year stay in Grant County he would have many opportunities to demonstrate his gunfighting prowess. By November 1881 a newspaperman traveling through Grant County would write that Deputy Sheriff Tucker had, in the course of his duties, dispatched no fewer than eleven bad men.[7] "Dan Tucker informs us," a Silver City paper reported a year later, "that in the course of his duty as deputy sheriff he has been obliged to kill eight men in this county, besides several in Lincoln and Dona Ana counties."[8] Wayne Whitehill, son of the sheriff, said that altogether Tucker killed twenty-one men.[9] Like most of the notch-sticks credited to Western gunfighters, Tucker's has no doubt been overcarved. But there can be little doubt that he was a very dangerous man, and the toughest, deadliest gunman in a very tough district.

"I, myself, saw him kill two different men," Wayne Whitehill recalled in 1949. The first of these shootings took place in 1876 outside of Johnny Ward's dance hall and saloon on Broadway in Silver City after two Mexicans got into a fight. One stabbed the other and "then ran out of the saloon and up the street. Dan Tucker happened to come along. I was standing right beside him. He drew his six-shooter and holding it with both hands fired just as the man turned the corner. The shot hit the Mexican in the neck and killed him instantly."[10]

Dan Rose, a youngster about Wayne's age, also witnessed this incident. Some sixty years later it was still vivid in his memory. The knife-wielding Mexican was running about "50 yards away and barely discernable in the dim light" when Tucker fired. "Spinning like a top," the man screamed and then toppled over, Rose said.[11]

He was dead, but the man he had stabbed, named Belmudas, although virtually disemboweled, still lived. Rose said that he watched while a Dr. Cocharan performed an extraordinary feat of surgery. "The Mexican had been slashed across the abdomen and his intestines were hanging out of his body, touching the ground. The doctor gathered them in his hands, washed and replaced them, then sewed up the wound. The Mexican, Belmudas, lived forty years longer."[12]

The other time Wayne Whitehill personally saw his father's deputy in action resulted from a report that a Mexican was throwing rocks at passersby. "Tucker went to investigate. I trotted after. Tucker just popped him through the window and killed him."[13]

Grant County troublemakers soon learned that Dan Tucker wasted little time in talk. Anyone who would "pop" a man through a window for throwing rocks was a dangerous customer indeed.

Dan Rose recalled other shooting affairs involving Tucker. There was the downing of "a Mexican thief who would not stop to be arrested," and the shooting of three suspected horse thieves in a Silver City saloon. When Tucker opened up with his six-gun, "two of them, mortally wounded, dropped to the bar room floor, while the other, made helpless by a bullet that grazed his skull and his desire to fight all gone, fell . . . by the side of his comrades."[14]

When two men were accused of looting the cabin of a prospector and stealing his money, provisions, weapons, and animals, Tucker took to the trail. He returned two days later, Rose said, with not only the stolen goods, but the horses, saddles, and guns of the suspects. "They didn't want to come back," Tucker told Sheriff Whitehill. "I left them with a rancher; he'll bury them all right."[15]

"Shortly after this incident," Rose relates, "the deputy was called to a house where a Mexican was murdering his wife and son. He had beaten them with a club, and had begun to demolish the furniture when Tucker arrived. Through a window the Mexican saw Tucker coming, and stepped behind the door. As Tucker, with his gun in his hand, entered the door, the Mexican brought his club down on the deputy's arm, knocking the gun to the floor. Quick as a flash Tucker picked up the gun with his left hand and shot the Mexican dead. 'I got him,' he told us afterwards, 'but I'm telling you it was a close shave.'"[16]

Late in 1877 Tucker became involved in the bloody conflict that erupted in the Rio Grande Valley of west Texas and came to be known as the El Paso Salt War. Beginning as an economic and political fight over conflicting claims to the commercially profitable salt beds lying 120 miles east of El Paso, the struggle degenerated into a bloody racial battle between Anglo Texans and Mexican Americans, supported by Mexican nationals. In December 1877 Mexicans killed three Texans in a vicious fight. Three other Texans who surrendered were executed by a Mexican mob at San Elizario. Racial passions were aroused, and neither U.S. troops from Fort Bayard nor a contingent of Texas Rangers seemed able to control the highly volatile situation. To provide assistance, Texas governor Richard Hubbard authorized El Paso County sheriff Charles Kerber to raise a posse of fighting men. Not-too-distant Silver City, New Mexico, was known to be well stocked with tough adventurers who would welcome an opportunity to do battle with Mexicans for forty dollars a month and forage, and it was there that Kerber turned for enlistees.

Dan Tucker was selected as captain, and with the aid of John Kinney, a notorious rustler and outlaw gang leader, he rounded up a platoon of about thirty "hard faced and battle scarred" warriors and headed for El Paso.[17] On December 22 the combined force of U.S. Army troopers, Texas Rangers, and New Mexico mercenaries moved on to San Elizario. There they killed several Mexicans suspected of being members of the mob. A mass exodus across the border into old Mexico followed, and the militant Mexican faction vanished.

The Anglo warriors went into camp at Ysleda. With no enemy to fight, the disparate elements began to turn on each other. "Quite an unfriendly feeling exists between the Rangers and United States troops stationed in El Paso county," understated a Silver City paper.[18] The smoldering enmity broke into violence on New Year's Day, 1878, when First Sergeant J. C. Ford killed Sergeant Fraser. Ten days later Sheriff Kerber disbanded his "posse," and the New Mexico mercenaries headed for home.[19]

In April 1878 Tucker, while still retaining his deputy sheriff commission, accepted appointment as city marshal at Silver City, the first to hold the position. By all accounts, during his several stints as city marshal of the town he kept the rough element under firm control. "Marshall [*sic*] Tucker, under the city government, has put a stop to the discharge of firearms upon our streets," commented a local paper.[20] The city fathers seemed to require an officer to police the town only during the summer months when festive cowboys flooded in. In November 1878 they let Tucker go and then rehired him again the following May.[21] He was still wearing the Silver City star the following December, however, when he narrowly escaped death at the hands of a drunk. "City Marshal Tucker was shot at last Tuesday night by a Mexican known as Carpio Rodriquez," said the *Grant County Herald*. "The ball passed through the marshal's clothing but fortunately did not touch his person. Rodriquez was intoxicated at the time and resisted arrest."[22]

In January 1880 Tucker turned in his municipal badge again to go to Shakespeare, a little town farther south in the county. Shakespeare was enjoying a small mining boom and had quickly become the favorite watering hole for cattle range outlaws and mining camp toughs from both southern New Mexico and eastern Arizona. John Kinney's rustlers and the San Simon outlaw gang of "Curly Bill" Brocious headquartered there. Sheriff Whitehill dispatched his top-gun deputy as a troubleshooter to cool things down a bit.[23]

In July 1880 Tucker caught prospecting fever and participated in a rush to a silver discovery in the Tres Hermanas Mountains. "Deputy Sheriff Tucker left off his official duties but not his guns and, regardless of all lawbreakers who might cross his path, came hurrying down the Old Copper Trail to hunt down the most elusive fugitive of all his experience," wrote another who took part in the rush.[24] The new strike excitement quickly abated, however, and Tucker soon returned to Shakespeare to resume his law-enforcement duties.

His adventures with the outlaws at Shakespeare have gone unrecorded except for his part in the termination of the careers of "Russian Bill"[25] and Sandy King,[26] members of the Curly Bill crowd. In early November 1881, when these two rode up and down the streets shooting off their pistols and making themselves obnoxious, Tucker arrested King and locked him up in the town's flimsy jail. Before he could collar Russian Bill, that worthy stole a horse and headed for Deming. Tucker rode in pursuit, and on November 7 caught the outlaw at

DEADLY DOZEN

Separ. He brought him back to Shakespeare and locked him up with his pal. At two in the morning on November 9 a vigilance committee took Russian Bill and Sandy King to John Evenson's Grant House, Shakespeare's stage station and eating house, and hanged them from the rafters.[27] The outlaws had been condemned to die, it was said, because Russian Bill "stole a horse and Sandy King was just a damned nuisance."[28] According to a newspaper report, "King died game, not deigning to open his mouth or say a word in his own defense. [Russian Bill] wanted to talk [but the mob] jerked him up with his words in his mouth."[29]

Dan Tucker participated in several legal hangings at Silver City. In August 1880 he assisted Sheriff Whitehill in a double hanging: the executions of Charles Williams (aka Barney O'Tool), convicted of a Georgetown murder, and Louis Gaines, the slayer of a fellow soldier at Fort Bayard. Williams was white and Gaines black, and integration of the two races was not popular in New Mexico in the 1880s, even on the scaffold. For scheduling the executions together, Whitehill came under intense verbal fire and threats of more deadly bombardment. But he and Tucker carried out the hangings without incident.[30] The following March Tucker assisted Sheriff Whitehill in the execution of Richard Remine. Four years earlier, Remine, in a drunken rage, had committed a particularly atrocious murder, hacking his partner to death with an axe as he slept in bed, and then crawling into bed beside the body of his victim to sleep off his brutal binge.[31] He had been convicted and condemned to death, but appeals delayed his execution until March 14, 1881. On that afternoon Whitehill and Tucker led Remine to the scaffold that had been erected outside the jail. As reported in the *Grant County Herald*, in a brief statement Remine said "that during the four years he had been in confinement he had been treated with uniform kindness by Sheriff Whitehill and his deputies. The Sheriff and Deputy Tucker stood upon the scaffold until the drop fell. . . . The body remained hanging some twenty minutes, when life was pronounced extinct."[32]

The double hanging at Shakespeare discouraged the outlaw element from convening there. The railroad town of Deming next became Grant County's meanest trouble spot. A gaggle of about forty shacks and shanties squatting near the newly laid Southern Pacific tracks, Deming drew toughs from all directions. Journalist C. M. Chase, stopping in Deming on November 27, 1881, wrote: "The cow-boys, or roughs and thieves, are so numerous that no man ventures any distance from the village without his Winchester rifle, ready to repeat 12 or 16 times without reloading. With this element constantly on the watch for plunder, a man's life goes for naught."[33]

Dan Tucker, Sheriff Whitehill's troubleshooting deputy, was dispatched to this new hellhole. "He was certainly the right man," said a visitor to Deming, "for if he wanted to arrest a desperado he was sure to either arrest or kill him." Tucker patrolled the streets with a double-barreled shotgun under his arm and, according to one report, within three days had killed three men and wounded two others.[34] In less than three weeks he arrested and jailed thirteen members of "the cowboy gang."[35]

As early as September 1881 Tucker had killed Jack (or Jake) Bond, a rustler from the San Simon Valley of Arizona. In order to break up a rustling gang operating between Deming and El Paso, Texas Ranger captain George W. Baylor had enlisted Bond and another outlaw named Chris Peveler[36] as spies, but the two soon proved unreliable and he discharged them both. Bond and Peveler promptly stole a pair of El Paso mayor Joseph McGoffin's fine carriage horses and fled to Mexico.

They turned up later in Deming and, joined by another of their kind, set out to hurrah the town. Yelling like wild Indians and firing their pistols, the three rode their horses through the office of the railroad hotel and into the dining room, scattering a crowd of men and women recently arrived on the train. As they emerged from the building, Bond dismounted,

> threw his Winchester rifle across the saddle and leveled it at the office. Just at this juncture [Tucker] appeared upon the scene . . . with a double-barreled shotgun and ordered Bond to throw up his hands. The command was not heeded and without further parleying the officer fired, landing nine buckshot in Bond's body. [The outlaw] instantly fell to the ground a corpse. The other two, seeing the fate of their comrade in crime, sought safety in flight, followed by a shower of bullets. It is not known whether or not either of them were injured. . . . [Deputy] Sheriff Tucker deserves great credit for courage in tackling the demons and but for his timely appearance they would have run the town

to suit themselves. The only thing to be regretted is the fact that the other two desperadoes did not share the fate that so fortunately befell their companion.[37]

According to another newspaper account, after Tucker shot Bond, "Peveler screamed and shoved both hands into the air just as Tucker unloaded the second barrel. Fortunately, the deputy twisted his gun aside at the last second and the buckshot buried itself in the wall, narrowly missing Peveler.[38] C. M. Chase visited Deming shortly after the shooting and said that the effect of Tucker's shotgun blast was plainly evident on the dining room door where it was "a reminder of Deming customs."[39]

The dead outlaw's body was carried a short distance out of town and buried without ceremony. Journalist Chase commented that Bond was "indebted to Deputy Sheriff Tucker for his change of abode, and ten other roughs are similarly indebted to that officer, who is still in the harness, and promises to rid the locality of the hateful element before long." Chase lamented the fact that men like Dan Tucker were in short supply: "What is needed in southern New Mexico is one or two such officers in every village, and traveling on every train. The great trouble is that too many officers are, for consideration or otherwise, in collusion with the roughs, and are conspicuously absent in the gambling hells and dance houses about the time the shooting begins.[40]

Reports reached Silver City from time to time that Dan Tucker had been bested in one of his gun battles. "There was a rumor on the streets yesterday that Deputy Sheriff Tucker had been shot and killed at Deming, but we were unable to have it confirmed," said the *Grant County New Southwest* of October 29, 1881. The *El Paso Lone Star* repeated the rumor a few days later but placed Tucker's demise at Benson, Arizona Territory.[41] There was no truth to the story, and the *Lone Star* could soon report that "Deputy Sheriff Tucker of Deming keeps that town free of rough characters."[42] In February 1882 he ran a gang of bunco men out of town,[43] and a few days later was back in Silver City to tell Sheriff Whitehill he was no longer needed in Deming. "Deputy Sheriff Tucker is in town and reports everything quiet in Deming," said the *New Southwest* of February 25, 1882.

Tucker augmented his income as deputy sheriff by riding shotgun on the Silver City to Deming stagecoach run. Recalled James H.

Cook, who came to southwestern New Mexico in 1882 to manage the WS Ranch near Alma: "The WS Ranch was at that time some distance from the railroad, Deming being the nearest railway point. A stage ran to Silver City each day, drawn by six horses. . . . One of the Wells, Fargo & Company's most noted shotgun messengers, Dan Tucker, helped guard the passengers and treasure carried by the stages. Tucker had some thrilling experiences with stage robbers in the Southwest. He had the reputation of being one of the bravest of the many gun-fighters of the southwest borderlands. Guarding treasure entrusted to the care of Wells, Fargo & Company was a pretty hazardous occupation in that bandit-infested country at that time."[44]

Later that year Tucker became embroiled in the most controversial incident of his law-enforcement career, a shooting involving no less than five peace officers or former officers. On Thursday, August 24, 1882, James D. Burns, a deputy sheriff from the Grant County mining camp at Paschal, rode into Silver City and went on a monumental drunk. He first attracted the attention of other officers that afternoon when he "made some show of his revolver,"[45] fast-drawing and twirling it in front of the Walcott & Mills saloon. Deputy Sheriff Cornelius A. Mahoney attempted to disarm him, but Burns refused to surrender his weapon, saying that as an officer he was entitled to carry it. Later City Marshal Glaudius W. Moore also threatened to arrest Burns if he continued to flourish his pistol. The Burns binge extended into the afternoon of the next day when he picked a fight with a man named Kerr in Sam Eckstein's saloon and at gunpoint drove him out of the establishment. Later in the evening he stopped in front of George H. Bell's Centennial Saloon and fired his pistol, evidently just to enjoy the sound. Hitching "his revolver around in front of his belt so that he would be able to pull it readily when he needed it,"[46] Burns walked through the barroom of the Centennial to the gaming rooms presided over by the house gambler Frank Thurmond.[47]

Marshal Moore, investigating the gunshot, found Burns seated at Thurmond's monte table. Also at the table were John W. Gilmo, former deputy sheriff at Paschal, and Dan Tucker. Marshal Moore told Burns he wanted to talk to him and asked him to step outside. Burns snapped that he would not leave the table until the game was completed. Moore then pulled his pistol and demanded that Burns surrender his weapon. "Go away, I have done nothing," Burns said.[48]

Centennial Saloon in Silver City, New Mexico. Site of Dan Tucker's
most controversial shooting scrape. Courtesy of the Silver City
Museum, John Harlan Collection.

Trying to ease the tension, John Gilmo implored Moore to holster
his pistol. The marshal complied, but immediately Burns leaped to his
feet, drew his own pistol, and stated emphatically that he would not
stand for arrest. Now Dan Tucker, behind Burns, made his move,
pulling his six-shooter and leveling it at the embattled deputy. With
Tucker having the drop on him and Gilmo reassuring him that he
would spend no time in jail, as someone could be found to go his
bonds, Burns put down his revolver. Marshal Moore went back outside
where he was joined by Deputy Sheriff William J. McClellan. The two
officers set out to obtain an arrest warrant for Burns.

Meanwhile in the back room of the Centennial Burns upbraided Tucker for involving himself in the earlier confrontation, while John Gilmo attempted to moderate the quarrel. Burns was still fuming when Moore and McClellan, having secured their warrant, entered the room by the rear door. They held revolvers in their hands, concealed under their coats. "Give up your gun. I have papers for you," McClellan told Burns.[49]

What then transpired is confused by conflicting testimony. According to early newspaper reports, Burns whipped out his pistol and fired a shot, hitting no one, and Tucker was the first to react. "The shot had hardly left his pistol before Tucker returned the fire, hitting Burns in the left ribs, just below the heart. The percussion from these two shots, fired almost simultaneously, extinguished all the lamps. McClellan then fired one shot and Moore four shots in rapid succession at Burns, every shot taking effect. The death of Burns must have been almost instantaneous."[50]

After hearing testimony the next morning, a coroner's jury concluded "that Tucker's shot had missed Burns, and that Wm. McClellan and G. W. Moore had caused his death."[51] At a later court hearing the verdict of the coroner's jury was upheld. Moore and McClellan were released to await the December session of the district court, and "as the principal accessories to the killing were dismissed, the prosecution decided not to bring any action against Tucker."[52]

James Burns had been very popular at Paschal, and indignant miners there held a protest meeting on August 30. A Silver City paper reported on "the best possible authority" that the meeting was called "to make arrangements for lynching the officers implicated in the affair." They would have carried out their designs "had not a gentleman arrived who persuaded them to adopt a more sensible plan of subscribing money to help prosecute the men." The miners finally drew up and published a resolution condemning the "cowardly, premeditated killing." Fearful that the killers would "go unpunished because of a lack of prosecution and because of the protection given them by unprincipled persons in authority," they declared their "intention to assist in prosecuting said murderers with all our ability and means."[53]

At Silver City on September 3 an attempt was made to arrest Moore and McClellan on a warrant issued by a Paschal judge, but, fearing a lynch mob in that hostile camp, they refused arrest. They went instead to Central City, where McClellan had been stationed and Burns was unknown, and surrendered to "Deputy Sheriff Baldonado, who summoned a large posse of Mexicans to defend the prisoners in case of any danger."[54]

Although it had earlier been reported that no charges would be brought against Tucker, he was also arrested and jailed with his fellow officers at Central City. A Silver City paper reported that the town experienced "no little excitement" on September 9 when Tucker, Moore, and McClellan arrived back from Central City, "heavily chained and under a strong guard," to be committed to jail without bond to await grand jury action.[55] The *El Paso Lone Star* noted that "in the course of his duty as deputy sheriff of Grant County, Dan Tucker killed eight men in that county and several in Lincoln," but this was "the first time he has ever been called to account."[56]

Authorities later released Tucker on $2,000 bond, and eventually dropped all charges in his case. By early October he had resumed riding shotgun on the Silver City to Deming stagecoach run. Lawyers for Moore and McClellan secured a change of venue, and at a trial held at Las Cruces on March 26, 1883, a jury acquitted both.[57]

The shooting in the Centennial Saloon on the night of August 25, 1882, was viewed by citizens of Silver City and Grant County as a sordid affair that revealed their peace officers as less than admirable characters. At least one contended that Moore, who hated and feared Burns, enlisted McClellan and Tucker to assist him in the cold-blooded assassination of the deputy from Paschal.[58] The later history of some of the principals tended to confirm this conclusion.

While still wearing a deputy's star, Bill McClellan was accused of rustling. Before he came to trial he got drunk, was thrown from his horse, and died.[59]

After being deposed as city marshal, G. W. Moore drifted up into Colorado, where he was reportedly killed in a shooting scrape a year later.[60]

John Gilmo, who had earlier killed a man in Silver City, ended up in Arizona. There he shot a man and was sentenced to four years in the Yuma prison for assault and attempted murder.[61]

The reputations of Sheriff Whitehill and his chief deputy, Dan Tucker, suffered as a result of the Burns shooting. Dan Coomer, a leading rancher of the region, remarking on Sheriff Whitehill's deputy appointments, said: "He had but one good deputy that I know of, and that was Tucker."[62] However, others in Grant County were not so sure the soft-spoken deputy with the quick gun was any better than his discredited fellow officers. In a letter to an El Paso paper, a Grant County resident said: "The general opinion here is that Tucker, as other of our officers, was disposed to use his pistol too freely and did not put a sufficient value on the average citizen's life."[63]

Whitehill was up for election the November following the controversial shooting, and he went down to defeat. Of course all his deputies, including Tucker, were discharged and replaced by men chosen by J. B. Woods, Whitehill's successor. Tucker continued his work as Wells, Fargo & Company shotgun messenger.

On December 14 he was almost killed in a Mexican brothel at Deming. According to newspaper reports, when he entered the house, "two women threw their arms around him. Thinking they were playing, Tucker struggled gently to free himself." But while he was being held, "a man jumped behind him and pulled his revolver from the scabbard on his belt. Tucker at once threw himself upon the man and a hand-to-hand conflict ensued. Tucker secured the weapon for a moment and fired it. Owing to his adversary's struggles, he missed, but slightly wounded one of the women. The other Mexicans present flung themselves upon him and the man with whom he was fighting secured the weapon and shot him in the shoulder, shattering the bone and inflicting a very painful wound. Some Americans, attracted by the noise, entered the house and prevented Tucker from being massacred."

This account, published a week after the incident, said that Tucker was "out of danger although still suffering considerably from his injuries."[64] Another Silver City paper, published two days later, said there were "conflicting stories" about the affair and it was "difficult to gather any particulars," but evidently Tucker "fell among those unfriendly to him." This account said that "two shots were fired at Tucker, one striking him in the arm, and the other, somewhere about the face, inflicting painful but not serious injuries."[65]

Dan Rose recalled that Tucker took a layoff from his messenger job and recuperated in Silver City. A bullet, he said, had broken a rib under Tucker's right arm and lodged under the skin of his back. At first Tucker planned on going east for medical attention, but before he left a new doctor arrived in town and successfully treated his wounds.[66]

One of the legends that spring up about characters like Dan Tucker grew out of this mending period. Dan Rose, who put it in print, said that several (three or four—Rose gave both figures) hardcase trouble-makers posted a note claiming Tucker was leaving town because he "had a streak of yeller" and knew that if he stayed they would "hang his hide." On hearing of this scurrility, Tucker is said to have arisen from his sick bed and sought out the men. "With his face drawn from constant pain, but still creased with its habitual slow, drawn smile, and his body bent to ease the pain, he stood menacingly before them" and ordered them out of town. The bad men looked into his "piercing blue eyes" and the hand hovering near his gun butt, mumbled something about a joke, and slunk off.[67]

His wounds healed, but Tucker found that he could no longer bear the daily jouncing stagecoach journey. He took a job as Special Officer for the Southern Pacific Railroad, finding rail travel much easier on his aging and battle-scarred body. He was acting in this capacity in November 1883 when he led a posse in pursuit of bandits who derailed and looted a Southern Pacific train and killed the engineer near Gage Station, fifteen miles west of Deming, on November 24, 1883.[68]

The following month he assisted Captain J. B. Hume of Wells Fargo in the arrest of York Kelly in Deming. Kelly was one of the gang who held up the Bisbee, Arizona, merchandising and banking firm of Castaneda & Company on December 7 and escaped after the brutal murders of three men and a woman eight months pregnant. Tucker and Hume arranged for the return of Kelly to Cochise County where he and four confederates were tried, convicted, and hanged the following March.[69]

By 1884 the indefatigable Tucker was involved in a variety of endeavors. He had taken employment as a cattle inspector for Grant County[70] and was also in the saloon business. "Old Dan Tucker has christened his new saloon at Deming 'The Eclipse,'" reported the *Southwest Sentinel* of May 31. "[He] has opened the corner saloon fronting the depot. . . . Tuck has many friends and is certain to do a good business. Visitors from Silver City may be relied on to drop in on him." Later that year he was a member of the Deming delegation to the Grant County Democratic convention. Together with a woman who called herself Maria Tucker, although there is no record that they were married, he was running a rooming house in Deming.[71] With the election of Grover Cleveland, a Democrat, to the presidency in 1884, jobs opened up for Democrats across the country, and in September 1885 Tucker received appointment as deputy U.S. marshal for Grant County.[72] He pinned on still another badge the following year when he was elected constable in Deming.[73]

With all his various duties Tucker still found time to do a little prospecting. One excursion in November 1885 almost cost him his life. Near Zuni siding, eleven miles east of Deming, he and a prospecting companion named William Graham ran into an Apache war party. In their buckboard, with the Indians in pursuit, they made a run for the railroad siding. There they took cover in a boxcar. Armed only with six-shooters, they held off the Apache warriors, who circled for some time, staying just beyond pistol range, before riding off.[74]

In October 1887 Tucker made an unusual arrest, nabbing a wanted fugitive as he walked beside the track while Tucker himself was aboard a moving train. As recounted in the *Deming Headlight*, Tucker had been on the lookout for a man named Dave Thurman, who had jumped bail in Sierra County on a horse-stealing charge. Expecting the fugitive to head for El Paso, Tucker had gone there but failed to locate his quarry. On his return trip he was in the engine cab when he spotted his man plodding alongside the track. Tucker had the engineer slow the train, "and before Mr. Thurman realized the situation, he had to make a choice between a bullet and surrender. He chose the latter, and is now safe in the Hillsboro jail."[75]

Shortly after this Tucker left Grant County, bound for California. He was reported to be a resident of Los Angeles when he made a visit to his old New Mexico haunts in May of 1892. "Dan Tucker, one of the best peace officers Grant County ever had, returned recently from California, and has been in Silver City during the present week, renewing acquaintances with old friends," announced the *Silver City Enterprise*. "He has grown so fleshy that his friends hardly knew him."[76]

When Harvey Whitehill died at Deming, September 8, 1906, he was honored and extolled for his service as sheriff of Grant County during those early, turbulent years. None of the laudatory accounts mentioned Dan Tucker, Whitehill's gunslick, troubleshooting deputy, who had contributed so much to the sheriff's success and who later reportedly died, his exploits forgotten, in a county hospital in San Bernardino.[77]

— 6 —

GEORGE GOODELL
(1853–1934)

"Laboring under great mental excitement"

Only dimly remembered by Western historians today and completely unknown to the general public is George Goodell, a small, wiry, red-headed man who, while wearing the peace officer's star in Kansas, Colorado, Washington, and Indian Territory, dispatched at least four men with his deadly six-shooter.

Born in Vermont in 1853 or 1854,[1] the son of chairmaker George F. Goodell and wife Lucy of Jamaica, Windham County, Vermont,[2] he came West with the railroad. In 1872 the west-stretching steel rails of the Atchison, Topeka & Santa Fe reached a little town in the center of the Kansas buffalo ranges that would later become famous as Dodge City. The great buffalo slaughter was just reaching its peak, and Goodell, together with many other AT&SF employees and construction workers, deserted the road to join in the lucrative enterprise. Here he met the Masterson brothers, Ed, Bat, and Jim, who were also working the buffalo ranges and would a few years later become the top-dog lawmen at Dodge. The Mastersons would become his idols and mentors and lead him into the dangerous work of frontier law enforcement and its concomitance, gunfighting.

By 1878, with the great hide-hunting bonanza over, Goodell was again working off and on for the railroad as a brakeman and sometime conductor, but he never strayed far from Dodge. The little community straddling the tracks of the AT&SF in western Kansas was now a cow town, the end of the longhorn trail from Texas, and fast gaining national notoriety as the "Beautiful Bibulous Babylon of the Plains."[3] Goodell's friends, the Masterson brothers, were the law in Dodge. Bat was sheriff of vast Ford County, headquartered in the town, Ed was city marshal, and young Jim took temporary appointments from his older brothers as deputy county sheriff or special city policeman.

Goodell, like Jim Masterson, also accepted law enforcement work whenever the opportunity arose. Married now to a girl named Addie, he became a father in 1878 when son George H. was born.[4] That year also saw Goodell's first mention in the papers as an officer, but the circumstances of that mention were embarrassing.

Sheriff Masterson had arrested two confidence operators, Bill Bell and "The Handsome Kid," and locked them up in the county jail. To assist his regular deputy and jailer, Bill Duffey, in guarding the prisoners, he enlisted the services of Red Goodell. During his watch Goodell evidently fell asleep, and the two con men escaped.

"The guard was not vigilant," said the *Dodge City Times*, "and while 'Red' was indulging in nature's sweet restorer, the prisoners saw the opportunity to escape justice and boldly 'lit out,' taking the 5 o'clock morning train for the west."[5]

"Who is 'Red'?" the *Ford County Globe* demanded to know. "Does anybody know him?" The paper suggested that perhaps he was one of the confidence gang and had finagled the jailer job for the sole purpose of aiding his friends in their escape.[6] Shady collaboration between confidence men and law officers was not uncommon in frontier towns— Goodell would later accuse Pat Desmond, the noted city marshal at Pueblo, Colorado, of "standing in" with a confidence gang led by J. J. Harlan, infamous throughout the West as the "Offwheeler"[7]—but there is no solid evidence that either Goodell or Desmond actively took part in this corruption.

Goodell's animosity toward Desmond may have stemmed from the Royal Gorge War of 1879 when they were on opposite sides. Goodell was one of the gunmen enlisted at Dodge City by Bat Masterson to defend the interests of the AT&SF in the railroad struggle, and Desmond was a leader of the Denver & Rio Grande forces.[8]

Drunken cowboys murdered Ed Masterson at Dodge in 1878. Bat lost his bid for re-election the next year and eventually moved on, following his friend Wyatt Earp to the booming new mining camp at

Tombstone, Arizona. One of the Masterson brothers still wore the star in Dodge, however; Jim was appointed city marshal the same month Bat was defeated.

In 1881 Jim Masterson became embroiled in a feud with Dodge City saloonmen A. J. Peacock and Al Updegraff, and murderous threats were exchanged. Someone wired Bat in Tombstone to hurry back, that Jim needed his support. Returning posthaste, Bat swung down off the train at Dodge to become engaged immediately in a gunfight with Peacock and Updegraff. In what has become known in Dodge City lore as the Battle of the Plaza, there were no fatalities, although Updegraff took a bullet through the lungs. Students of Western gunsmoke history have long wondered who sent the telegram to Bat, calling him back to Dodge. George Goodell told family members in later years that he was that man.[9]

The Mastersons and their friends lost much of their popularity in Dodge as a consequence of the Battle of the Plaza, and the town saw an exodus of former law officers and sporting men. Among those taking up new residence in Trinidad, Colorado, were Bat and Jim Masterson, saloonkeeper P. L. Beatty, professional gamblers Charlie Ronan, Jack Allen, and "Cock-Eyed Frank" Loving, and aspiring lawman George Goodell. Bat Masterson, who counted among his many powerful political friends Trinidad mayor John Conkie and *Trinidad Daily News* editor Olney Newell, soon secured appointment as city marshal, replacing a popular incumbent named Lou Kreeger. Jim Masterson, too, quickly found law work, first as a city policeman, then as a deputy sheriff. Goodell pinned on a badge as deputy to another popular local figure, Las Animas County sheriff Juan Vigil.

It soon became evident to Goodell that Sheriff Vigil was a politician and no fighting man. This work he had turned over to his undersheriff, a fiery, hot-tempered Irishman named M. B. McGraw. Goodell and McGraw took an instant dislike to one another. This antipathy was destined to lead to gunfire and blood spilled on a Trinidad street.

Goodell first attracted attention as a peacekeeper in June 1882 when he interceded in a lunch counter disturbance. A woman was "belaboring unmercifully a muscular youth of about 200 pounds," reported a paper, "when Goodell intervened, whereupon another man stepped in and "let his giant powder loose upon Mr. Goodell, who arose and brought his assailant to the ground with a blow from his gun."[10]

A month later, when an opening developed on the city police force, Goodell, eager to work again for his old pal, Bat Masterson, and at the same time escape the baleful influence of M. B. McGraw, quickly applied for the job. Editor Newell supported his candidacy and City Marshal Masterson made the appointment.[11] The *Trinidad Daily Democrat* noted that Goodell wasted no time in setting to work, issuing "mandates" to J. J. Harlan, the "Offwheeler," and his confederates to "pack their pie boxes" and get out of town.[12] In his new position Goodell sported a new uniform, and the paper, echoing a faddish phrase popularized by English fop Oscar Wilde in a tour of western America, commented that the new officer looked "too utterly too" in his getup.[13]

One of Goodell's arrests proved to be very painful when his prisoner bit a chunk out of his finger. Olney Newell reported in the *News* that "this enraged Goodell to such an extent that he banged his man over the head with his revolver [felling] him like he had been hit with a pile driver." Newell went on to editorialize that it took tough men to administer the law in a frontier town like Trinidad and the tender-hearted need not apply. "Men are required for these positions," he said, "who are willing to take their lives in their hands and who expect not only to get hurt, but to give hard knocks."[14]

Goodell was called upon to display that toughness in a life-and-death struggle only two weeks later when his difficulty with M. B. McGraw erupted into six-shooter violence. A paper had quoted Undersheriff McGraw a few months before as lamenting the absence of gunplay in Trinidad. "There has been no one killed for a long time," he said, "but there are lots of them that ought to be."[15] He was about to get his wish.

The trouble began with an exchange of newspaper broadsides. After Editor Newell, in an August 11, 1882, *News* editorial, accused the county officers of negligence in the operation of the jail and responsibility for the escape of several prisoners, McGraw took the criticism personally and responded with a "card" in the pages of the opposition paper: "Allow me space in your column to reply to the article published in yesterday morning's *News* in regard to the escape of prisoners from the county jail. Mr. Newell does, and always did, pick me out for a mark for some reason unknown to Me. . . . Olney Newell, all you have said I think was intended for me; but I am like the man that the ass kicked—I consider the source and I think the people of Las Animas County will do the same."[16]

Since McGraw had chosen to personalize the controversy, Newell struck back in response to what he called "a rather remarkable card from Undersheriff McGraw" and aimed his fire directly at that officer. He challenged him to answer questions relating to a particular case, one in which it had been alleged that a man, sentenced by a magistrate to thirty days in jail, had been released by McGraw after paying the undersheriff fifty dollars.[17]

McGraw explained with another "card," saying that in the referenced case he had been out of town. In his absence George Goodell had accepted fifty dollars from the prisoner, he said, but had turned the money over to him when he returned and he used it to pay the magistrate's fees and other costs. Then McGraw turned bitter and vituperative: "I met Mr. Newell yesterday and asked him the name of the author of the article published by him, but he refused to give it. The charging me with being bribed is a COWARDLY, WILLFUL LIE! Let the author be who he may."[18]

Newell responded by lecturing McGraw on politics, saying that the News, while Democratic, would not countenance improper acts by Democratic officials and reminded him that charges had been made and never adequately refuted.[19]

McGraw's next card, which he said was his last, lowered the level of rhetorical debate to invective: "In regard to the articles that Olney Newell had published about me, all I wish to say is that they are a lot of COWARDLY and WILLFUL LIES! And if he refuses to give me the name of the author, I consider him, Olney Newell, a COWARDLY, MALICIOUS LIAR and the author of the articles referred to is a dirty, lowbred PIMP and a COWARD, and now if you are any part of a man, put on your 'fighting clothes' and come to the front and take your part."[20]

It was apparent to McGraw now that Goodell was the informant feeding Newell the information to which the undersheriff was so sensitive. On August 17 the News published Goodell's sworn affidavit stating that while acting as a county deputy under McGraw he had released a prisoner named Joseph Bryant upon payment of fifty dollars by Bryant's brother, but that he had done this on the specific instruction of McGraw. The undersheriff, he said, turned over fourteen dollars of the money to the magistrate only after being questioned by that officer regarding the prisoner's release. Goodell did not mention the balance of the money, but his statement left the clear inference that McGraw had kept it. In a comment following the affidavit, Newell said that McGraw's explanation had been feeble and inadequate, and that his vituperative "cards" revealed an uncontrollable temper entirely inappropriate for an officer of the law.

Although he had said he had written his last "card," McGraw was back in the columns of the *Democrat* the next day with a scurrilous attack on Goodell. Shrugging off the sworn affidavit as "a willful lie," he set out to destroy the reputation of Goodell. The man, he said, "lived in Dodge City previous to his coming to Trinidad, and for one year he acted as a pimp for his own wife, and, I am told on good authority, that he has done the same thing here in Trinidad, and after his wife would make money in that way, he would take the money and gamble it off. This is the true character of George Goodell. I do not ask anyone to take my word for it, but let Mr. Goodell come forward and demand the proof and I will furnish it. I will state further that the first time I was satisfied of these facts was the day I discharged him from the Sheriff's office."[21]

Newell's response was brief. His charge that prisoners had escaped from the county jail through the negligence of the officers had not been refuted, he said. In the Bryant affair the public could weigh Goodell's affidavit against McGraw's denial and reach its own conclusion. As for McGraw's threats, he said that "the editor of the *News* has no time for street broils, but is generally to be found doing business in the old stand where he will be pleased at any time to see people who have matters to settle."[22]

M. B. McGraw was no longer interested in Olney Newell, however. It was George Goodell upon whom he was now focusing all his ire. The next morning, August 19, the showdown came at ten minutes after nine. Approaching Goodell as he stood on the plank sidewalk in front of Jaffa's Opera House, McGraw stepped up close, slapped Goodell in the face with his left hand, and reached for his pistol with his right. But Goodell's six-shooter was out and leveled before McGraw's gun cleared the scabbard.

His first shot hit the undersheriff in the pistol arm and his weapon clattered to the walk. A second shot struck McGraw in the side, and he tumbled into Jaffa's open doorway. Goodell worked his six-shooter furiously, pumping two more bullets into McGraw's body. "For God's sake, hand me my gun!" McGraw screamed.

Deputy Sheriff H. E. Hardy came running and threw both arms around Goodell. Although he was a little man, weighing barely 130 pounds, Goodell was in a fighting frenzy and seemed to possess amazing strength. Carrying Hardy on his back, he stooped and snatched up McGraw's revolver. With a pistol in each hand and his upper arms pinned to his sides by Hardy's grip, he continued shooting at his prostrate adversary until both guns were empty.

McGraw's body was like a sieve, with ten holes where .45-caliber bullets had entered or exited, but, amazingly, he survived for two days. He finally died on August 21. At an inquest, a coroner's jury found that the killing was done without felonious intent and no charges were brought against George Goodell.[23]

Although he had been legally cleared in the killing, many in Trinidad were appalled at the ferocity of Goodell's pistol work, and he lost much of his popularity. For police officers in small frontier communities, the continuing good will and support of the citizenry was necessary. City Marshal Bat Masterson, recognizing that his deputy had lost his effectiveness, relieved him of his badge. Within two months Goodell left town.

Once he was gone, A. K. Cutting, editor of the *Daily Democrat*, the paper that had published McGraw's "cards" and supported him in the controversy, began an accusatory campaign against the former city policeman. McGraw, he said, had been the victim of premeditated murder committed by Goodell and an unnamed accomplice. Goodell had then left town with stolen city funds. Quoting unidentified "knowing" sources, Cutting charged that "George Goodell, one of the murderers of Undersheriff McGraw, left Trinidad several hundred dollars ahead, from fines collected and not turned over to the proper authorities. His accomplice will count ties when he skips," he added, implying that Goodell had gotten away with all the loot, leaving his alleged accomplice without railroad fare.[24]

Two days later Cutting wrote that Goodell was in Dodge City, and "the woman who passes for his wife" was in Kinsley, Kansas. Upon his arrival at Dodge City, he said, Goodell "was arrested and put in the 'dog house' for carrying concealed weapons. The revolver was taken from him and he was fined $50 and given 12 hours to shake the dust of Dodge from his sandals. The matter of holding him on an old crime committed in 1879 was considered, but finally he was given the alternative of skedaddling, which was accepted."[25]

Goodell returned to Trinidad at least once more. In February 1883 a local paper noted that he and gambler "Texas George" had accompanied Bat and Jim Masterson to Springer, New Mexico, to witness the hanging of an eighteen-year-old convicted murderer, Damian Romero.[26]

By 1885 Goodell was living in Leavenworth, Kansas, where he was employed as a guard at the construction site of the Soldiers' Home, a large complex built to provide for the needs of aging Civil War veterans. The following year he served as a city constable and deputy sheriff, and in 1887 he pinned on yet another star when he took appointment as a federal deputy under Colonel William C. Jones, U.S. marshal for the Kansas Judicial District.[27]

He was acting as a city police officer when his next recorded shooting affray occurred in May 1888. His adversary was Ben Black, a fifty-three-year-old native of England who kept a saloon in Leavenworth and had developed a reputation as a "bold, bad, desperate, vicious man," in the words of one who claimed to know him well.[28]

Five months earlier Black's wife, Lillie, had left him and opened a brothel. After being harassed and threatened by her husband, Lillie had filed complaints with the city police, and all the officers, including Goodell, were well aware of the ongoing Black marital difficulty. Evidence later suggested that Officer Goodell had more than a professional interest in the affair, that he had a personal involvement with Lillie Black.

On the evening of May 24 Black went on a drunken rampage during which he accosted his wife in the street and verbally abused at least one city policeman, Officer W. O. Tillery, slapping him in the face and inflicting damage to one of his eyes.[29] Years later Goodell would claim that Black humiliated two Leavenworth policemen that night, "took their guns away from them and said he would run the town to suit himself," but this appears to be an example of the exaggeration to which he was prone.[30]

About 1:30 on the morning of the 25th Black appeared at his wife's bordello and demanded that she leave with him. "If you do not come with me now," he threatened, "I'll kill you and if you send for a police-man, I'll kill the first one that comes."[31] Carrie Smith, one of the inmates of the house, heard the violent threats and ran into the street, screaming for the police.

Hearing the cries of a woman, Officer Goodell came on the run. Remembering the trouble existing in this family," he said, "I supposed the cry came from [Mrs. Black]." As he neared the place he passed Carrie Smith and heard Lillie screaming in the house and beseeching Black not to shoot her.

> I then rapped on the door and got no response. I . . . stated that I was a police officer and demanded admission. I stood for a few seconds at the door with my left hand on the knob. The key was turned and the door opened. . . . I then got a look at him. He was standing within three feet of me, his hands in his pants pockets, and as quickly as it was possible for him to fire, he drew his pistol and put it to my stomach and fired. . . . It set me back one step from the force of the ball striking a button on my vest. . . . Glancing to the right, [it went] through the vest, pants and two shirts before it left my person. I then drew my pistol and before he had time to fire a second time at me, I fired . . . three shots and he fell.[32]

Not pausing to see the effectiveness of his shooting, Goodell jumped back out of the doorway and ran around to the rear of the building. He re-entered through the back door of a house that was now a bedlam of screaming, hysterical women. His intention, he later said, was to attack his adversary from the rear if the man was still on his feet. He found Ben Black sprawled on his back, legs stretched toward the door. He was not moving. After telling the women to send for a doctor and other police, Goodell left to have his own wound treated.

Dr. J. A. Lane arrived and after examining Black, pronounced him dead. The doctor found entrance wounds of three bullets, one in the chest, one in the abdomen, and another in the upper leg. There were two exit wounds. The shot in the chest was the immediate cause of death.[33]

After leaving Lillie Black's whorehouse, Goodell walked to the home of a Doctor Walters, with whom he was acquainted. Complaining that he had been shot, he got the doctor out of bed. Upon examination, Walters found a contusion on Goodell's abdomen. It was a welt about three-fourths of an inch long and looked, said the doctor, "red and angry." The bullet holes through Goodell's clothing and the slight wound were consistent with the officer's story about the shooting.[34]

At a hearing before Coroner James C. Lynch, Goodell was cleared of any wrongdoing in the death of Black. A six-member jury found that he had fired "in self defense and while executing his duty as a police officer of this city."[35] But an attorney named Henry Shindler, hearing saloon talk of a liaison between Goodell and Lillie Black, filed murder charges against the policeman and a charge of accessory to murder against the woman. At a preliminary hearing on May 29 before Judge Wendorf, the state was represented by County Attorney John H. Atwood, assisted by Henry Shindler. Goodell obtained first-class counsel; he enlisted the services of Lucien Baker, a prominent attorney in Leavenworth who would later be elected to the Kansas legislature and the U.S. Senate.

Witnesses Rosa DeCamp and Henry Crouse gave the most damaging testimony against the defendants at this hearing. Mrs. DeCamp recalled walking with Lillie Black on the street and Lillie exclaiming, "There's my baby!" when George Goodell came into view. On another occasion, Mrs. DeCamp said, Lillie told her that if Ben Black did not cease his harassment, "she would have Goodell fix him." Crouse testified that he heard Lillie say: "To hell with Black, he's no good. I'm Lady Goodell now."

The *Leavenworth Times* thought the evidence against Goodell and Mrs. Black so skimpy that it headlined its story "Very, Very Thin." Sufficient doubt was raised by the hearing, however, for the defendants to be bound over for trial.[36]

At that proceeding, held the following September, prosecutors produced little in the way of new evidence against the defendants. Lucien Baker for the defense had little difficulty in depicting the case as one of those melodramas so popular at the time, with Lillie as the beautiful heroine, Ben Black as the dastardly villain, and Goodell as the gallant hero arriving just in time to rescue the innocent maiden from his evil designs. Baker trotted out a string of witnesses, including City Marshal W. W. Roberts and Officers W. O. Tillery and Ed Murphy, who testified to Black's well-known reputation as a dangerous, desperate man. The jury was out only twenty minutes before returning a verdict of "not guilty."[37]

Goodell had escaped punishment for the Ben Black killing, but the story of his unsavory dalliance with a whorehouse madam may have cost him his marriage. Within months he departed Leavenworth, leaving his wife, Addie, behind. The separation led to a divorce, and some time later Goodell married a woman named Bertha.[38]

In newspaper interviews many years later Goodell said he went from Leavenworth to Tacoma, Washington, where he held important positions in the police department and remained three years. He was quoted as saying he served as chief of police or inspector of police at Tacoma under three different mayors.[39] This is another of Goodell's exaggerations. There was, indeed, a succession of mayors at Tacoma during this period when the mayoral term was only a year and voters seemed inclined to change. Each new mayor appointed his own police chief, and a total of five held the position between the years 1888 and 1891. None of them, however, was George "Red" Goodell. He did serve on the police force at Tacoma for a time, but it appears from the records that he held no position above that of patrolman.[40]

By 1897 Goodell was back in Kansas. When he heard that the businessmen of Nowata, a small community in the northwest corner of the old Cherokee Nation were looking for a town marshal, he applied for the job and was appointed.

Situated about twenty-five miles south of Coffeyville, Kansas, on the newly built St. Louis & Iron Mountain Railroad running from Coffeyville to Fort Smith, Arkansas, Nowata was a supply point for the surrounding farms and ranches and the seat of Nowata County, Indian Territory. A townsite had been platted and incorporated in 1892 by the Cherokee Nation and lots auctioned off. Most of the purchasers were whites who campaigned to bring the area under the laws and jurisdiction of the federal government. During the middle 1890s the congressional Dawes Commission initiated a series of agreements with the Five Civilized Tribes that greatly expanded federal authority in the Indian Territory. The passage of the Curtis Act in 1898 established a universal U.S. legal code for the Indian Territory and virtually brought tribal government to an end. But during these transitional years two separate municipal governments operated in Nowata, one under the laws of the Cherokee Indian Nation, and another as an incorporated municipality under the authority of District Judge William M.

Springer. Each government had its own city officials, including town marshal. It was a situation primed for trouble.[41]

Leo C. Bennett, U.S. marshal for the Northern District of the Indian Territory, in a 1901 letter to President McKinley, described the perilous situation at the time: "It is not possible for one who is not familiar with conditions existing in . . . Cherokee Nation in 1897–8 to understand the bitterness and deadly animosities which existed between the two municipal organizations; one the so-called Cherokee government, almost invariably corrupt, inefficient and turbulent, without standing in the Courts, and generally disregarded by the better class of the Indian citizens; the other, the newly organized municipal government authorized by the existing laws of Congress."[42]

At the time of Goodell's appointment as Nowata city marshal by the white town government, a Choctaw Indian named Push-ta-ha, or "Push," also known as Johnson Fulsom, held a similar position under the Cherokee tribal laws. James Fulsom, alias Willie Hickey or Hicker, a half brother to the Indian marshal, served as his deputy. According to Marshal Bennett, "the Fulsoms were rough, quarrelsome, drinking men who made it a general practice to bulldoze and overawe the people of Nowata. . . . These Fulsoms repeatedly boasted in public that if ever City Marshal Goodell attempted to arrest them or otherwise interfered with them they would shoot him down like a dog; they even rode the streets of Nowata when Goodell was absent and loudly proclaimed that they were 'laying for' Goodell, and, with an exhibition of their Winchesters and pistols, would explain how they would bore Goodell full of holes."[43]

H. O. Dooley, a Nowata attorney who later represented a Kansas district in the U.S. Congress, attested to the infamy of Johnson Fulsom, a "desperately wicked character" who once threatened him with a weapon. "To my knowledge," he said, "he has assaulted others and many times attempted to shoot up the town of Nowata."[44]

Marshal Bennett said that he commissioned Goodell a deputy U.S. marshal "upon the earnest solicitations of the best citizens of Nowata and the surrounding country for ten or twenty miles." Headquartered at Nowata, Goodell was responsible for fieldwork in an area extending twenty miles to the Kansas line and twenty-five miles to the Osage Reservation. "Goodell made a splendid officer," said Bennett, "being faithful and painstaking, as well as wholly without fear."[45]

Shortly after Goodell's arrival in Nowata, it became apparent that he and Fulsom would tangle. Marshal Bennett, J. E. Campbell, president of the bank in Nowata, and other businessmen of the town all later testified that the Fulsoms not only threatened Goodell's life, but tried to bushwhack him on several occasions. Goodell, they said, made every effort to avoid the brothers, but tensions continued to mount until November 1897 when the clash finally came.

The incident triggering the explosion was Goodell's arrest of "Push" Fulsom on a charge of public drunkenness. Goodell claimed later that he also decided to make the arrest when he learned the Fulsom brothers had set an ambush for him. James Fulsom and other supporters soon broke into the flimsy Nowata jail and freed the Indian marshal. The town tensed for the blowup that now seemed unavoidable and imminent.

Goodell was making his rounds in the early hours of Saturday morning, November 13, when he spotted Willie Hickey (James Fulsom) hiding in a stairway. Certain that Hickey was waiting to shoot him as he passed by, Goodell slipped around behind the man, got the drop on him, disarmed him, and placed him under arrest. He was marching his prisoner to the jail when Hickey suddenly broke and ran, heading out of town. Mounting a horse, Goodell followed and shot Hickey down in the road. Townsmen, aroused by the gunfire, carried the mortally wounded Hickey to a hardware store. When Johnson "Push" Fulsom learned of the shooting, he ran into the street where a bullet from Goodell's gun dropped him. Fulsom managed to drag himself into the store where his half brother lay dying. Goodell strode into the building behind him. There, according to some accounts, Fulsom begged for his life, but an implacable George Goodell mercilessly shot him dead.[46]

The town was in an uproar, of course, and further violence was threatened. Goodell surrendered to Nowata's mayor, who had to protect him until Marshal Bennett arrived to take him to Muskogee. Following a hearing before U.S. Commissioner Q. C. Jackson, he was charged with two counts of murder and released on $10,000 bond.[47]

As might be expected, adherents of the two governments viewed the shootings from diametrically opposed perspectives. The *Vinita Indian Chieftain*, a newspaper sympathetic to the cause of the Cherokee Nation, called Goodell "most brutal" and said his actions were "denounced by all the best people of the town."[48] But a contrary opinion was held by most of the white citizens. Nowata bank president J. E. Campbell argued that although Goodell might have been "technically at fault, yet the best people of Nowata without exception believe that he was justified in doing what he did, that he not only saved his own life, but he relieved the town of two lawless, desperate characters."[49]

"The truth is," wrote P. L. Soper, federal prosecutor for the Northern District of Indian Territory,

> that there was intense jealousy between the Arkansas corporation
> of the town of Nowata . . . and the Cherokee corporation. . . .
> The larger portion of the population consisted of non-citizens,
> that is, people who do not belong to any Indian nation. Long
> prior to the killing, I had been advised that it was only a question
> of time before either Goodell would be killed or Fulsom. . . .
> Only people who have lived in this country can appreciate the
> bitterness that existed in the hearts of a large number of the
> Indians against white men, and this feeling was intensified in the
> town of Nowata by the establishment of a separate and distinct
> town municipality. . . . George Goodell firmly believed that he
> had to be continually on his guard to preserve his own life. . . .
> Viewed in this light, the conduct of George Goodell at the time
> of the killing was explainable. . . . The tension at the time of this
> killing was more than great. The town was divided into factions.
> One half saw nothing wrong in what Goodell had done, and the
> other half saw only the blackest crime.[50]

Marshal Bennett, fully supporting his deputy, urged Goodell to fight the charges against him. U.S. Attorney Soper, however, fearful that a trial would exacerbate the potentially explosive situation and result in more violence, persuaded Goodell and his court-appointed counsel to plead guilty to a manslaughter charge. He assured them that on his recommendation Goodell would receive a light sentence. Goodell waited a year for his sentencing, and during that time his penchant for exaggeration probably did not help his cause. The editor of the *Fort Smith Elevator* reported: "We understand Goodell boasts of having killed a dozen men during his life besides these two."[51]

On November 23, 1898, Goodell stood before Judge Springer to hear his sentence. Ignoring Soper's recommendation, Springer imposed severe punishment, ten years imprisonment on each count, the terms to run consecutively. Goodell's enemies, including the partisan *Vinita*

Indian Chieftain, thought he got off too lightly and wanted to see him hang. The sentence, noted the *Chieftain* sourly, "indicates that the days of capital punishment for crimes are about over in this country."[52]

Federal prisons at Leavenworth and Atlanta were full at the time, and the Ohio State Penitentiary at Columbus was accepting U.S. convicts under a government contract. On December 27, 1898, this facility received George Goodell as Convict Number 31386. According to the prison records, he weighed 130 pounds, was five feet, six and a quarter inches tall, had "frank" slate blue eyes and auburn-brown hair and beard. His habits were "intemperate" and his education "none." Prison doctors measured and described a number of scars on his body, including a prominent one on his wrist that he said was a souvenir of a fight with an Indian on the Canadian River in Texas. His nearest relative was his wife, Bertha, then residing in Arkansas City, Kansas.[53]

For Goodell, a former lawman now condemned to incarceration among the criminal class he had opposed, the coming years were fraught with danger. In recognition of this, Warden E. G. Coffin assigned Goodell to a job as a clerk in the transfer office where contact with the general prison population was minimal.

The Ohio pen held several noteworthy convicts at this time. Convicted bank embezzler William Sydney Porter, destined to achieve fame as short-story writer O. Henry, was there. Al Jennings, a minor Indian Territory bandit who would later capitalize on his notoriety to publish several books and run for governor of Oklahoma, was an inmate. Also there was a genuine Indian Territory desperado, William F. "Little Bill" Raidler, a former member of the Bill Doolin gang.

In later accounts of his prison experience Al Jennings claimed to have led a breakout attempt in which saw blades were smuggled in, bars cut, and final plans made when prison officials, tipped off by another convict, thwarted the escape.[54] Although Jennings and his confederates never learned the identity of the convict who informed on them, Warden Coffin named George Goodell as that man. In a letter to the president of the United States, Coffin wrote that when Goodell learned of the breakout attempt, "planned and consummated by the notorious Al Jennings and other United States prisoners, [the information was] imparted by him to me at . . . the peril of his life. . . . The act was voluntary and without hope of reward in any manner, whatsoever, except that which his sense of duty prompted him to do as a matter of justice."[55]

In 1901 a prodigious effort was mounted and a petition circulated to obtain an executive pardon for Goodell. President William McKinley received letters recommending clemency from former Ohio State Penitentiary warden Coffin, current warden William N. Darby, and Superintendent W. F. Bryant, Goodell's immediate overseer, all of whom testified to the petitioner's exemplary behavior in prison. Coffin cited Goodell's key role in preventing the escape of Jennings and his cohorts. Soper and Springer, the men who had prosecuted and sentenced Goodell, also wrote letters supporting the petition, as did Marshal Bennett. Dozens of other lawmen and Nowata citizens signed the petition, and many included personal letters of support.

The campaign to secure a presidential pardon for Goodell was conducted in the summer of 1901. But before pardon attorney J. S. Easby-Smith had an opportunity to make a formal presentation of the case, disaster struck. On September 6 President William McKinley, while attending the Pan-American Exposition at Buffalo, New York, was shot down by an assassin and died six days later. The Goodell executive clemency appeal was put on hold during the hectic period of transition to a new presidency.

Finally, on May 28, 1902, Easby-Smith submitted all documents and a ten-page summation of the case to Attorney General Philander C. Knox. After studying the file, Knox on June 10 added his recommendation for clemency and passed it along to President Theodore Roosevelt. Three days later Roosevelt scribbled "Pardon" and the letter "R" across the face of the file. A telegram went out that same day to Warden Darby at the Ohio State Penitentiary. On June 14, 1902, George Goodell walked out of the gate a free man. He had served just under three and a half years behind bars.[56]

After his release Goodell continued his drifting ways. He returned for a time to Oklahoma and Indian Territories where he took a job guarding federal prisoners at the so-called Bull Pen at Muskogee. He later claimed that he went back to the state of Washington where he acted as a special bodyguard for President Roosevelt during the campaign of 1904. He lived for periods in Chicago, Kansas City, and Milwaukee. By the 1920s he was working as a railroad policeman for the Chicago, Milwaukee & St. Paul Railway.[57]

George Goodell in his sixties and working as a railroad policeman. From the author's collection.

Responding to renewed public interest in the recently tamed Wild West and its colorful characters, newspaper reporters in various cities he visited during this period interviewed Goodell, an authentic frontier veteran and gunfighter. He regaled them with tales that were a strange mixture of truth, half-truth, and total falsehood. He told a Bartlesville, Oklahoma, newsman in January 1922 that he had killed nineteen men and had a notched six-gun to prove it. He described his killings of McGraw, Ben Black, and the Fulsom brothers in fairly accurate detail, but grossly exaggerated some of his experiences, saying, for instance, that he had been city marshal at Dodge City when Bat Masterson was sheriff and that he and Bat had killed six cowboys in one gun battle. He falsely claimed to have been city marshal at Pueblo, Colorado, and Albuquerque and Las Vegas, New Mexico, and to have been chief of police at Tacoma.[58]

Interviewed by a writer for the *Denver Post* in November 1923, he repeated many of the same tales, some of them true, some barefaced lies. The notches on his old gun now totaled twenty-one. The tally included another Indian policeman, a mythical "John Wilson" whom he said backed the Fulsoms at Nowata. When they "challenged his authority," he said, he killed all three.[59]

By July 1924 when he was interviewed by a reporter in Kansas City, those extra nicks in his gun butt had strangely disappeared: "His Gun Has 19 Notches," read the headline. Although Goodell was quoted as saying he remembered every one of those killings in detail, he described only the Leavenworth and Nowata shootings. He told this newsman that he had participated in the famous Battle of Adobe Walls between buffalo hunters and Indians in the Texas Panhandle in 1874. Of course, his old friend Bat Masterson had been there, but not Goodell. He also chopped a decade off his age, saying he was fifty-seven, which would have made him seven years old at the time of the Adobe Walls fight, a fact missed entirely by the credulous reporter.[60]

Sometime after his release from prison Goodell divorced his wife, Bertha. In Chicago on February 28, 1904, he married again and lived with Ida, his third wife, until April 10, 1921, when they separated at Los Angeles. A divorce was granted on September 29, 1922. Goodell fathered children by each of his several wives. He is believed by family members to have died at Los Angeles on March 23, 1928, but like many events in his colorful life, the place and time of his passing is wrapped in uncertainty.[61]

— 7 —

BILL STANDIFER
(1853–1902)

"Caused a flutter among the thieves"

To combat the plague of rustling during the days of the great open unfenced cattle ranges, large ranchers employed what they called "protection men," hardcase fighters of demonstrated fearlessness, skill with guns, and a willingness to use them. Protection men rode the range, keeping a sharp eye out for the illegally branded calf or butchered beef. At roundup time, when cowboys from the various ranches drove the free-ranging cattle to a central location for sorting and branding, it was the job of the protection man to represent his employer and protect his interests. Later, ranchers formed associations to share the expenses of these range riders and carried them on their books as "cattle detectives," "stock inspectors," or simply "association men." Small ranchers and settlers, often harassed as suspected cow thieves by the protection men, called them "killers" or "scalpers."

The protection man, as an early cattle country historian wrote, "carried his only authority in his holsters," but he was paid "to patrol the ranges, find as many rustlers as he could, and kill them where he found them."[1] How he accomplished his mission was rarely questioned in the early days, and protection men were responsible for the unmarked prairie grave of many a suspected rustler.

These enforcers of range law acted as sole judge on behalf of their employers when disputes over cattle ownership arose at roundups. Old-time cowboy A. P. Black wrote that "association men always traveled around the country settling arguments over stolen cattle and burnt brands. Not a day passed at one of those roundups but what there was some argument about burnt cattle. An association man was just the same thing as a detective, and was paid by the association to keep a little order. He wasn't allowed to gamble with any of the cowpunchers and had to keep his head clear and his gun on the danger side. I've never seen one at a roundup with gloves on; he always had his gun hand bare."[2]

Some celebrated gunfighters, including George Scarborough and Tom Horn, worked at various times as range detectives. Scarborough was killed by outlaws in 1900 while working for a New Mexico cattlemen's association, and Horn, convicted of a murder committed in the interest of his Wyoming employers, was hanged in 1903.

In the Texas Panhandle during the 1880s and 1890s none of the breed was better known than J. William "Bill" Standifer, a dark-haired, brown-eyed man of small stature but large reputation. Standifer was born about 1853 in central Texas[3] and grew up in Lampasas County where his father, William J. Standifer, owned a mercantile business.[4] He was still a toddler when his mother, Mary E. Standifer (née Lawhon), died in Burnet County on April 17, 1857. His father remarried in 1859, taking as his second wife Sarah M. Wolf,[5] reportedly a relative of the Horrells, a clan of fighting men who during the 1870s became engaged in a long and bloody feud with the Higgins family of Lampasas.[6] It has been suggested that his stepmother's family connections had much to do with Bill Standifer's sudden demise at the hands of Pink Higgins many years later.[7]

Like many young male Texans of the 1870s, little Bill Standifer—he never weighed as much as 140 pounds[8]—became a cowboy and in the summer of 1879 was working on the ranch of Ike Mullins in Tom Green County. A shooting incident occurred that became the foundation for Standifer's widespread reputation as a deadly gunman who would brook no insult or back down to any man.

One of the cowpunchers working the roundup that summer was a man from Gonzales named John Mahan. Standifer, working alone, was holding some Mullins cattle in a pasture when Mahan attempted to drive some strays he had rounded up through the herd. Standifer objected and a bitter argument ensued. Finally, Mahan, infuriated by the obstinacy of the little Mullins hand, uncoiled a blacksnake whip and, while a companion held a Winchester on Standifer, lashed him brutally.

Dripping blood and seething with rage, Standifer rode to the Mullins house, asked for his wages, and told Ike Mullins he was quitting because he had to kill a man. Rejoining the roundup working up into Runnels County, he went from one crew to another in search of the man from Gonzales. He found him at a camp near Pony Creek. Mahan was mounted, talking with a group of punchers, when Standifer rode up. One glance at the angry and determined face of the little man told Mahan this was showdown time. He jerked out his six-shooter and fired off a wild shot. Standifer, with what everybody agreed was a lucky shot, put an answering bullet through the gunhand wrist of the man from Gonzales.

With a shriek of pain, Mahan dropped his pistol and dug spurs into his horse. Standifer galloped in pursuit, ripping off shots. After 600 yards one of his bullets struck Mahan's horse and it went down. Mahan leaped to his feet and began to run, but another bullet from Standifer's gun slammed into his back, and he was dead when he hit the ground.[9]

Bill Standifer pulled out that night with a trail herd heading for Marfa. He worked cattle in west Texas until another violent episode forced him to move on again. In a Fort Davis restaurant he got into a fight with three black U.S. Army troopers. Guns roared, and when the smoke cleared two of the cavalrymen lay bleeding on the floor.[10]

Standifer headed back east, but the Texas Rangers caught up with him and he had to stand trial in Coleman County for the Mahan killing. His self-defense plea held up, and he was acquitted. Since neither of the black troopers he had shot in Fort Davis died, no charges were filed in that case.[11]

His gunplay in west Texas established Standifer's reputation among cattlemen as a cool, straight-shooting fighting man of the first order. He knew cattle, could not be bluffed, and was skilled with a gun. With qualifications like that he was soon in demand as a roundup foreman. In 1882 he bossed the C. C. Slaughter roundup in Scurry County that longtime cowpuncher Hiram C. Craig called the largest he "ever saw or heard speak of." When the cattle were finally gathered, they numbered 10,000 head and covered the prairie one-half mile in every direction.[12]

Despite his diminutive size, little Bill Standifer was a dominating presence on the cattle ranges, as demonstrated in another roundup story that cowmen were retelling half a century later. A big roundup in the spring of 1883 brought 150 cowboys toward Snyder, a tiny community of several houses and a single saloon in Scurry County. In anticipation of an invasion of parch-throated cowpunchers, the saloon proprietor freighted in large stocks of liquid refreshment and waited to reap a financial bonanza. Bill Meador,[13] a puncher working the roundup for the JD outfit, was early on the scene and described what happened.

Felix Franklin and his crew won the race from the roundup grounds to the Snyder saloon. The Frank Cooksey and Bill Standifer wagons arrived some time later. Horses were jammed at the hitch rail in front of the saloon, when Franklin staggered out, roaring oaths, and began firing his revolver under the animals' hooves. Frightened, several broke loose from the rail and ran off.

Bill Standifer, who had just arrived, stepped off his horse and approached Franklin. He told him to stop his hell-raising and reminded him that respectable women and children lived in the houses nearby. Franklin, reloading his pistol, glared at Standifer for a moment, and then

> he started walking toward Bill, gun in hand. The crowd grew tense, and there wasn't a man in all that round-up crew that didn't edge back a step or two. But Standifer held his ground, his elbow slightly crooked.
>
> "Felix," he said, as calm as a man in church, "don't you have a mother and sisters?"
>
> "Yes."
>
> "Then you don't respect them if you don't respect the women in that house over there."
>
> A hundred men stood waiting . . . and then Felix turned on his boot heel and walked away. But he did not re-enter the saloon; he walked toward his wagon.

The scene had a remarkable effect on the assembled cowboys. "I went into the saloon with the rest of the JD boys," recalled Bill Meador, "but not a word was spoken. We lined up to the bar and had a round of drinks, and then we all walked out again to go to our own wagons. And there was no drinking in the bar that night. I don't think there was anything quite like it, before or since. There was something in what Billy Standifer said that went right through that whole crowd. . . . Something that made them think of home . . . or when they were kids. . . . And I'll tell you it was pretty lonesome out there on the plains that night."[14]

Standifer's little lecture no doubt saved a lot of hangovers and perhaps some shooting. The incident added to his growing rangeland legend, but the Snyder saloonkeeper, after missing out of his big sales day, probably was not one of his admirers.

It was during this period that ranchers began to seek Standifer's services as a protection man. After he reportedly killed a rustler near Estacado in northwest Crosby County,[15] his reputation became so formidable that cattle thieves quit the country as soon as they heard he had been hired to patrol a certain range. "Bill, more often than not, worked himself out of a job without ever 'bustin' a cartridge.'"[16]

This kind of ability caught the attention of Crosby County politicos, who induced Standifer to run for sheriff. When Crosby County was created in 1886, Felix Franklin, the roundup boss Standifer had faced down five years before, became the first sheriff. In November 1888 Standifer ran for the office and was elected. He would be re-elected twice and hold the position for six years.[17]

"There were great sheriffs in those days," testified J. F. Cunningham, who was elected district attorney for the Thirty-ninth Judicial District that same year and worked with law officers in over thirty Texas counties. "Bill Standifer of Crosby County and George Scarborough of Anson were among the best—as game as any men I ever knew. On one occasion Standifer went three hundred miles, clear into New Mexico, after a thief, and brought him back."[18]

Actually, while serving as Crosby County sheriff, Standifer made several trips into New Mexico after wanted men. One expedition, made shortly after he took office, turned out to be a harrowing experience for both the new sheriff and Charlie Quillen, a deputy who accompanied him.

In pursuit of Brude Brookins and his partner, who had stolen thirty Texas horses, Standifer and Quillen rode into Lincoln County, New Mexico, and caught up with the thieves near the notorious outlaw hangout at Seven Rivers. Ignoring jurisdictional restrictions, they arrested the pair and started on the long ride home with the stolen

Bill Standifer (*back row on left*) and a group of Texas Panhandle cattlemen in the 1890s. Courtesy of the Panhandle-Plains Historical Museum, 160/77 Hank Smith Collection.

horses and the prisoners in shackles. On the evening of the first day of the return trip they stopped at the VVN Ranch and asked manager George Neal, who lived there with his wife and children, if they could spend the night.

The next morning,[19] while Neal and Quillen were outside tending to the horses, Standifer removed the prisoners' shackles so that they could wash and dress. As the sheriff stooped to pick up a live coal from the fire to light his pipe, Brookins suddenly attacked him, smashing him in the face. Standifer fell to the floor, momentarily stunned. Quillen was just coming in the door. Brookins grabbed Standifer's rifle and shot the deputy in the chest. Another bullet struck Mrs. Neal in the leg, inflicting a painful but minor wound.[20]

DEADLY DOZEN

The other outlaw, meanwhile, grabbed up Standifer's shotgun and swung the muzzle toward the sheriff. For one awful instant Standifer looked into that gaping barrel and instinctively braced himself to receive the full blast of a shotgun charge at short range. He watched the man's finger tighten on the trigger and saw the hammer fall.

There was a click. The gun, loaded with shells Standifer had prepared himself, had misfired. The two outlaws ran from the building to find the shooting had scattered the horses. In a panic they took to the sandhills but were soon run down and recaptured.[21]

Standifer considered his escape from death by his own shotgun nothing less than miraculous. "There are men living today," a range historian wrote fifty years later, "who will tell you that Bill never ceased to marvel at that miracle . . . , that even if the fault saved his life, his inefficiency in loading the shell hurt his pride."[22]

Deputy Quillen was seriously wounded. The rifle bullet had struck him just above the heart. Standifer and Neal patched him up as best they could, and then Standifer left to get medical help. Leaving the stolen horses temporarily on the VVN range, he set out with his prisoners. He found a doctor and sent him back to attend to Quillen, and continued on to Crosby County.

Almost as miraculously as Standifer's shotgun misfiring, Charlie Quillen survived. "He often wore the coat with the bullet hole in the left breast," old-timer R. P. Smyth recalled. "I've looked across the table at that coat many a time . . . , and I always wondered at Charlie being alive."[23]

Returning with a prisoner from another New Mexico manhunting excursion, Standifer spent a night at the camp of a line rider in Hockley County, who later recalled: "Billy wanted me to guard the prisoner while he got some sleep. I remember how the fellow cussed Standifer and called him a coward, and how Billy left his bed, came over to the prisoner. Looked down at him and said: 'So I'm a coward, am I? I suppose you're a brave man, because when I walked up to your dugout where you were hiding with four buckets of water and half a dozen guns, you came out when I told you to . . . , and you came out with your hands up.' Bill Standifer was a brave man—as fearless as they come."[24] This testimony should carry special weight, as the young line rider was J. Frank Norfleet, a singularly courageous, determined man in his own right, who later spent several years and a great deal of money hunting down and hounding to conviction a gang of confidence operators who had bilked him.[25]

Bill Standifer's spreading reputation as a straight-shooting, swift-handed gunfighter sometimes was enough to defuse potentially violent confrontations, as in the summer of 1889 when IOA Ranch manager Rollie Burns came to the sheriff with a problem. A tough trail boss from south Texas had driven a herd through the IOA pasture, killed an IOA calf for beef, and deliberately ripped out a section of ranch fence rather than go a little way around to the gate. As a veteran cowman, Burns had seen and handled his share of hard cases, but the south Texas drover, whom he described as "a big, muscular fellow with a heavy, drooping mustache [and] one of the biggest guns I ever saw," gave him pause. Burns rode hard for Estacado, swore out a warrant against the man, and enlisted the services of Standifer to serve it. "Standifer had a reputation as a daring man; he later died with his boots on in a duel with another one of his kind," said Burns. When he and the sheriff overtook the trail boss and told him he was under arrest and would have to go back to Estacado with Standifer, he gave them "one hard look" as if he were making up his mind whether to comply or go to shooting. After consideration of Standifer's record as a gunfighter, he decided not to challenge the little lawman and meekly rode back to town with him. The affair cost the trail driver a day's lost time, as well as payment for the damaged fence and twenty-five dollars for the calf. Later Burns learned that the fellow was considered a very bad hombre down on the border. "He had a couple of notches on his gun for white men, and he had gotten several Mexicans, but he didn't count notches for them."[26]

In 1890 Standifer and a Spur Ranch cowboy named Hosea tracked down a horse thief who had been preying on the Spur herds. When the owners of the vast Spur spread authorized a fifty dollar reward to Hosea, but ignored Sheriff Standifer's contribution to the capture, Fred Horsbrugh, Spur Ranch manager, objected: "I would further like to reward Standifer, the sheriff at Estacado, who volunteered to go with Hosea and without whom the thief in all probability would not have been taken. They had a very close shave getting the thief, and if they had been caught by the mob of outlaws they would have been hanged if they let themselves be taken alive, which they were not going to do; and the prisoner was the first they were going to kill."[27]

The voters of Crosby County were pleased with Standifer's performance as sheriff and re-elected him in 1890 and again in 1892. But the stressful years of chasing outlaws took their toll on the diminutive gunman. Increasingly he relied on the bottle for relief and became more quarrelsome and erratic in behavior. "He was a drinking man and a hell-raiser," one old-timer said. "If he got it in for you, he'd go out of his way to make trouble for you."[28] Voters rejected his bid for re-election in 1894, but Spur Ranch manager Fred Horsbrugh, a great admirer of Standifer, quickly saw that he received an appointment as stock inspector for the Northwest Texas Stock Raisers Association and hired him as a protection man.

The Spur Ranch was so huge, extending over more than 400,000 acres and covering large sections of Dickens, Kent, Crosby, and Garza Counties, that Horsbrugh had to hire additional men to assist "the famous Standifer," as he referred to his top gunman in reports to absentee owners.[29] He also contracted with a Denver detective firm for an operative to spy on settlers who had filed on Spur pastureland and were suspected of harboring rustlers.

In August 1896 Horsbrugh dispatched Standifer and an associate named Britt to check out a suspicious settler who was pulling out, headed east. He wanted to be sure the man didn't take any Spur stock with him. "They will follow to the Indian Territory if necessary," Horsbrugh reported, "and if there is anything crooked will either take this man or kill him." Both Standifer and Britt, he assured the owners, were "very determined men and of course well armed."[30]

Clairemont, seat of Kent County, was a favorite rendezvous for rustlers, and Standifer gave it special attention. Little more than a village, with only a few homes and commercial buildings surrounding the courthouse and jail, Clairemont was a very rough town during the turn-of-the-century years and was said to average a killing a week.[31] This was an exaggeration, no doubt, but a great deal of violence did occur there. A feud over ownership of a single cow resulted in the deaths of nine men, a district judge was gunned down in a Clairemont hotel, and a younger brother of the premier Texas gunfighter John Wesley Hardin was killed there.[32]

Bill Standifer contributed to the town's reputation for gunsmoke violence when in June 1898 he killed a rustler named Kiggings in a Clairemont saloon. Fred Horsbrugh reported the killing to his superiors as "a piece of good news." Kiggings, he said, was "one of the worst cowthieves that ever came to these parts. . . . He lived over on Catfish in our pasture, and was about the worst we had. His sudden taking off has, I think, rather disconcerted some of our neighbors and caused a halt, or rearrangement in their programs, as I believe a great deal of quiet stealing was intended to be done through this man, who was a reckless, improvident sort of individual who delighted in stealing, and who stole for the love of it, and for a very small reward would 'maverick' an unbranded calf for another man, and kill the cow to prevent the calf following, if necessary."[33]

Standifer was charged with murder in the Kiggings shooting and released on $5,000 bail. At a hearing in October his lawyers requested a change of venue, and the judge agreed, saying that there were "not enough qualified jurors in [Kent] county to try said cause." The case was transferred to the district court at Fisher County, where the following year a jury acquitted the defendant in a quick trial.[34]

The Matador Ranch, neighboring the Spur, was suffering greatly from rustler activity at this time. The desperate managers hired Standifer away from the Spur with offers of higher pay. Fred Horsbrugh at the Spur kept trying to get his best protection man back. On May 19, 1899, he advised his home office: "I have also written to Standifer who is greatly feared by the thieves, and who killed one of the worst last year, but I have not much hopes of getting him as he is employed . . . in a similar capacity by the ranche to the south-east of us."[35] Horsbrugh kept working at it, however, and less than two weeks later was able to advise his superiors that he had worked out a deal with the Matador to share the work of

the famous Standifer, who has lately been acquitted in the case in which he killed the worst thief we had down at Clairemont last year. He is at work for the ranche south of us who have been having a lot of trouble with thieves, and he has made a lot of those gentry move out of there, [but] he has some time at his disposal, and has come up here to see if he cannot help me with our neighbors. He cannot give me all his time, but I have him riding and he will be able to stay a while and I give him $40 a month in the meantime. The ranchers who really have him hired are agreeable to his assisting up here, and in fact it is not known that he is working here for good and all. He is very well

DEADLY DOZEN

known, and is worth a lot of ordinary men; and already has caused a flutter among the thieves. I understand that the departure of the gentleman who we tried unsuccessfully to send to the penitentiary . . . has been hastened by the advent of Standifer, and has gone to New Mexico.[36]

One of those Standifer suspected of cattle theft was Bee Hardin, a cousin of the redoubtable John Wesley and considered a dangerous man in his own right. Many in Kent County predicted a violent meeting between the two. During this period three horsemen, led by Jim Gober, former sheriff of Potter County in the Texas Panhandle, rode into Kent County in pursuit of outlaws who had driven some stolen cattle from Arapaho, Oklahoma. At Clairemont, Gober talked to Kent County sheriff Norman N. Rodgers, who told him that the wanted men had come through the country with the cattle and that Bee Hardin had provided them fresh horses. Rodgers recommended that Gober get Bill Standifer to help in the chase, but warned: "Don't mention young Hardin taking horses to these men. . . . He and Billy Stantifer [sic] are at loggerheads, and I have been keeping down a killing between them for some time. If Stantifer heard of this kid assisting those fellows for sure it would cause trouble to start anew."[37]

After receiving very little cooperation from others in his long pursuit, Gober was glad to get the assistance of Standifer, whom he knew. "I felt considerable relief," he said, "to know that I was going to find one man that was not obligated or intimidated by thieves and outlaws, so I asked Rodgers where I could find Billy. Rodgers then went with me, and we found Billy and arranged for him to go with us after the cattle the next morning." With the help of Standifer and Rodgers, the Oklahomans recovered the stolen cattle, but the outlaws had flown.[38] No one mentioned Bee Hardin's part in the affair, and apparently he and Standifer never tangled.

Late in 1899 Horsbrugh hired another renowned gunfighter as a Spur Ranch protection man. John Calhoun Pinckney Higgins, known to everyone as "Pink," was a recent arrival in the lower Panhandle country. He had come from Lampasas, Standifer's original home, and it is quite likely that he and Standifer knew each other many years earlier. Although some said that at one time the two men had been close friends,[39] others thought the enmity between them had its origins in those earlier times.

Pink Higgins had seen a great deal of violence and contributed more than his share in his forty-eight years. He had been a major figure in the Higgins-Horrell feud that plagued Lampasas County a quarter century earlier. His reputation was even more fearsome than Standifer's; he had reportedly killed more than a dozen men. When shown a list of fourteen men he was said to have killed, Higgins is quoted as remarking: "I didn't kill them all, but then I got some that wasn't on the bill, so I guess it just about evens up."[40]

One story told about Higgins may be apocryphal—its setting has been placed both at Lampasas County at the time of the 1870s feud[41] and during his turn-of-the-century sojourn in the lower Panhandle[42]— but it illustrates the man's reputation for brutality. It seems Higgins came on a rustler butchering a cow that was not his own. After dispatching the thief with a single rifle shot, Higgins disemboweled the cow, stuffed the dead man inside, and rode to town to announce that everyone should take a ride out onto the prairie and witness a miracle— a cow giving birth to a man. True or not, it is significant that people who knew Pink Higgins believed he was fully capable of such a morbid joke.

As long as the two gunmen were able to work together on the Spur they achieved much success in ridding the range of rustlers. There is no record that they killed any, but they scared them out of the country. Horsbrugh was able to report in the summer of 1900: "Standifer and Higgins . . . have already done us a great deal of good, there being only two or three of the suspected ones left living inside of our fence, and they are very careful what they do. New Mexico has received some of our toughest specimens, and there is a chance that before the year is out that territory will be still further enriched in the same way."[43]

But in time it became apparent to the ranch manager that trouble, which he only defined as "an old grudge," was brewing between his two hired gunfighters. "When I found it out," he later wrote, "I made them understand that they were no good to me if they were unfriendly to each other, as their usefulness depended on their relations, one to the other. They promised to make it all up and let by-gones be by-gones."[44]

The basis for the animosity between Standifer and Higgins has never been adequately explained, although many suggestions have

Deadly Dozen

been offered. Some, including Clifford B. Jones, a later Spur manager who discussed the matter with Higgins, believed Standifer's connection to the Horrell clan through his stepmother and vestiges of hatred remaining from the decades-old family feud in Lampasas were the roots of the "old grudge" mentioned by Horsbrugh and led to the clash between the gunmen.[45]

Others pointed to more current provocations. Another longtime Spur employee, W. J. Elliott, speculated that the trouble grew out of a clash over Pink's son. Standifer was going through a bitter divorce from his third wife during this period, and Cullen Higgins, lawyer son of Pink Higgins, represented Mrs. Standifer in the messy affair. Standifer is said to given young Cullen public tongue-lashings on several occasions. Hearing of this, Pink came to his son's defense and warned Standifer that if it happened again he would be backing his son with a gun. Standifer, never one to be easily bulldozed, reportedly challenged Higgins to name the time and place. Thereafter, Elliott said, "Billy had a chip on his shoulder when Pink Higgins was near or his name mentioned."[46]

A story circulated later that Higgins accused a friend of Standifer's named Bill McComas of stealing Spur stock, and intimated that the dirty work was being done with Standifer's knowledge and possible assistance. Higgins was said to have pistol-whipped a Standifer friend, who may have been McComas. Standifer, furious, then declared war on Higgins.[47]

Any one or all of these reported causes may have brought about the difficulty between the two veteran gunfighters.

Once the two gunmen came face to face in a Clairemont saloon. Higgins, learning that his enemy had spent several hours tipping the bottle, may have deliberately planned the confrontation, knowing that if it came to a gun battle, he, being cold sober, would have a distinct advantage over the inebriated Standifer. But little Billy was not so drunk that he did not recognize the ploy. He refused to draw on Higgins, but dared him to meet him on the town's main street the next day to settle their differences. Higgins nodded agreement and the next morning rode slowly into town with his Winchester in his hand. Standifer, who apparently had second thoughts, was not to be found.[48]

Despite their promise to the Spur manager that they would bury their grievances, Standifer and Higgins must have known that the problem between them could never be resolved until one or the other died or left the country. Horsbrugh, when he saw they could not reconcile their differences, fired his two best protection men in the late summer of 1902. "It broke out again," he reported, "and I turned them both off. Standifer I turned off in August and Higgins later. Higgins asked me to let him stay until the end of September as he had some arrangements to make about moving his family and children to a place where they could attend school. I told him a month did not matter."[49]

It may have mattered a great deal to Bill Standifer, however. Having lost the job he did best, while the man who had become his archenemy still worked for the Spur, he was outraged. Higgins later claimed that during that month of September Standifer several times tried to bushwhack him.

Standifer had been using man-trapping techniques for years, but Pink Higgins had not survived the bloody war with the Horrells and been a protection man himself without learning a few self-survival tricks. When someone told him cow thieves were at work in a certain Spur pasture, the wily old gunman made a circular approach to the section, found a high point of ground, and combed the area with field glasses. Spotting Standifer waiting in ambush, Higgins went home. He said that on another occasion as he started out to corral his horses he caught a glimpse of Standifer hiding behind a rock pile within rifle shot of the pasture. Again he went home without pushing the fight. He claimed that another time Standifer and McComas tried to cut him off as he walked unarmed into his pasture. He ran back to his house, seized his rifle, and rushed out into the yard, but his enemies had melted away. It got so bad, Pink said, that for two days he stayed inside his house, but making up his mind that he would not "live holed up like a rat any longer," and that he must kill his enemy before his enemy killed him, he went looking for Standifer.[50]

These stories, of course, are Pink Higgins's version of events leading up to the final confrontation. Bill Standifer left no accounts. It is known, however, that for several days the two crafty old gunfighters played a deadly game of cat and mouse, with each trying to be the cat.

Finally, on the morning of Wednesday, October 1, 1902, Higgins spotted Standifer, astride "a big beautiful bay horse," and still some distance away, slowly riding toward his house. Saddling his favorite horse, Sandy, Higgins slid his Winchester into the scabbard, mounted up, and rode out to meet him. Like two medieval knights, the two bitter enemies closed for combat.

As they approached, each turned his horse a little to the left, so that his right side would be toward his adversary as they passed. In graphic detail, Higgins later described what happened then:

> He was a little on my right, and I was sure he would not get off his horse on my side, but would use his horse for protection. So I made up my mind to keep my eye on his left foot, and the minute that foot left the stirrup I would get off and go for my gun. When we were less than a hundred yards apart and getting closer every step our horses took, he slipped her out and off I went. My rifle sorter hung in the saddle scabbard, and as I got it out Standifer shot, hitting old Sandy. He jumped against me and made me shoot wild—I always hated to lose the first shot.
>
> Standifer was shooting, but he was jumping around like a Comanche and his shots were going wild. He was sideways to me, and so thin I knew I had to shoot mighty accurate to get him. I knew he couldn't do any good with his gun till he stopped jumping. So I dropped on my knee, trying to get a bead on him, and when he slowed down I let him have it. I knew I had got him when the dust flew out of his sleeve above the elbow and he started to buckle. He dropped his gun into the crook of his other arm and tried to trot off. I called to him, saying if he had had enough I wouldn't shoot again and would come to him, but he fell face forward, his feet flopped up, and he didn't speak.
>
> I was afraid to go to him, fearing he was playing possum after being shot, so I got on my horse and started home.[51]

As he reached his yard, Sandy fell dead. Higgins got another horse, rode to a telephone, and called Sheriff Rodgers at Clairemont. He said he had thought he had killed Bill Standifer and was coming to town to turn himself in. As Higgins told it, Rodgers was no admirer of Standifer: "He said if I wasn't sure I had better go back and finish."[52]

But Standifer was dead all right. Higgins's bullet had passed through his right elbow and into his heart. When Pink recounted the story of the gun battle to Charles Adam Jones several years later, Jones asked if Standifer was buried where he fell. "'Damn him, no!' Higgins exclaimed. 'Do you think I'd let him stay on my place?'"[53]

But actually Bill Standifer is buried not far from the site of his last gunfight, in an area that was then part of the Higgins ranch and later came to be called Standifer's Thicket. About 1959 a headstone was placed over his grave. Its inscription reads: "Billy Standifer Killed by Pink Higgins Oct. 1, 1902."[54]

In his report to the Spur owners of October 6, Fred Horsbrugh described what he called "a premeditated (and mutually arranged for) duel" between "fearless, determined men."

There were two witnesses to the shooting: Bill McComas, who rode to the scene with Standifer and viewed the gunfight from a nearby knoll, and Pink's eldest daughter, who climbed to the roof of the Higgins house to watch the drama unfold. A grand jury, after listening to their testimony and that of Higgins, and considering the physical evidence at the scene, found the killing justifiable and refused to indict Higgins.[55]

Before he died of a heart attack on December 18, 1913,[56] Pink Higgins spoke often of the Standifer killing. Interviewer Charles Adam Jones found that he discussed the affair matter-of-factly, exhibiting no sign of regret or remorse. "With anyone who was interested, Higgins would discuss this shooting just as though it had been a wolf hunt, and with no more feeling, which is understandable enough when one considers that a human wolf was the victim."[57]

— 8 —

CHARLEY PERRY
(1855–?)

"His eyes flashed like the rays of a revolving light."

Charley Perry might have entered Old West legend as an intrepid, determined, gunfighting frontier lawman, a bold and resolute nemesis of the toughest class of border outlaw. He had the necessary attributes of daring, gun-handling skill, and native cunning, and he acquitted himself well enough in several well-publicized cases to catch the attention of the national press. He gloried in the publicity and seemed well on his way to joining his friend Pat Garrett in the upper ranks of legendary gunfighters and lawmen. But Perry had a fatal flaw; as much as he loved the limelight and the admiration of others, he loved money more. That defect would destroy his reputation and erase the memory of his hard-won celebrity as a manhunter. He would be remembered, if at all, as a thief.

Born in Texas in 1855,[1] he was named Christopher Columbus Perry by his parents,[2] but preferred the name "Charles" and used it throughout his adult life. About 1876 he went to Lincoln County, New Mexico, to live with relatives, the Charles J. Ballard family, and take work as a cowboy. He was twenty-two years old in 1877 when he played a minor role in what became known as the Pecos War, a violent range dispute between the big cattlemen of the region and a group of cowboys who, the ranchers charged, were trying to build private herds by stealing from their employers. To protect their interests, John S. Chisum and Robert K. Wylie, the major ranchers, employed a tough crew of gunmen, headed by James M. Highsaw, described by a contemporary as "quick as lightning on the draw [and] cool under any circumstances."[3] The suspected rustlers, centered in the Seven Rivers region, a notorious hangout for outlaws, included "such Seven Rivers hotheads as [Buck] Powell, [Dick] Smith, Andy Boyle, the Beckwith clan, W. H. Johnson, Jake Owen, Lewis Paxton, Nathan Underwood, Milo Pierce, Charlie Woltz, Charlie Perry, and Robert and Wallace Olinger."[4] At least five of those named would die violently in the Pecos War or the more famous Lincoln County War immediately following it.

On March 10, 1877,[5] Jim Highsaw, having obtained solid evidence connecting Seven Rivers cowboy Dick Smith to rustling activity, rode to a cow camp on Loving's Bend of the Pecos and confronted Smith. When Smith went for his gun, "quick as lightning" Highsaw outdrew him and shot him dead. Charley Perry and Jake Owen, two of Smith's pals, were nearby and witnessed the shooting but made no effort to interfere. They later testified before a grand jury that indicted Highsaw for murder, but the gunman came clear on the age-old self-defense plea.[6]

Three months later Perry appeared in another court case. This time the Seven Rivers bunch accused the big cattlemen of thievery. In a June 20, 1877, indictment, they charged Chisum and Wylie and two of their hands, Highsaw and Thad Hendricks, with stealing livestock valued at $1500 from Hugh Beckwith. Charley Perry, Jake Owen, and Buck Powell supported Beckwith in the indictment. The charges were later dropped as the Pecos War ground to a halt, but the stage was set for an even deadlier conflict to follow, the Lincoln County War.[7] Charley Perry played no part in that war, and, although newspapers later reported that he served in posses under Sheriff Pat Garrett that ran down and killed members of the Billy the Kid gang,[8] no evidence corroborates this.

Until 1883 Perry was just another cowboy riding the New Mexico ranges, but a chain of events beginning in the fall of that year changed the course of his life. On November 24 bandits derailed and robbed an eastbound Southern Pacific train near Gage Station in neighboring Grant County. In the course of the robbery they shot and killed T. C. Webster, the engineer. Clever detective work by Silver City marshal Harvey Whitehill and Wells, Fargo & Company chief of detectives James B. Hume soon identified the outlaws as Christopher "Kit" Joy,

Frank Taggart, A. M. "Mitch" Lee, and George Cleveland, all cowboys from the area. When the express company posted a reward of $1,000 for the arrest and conviction of each member of the gang, the Southern Pacific Railroad announced it would match that figure. Responding to the lure of a pot of gold totaling $8,000, lawmen and bounty hunters were soon in the saddle, combing the hills of southwestern New Mexico for the fugitives. On December 28 Whitehill and Socorro County sheriff Pete Simpson captured George Cleveland in the town of Socorro. Ten days later Deputy Sheriff John W. Gilmo of Grant County nabbed Frank Taggart.[9]

The large reward offered for the robbers was the talk of the territory. Even lonely riders like Charley Perry, at a remote line camp of the Lyons and Campbell outfit at Horse Springs, 120 miles west of Socorro, had heard about it. When two well mounted and heavily armed strangers rode into his camp one day in January, saying they were cowboys from White Oaks looking for work, Perry eyed them carefully. He told them he was just a line rider and did no hiring, and the two rode on. Convinced that the men matched the descriptions of Kit Joy and Mitch Lee, the two remaining fugitives, but aware he could not arrest and guard them all alone, Perry hunted up Deputy Sheriff Andrew J. Best and enlisted his aid in pursuing the suspects.

Even for two men, getting Joy and Lee back to Socorro presented a problem. Hounded and desperate, the fugitives would undoubtedly greet any approaching horsemen with leveled guns. Any attempt by Best and Perry at forcible arrest without the "drop" could be suicidal. By the time they overtook the fugitives, Perry and Best had come up with a clever scheme to trick the two into returning voluntarily with them to Socorro. At the outlaw night camp they presented a proposal designed to tempt young desperadoes eager for quick money and daring adventure; they offered an opportunity to help spring Joel Fowler from jail.

That winter the Joel Fowler murder case had vied with the hunt for the Gage Station robbers for the rapt attention of folks in southern New Mexico. Fowler, a prosperous cattleman and notorious gunman, had been convicted and sentenced to hang for the brutal murder of a man named Cale. He remained locked up in the jail at Socorro while his lawyers fought a delaying action in the appeals courts, but the town had a history of active vigilantism and rumors were rife that the "Socorro Stranglers" planned a midnight necktie party for him.

Perry and Best asked the suspected robbers if they were interested in joining a party being organized to rescue Fowler. Participants in such a rescue, they said, could expect to receive handsome payment for their help from wealthy friends of Fowler. For Kit Joy and Mitch Lee, the temptation was irresistible, and they agreed to return to Horse Springs with their new acquaintances. But that night, after they were asleep, Perry and Best disarmed and arrested them. On January 21 the bounty hunters arrived in Socorro and lodged their prisoners in jail to await transfer to Grant County.[10]

The very next night the recurrent Fowler lynching rumors proved accurate. A mob entered the jail, removed Joel Fowler, and strung him up while the young bandits, Kit Joy and Mitch Lee, watched in horror from their cells.[11]

After joining their pals, Cleveland and Taggart, in the Silver City jail, Joy and Lee, still in mortal fear of midnight vigilante justice, engineered a daring breakout. On March 10 the four bandits, together with prisoners Spencer and Chavez, overpowered their guards, secured guns and horses, and galloped out of town, closely pursued by a hastily formed posse of citizens. In a bitterly fought gun battle, Cleveland, Chavez, and posseman Joe Lafferr were killed and Mitch Lee severely wounded. Lee, Taggart, and Spencer finally surrendered. Only Kit Joy escaped. The citizens, enraged over the death of the popular Lafferr, held a summary court right there. They voted to return Spencer to jail but to execute Lee and Taggart on the spot, and carried out the sentences at once. A reporter for a Silver City paper was on the scene and wrote that Mitch Lee "died almost immediately, being weak from loss of blood," but that "Taggart died hard of strangulation—a throat disease that is extremely common among their ilk in this section."[12]

Kit Joy's freedom was short-lived. Ten days later a farmer named Erichus "Rackety" Smith shot Joy in the leg and captured him on the Upper Gila River. Returned to Silver City where his badly infected leg was amputated, Joy remained in jail awaiting trial. The following November a jury convicted him of the murder of Engineer Webster and sentenced him to a life term.[13]

Charley Perry, meanwhile, was involved in another legal battle, the fight over division of the rewards for the capture of the train robbers. Those who had made the original arrests, Harvey Whitehill and Pete Simpson for nabbing Cleveland; John Gilmo for Taggart; and Charley

Perry and Andy Best for Joy and Lee, all had a claim on the reward money. But the escape of the robbers from the jail complicated matters. Four of the posse that had fought the gang and killed three of them felt they deserved a share. So did Rackety Smith, who had captured Kit Joy, and a man named A. C. Eaton, who claimed he had provided vital information to Whitehill that led to the identification of the bandits. There were eleven claimants in all. The claim of the posse members posed a legal question, since the rewards had been offered for "arrest and conviction," and Lee, Taggart, and Cleveland had never gone to trial.

Judge Warren Bristol, after protracted hearings, announced his decision on September 8, 1884. Distribution of Kit Joy reward money he postponed until after Joy's trial. He ruled that rewards for the other three robbers should be divided as follows: $1,333.33 to Harvey Whitehill; $1,333.33 to Perry and Best, jointly; $444.44 to Simpson; $888.88 to Gilmo; and $500 each to the four posse members who had pursued and killed three of the gang after the escape. He rejected Eaton's claim. Court costs were to be deducted from the rewards on a pro rata basis.[14]

At the November 1884 term of court a Sierra County jury convicted Kit Joy of second-degree murder and a judge sentenced him to a life term in the territorial prison. Nine months later, on August 3, 1885, "Special Master" John M. Wright awarded Perry and Best $590.60 for their part in the original capture, and Rackety Smith $295.30 for his recapture of Joy. The $114.10 balance from the $1,000 Southern Pacific reward money went to defray court costs, including $100 for the special master. Somehow Wells, Fargo & Company avoided payment of the reward for Joy, and only $7,000 of the original $8,000 posted for the four bandits was paid.[15]

So, for his part in the capture of Kit Joy and Mitch Lee, Charley Perry cleared almost a thousand dollars. For a cowboy in the 1880s it took two years of hard saddle work to earn that much money. Perry did not miss the lesson: money could be made a lot quicker corralling bad men than corralling livestock. He knew that it was only luck that led Joy and Lee into his camp at Horse Springs, but he also knew he had been sharp enough to recognize them and clever enough to take them into custody. He decided to be a lawman. Wearing the star, he would have the opportunity to nab wanted felons and perhaps enjoy another big payday. Maybe in the process he would see himself lauded in the papers. He liked that.

He quit his job with Lyons and Campbell and returned to Lincoln County where he became a deputy under Sheriff John W. Poe, who had sided Pat Garrett in the Billy the Kid hunt several years earlier. Garrett himself became Perry's idol and mentor.

The first published account of his law enforcement work hardly contributed to the heroic image he sought to create. In January 1890 he and Deputy Sheriff John Berkely, holding a warrant for the arrest of a man named Jeff Kent, trailed their man down the Pecos toward the notorious outlaw hangout of Seven Rivers. At Si Hogg's trading post at the mouth of the Peñasco they stopped to eat and learned that Kent had also eaten there only recently. He was a tough one who would not be taken, Hogg said, and advised the officers to let him go. Perry considered that for a moment. "But if I don't arrest him," he said, "I might as well give up my badge and quit."[16]

On Saturday, January 11, 1890, the lawmen cautiously approached Seven Rivers after dark. Hiding behind a crumbling adobe wall, they watched Kent walk out of Les Dow's saloon and enter a nearby store. They followed him.

"Throw up your hands, Kent; you're under arrest," Perry commanded.

"I'll consider myself under arrest," Kent retorted, "but I won't throw up my hands for any man."

Berkely stepped forward to disarm him, but Kent grabbed the deputy by the coat, spun him around, and, using his body as a shield, thrust his pistol in Perry's face and fired. Momentarily blinded by the blast as the bullet seared along his cheek, Perry staggered backward as a second bullet flew over his head. "He came out of the door on all fours,"[17] and lay as if dead.

Berkely and Kent wrestled, locked in a fierce death struggle. Each managed to get off a shot. As Kent took a bullet through the chest, he shot his adversary just under the left eye, and the deputy sank to the floor. Kent stepped over the body of Berkely and staggered through the doorway. Outside, Perry still lay unmoving. Kent made it to the saloon and asked Les Dow to get him a mount.

When the saloonkeeper got back with a horse, Kent was nowhere to be seen. He had wandered off into the darkness and collapsed. Dow located him by the sound of his groans. With the help of others, Dow

Deadly Dozen

carried Kent to the house of Joe Woods and sent for Barbara Jones. There were no doctors in Seven Rivers, and someone started for Eddy to get one, but Ma'am Jones had plenty of experience ministering to gunshot victims.

A little later Charley Perry, not seriously hurt and his sight restored, appeared at the Woods house and asked if Kent would live. Not likely, Woods replied. Perry demanded to see the dying man. Hearing the exchange, Kent, still defiant on his deathbed, called out: "Joe, give me my gun and tell him to come in." Perry elected to leave. Both Jeff Kent and John Berkely died from their wounds.[18]

Charley Perry's performance in the gunfight at Seven Rivers did not greatly enhance his stature as an officer, but the affair did not deter him from acquiring other badges. In addition to his deputy sheriff's job, he secured a commission as deputy U.S. marshal and appointment as city marshal at Roswell. He was acting in the latter capacity later that year when he was again involved in gunplay, and this time came off to better advantage.

Heavy rains in late August caused cowboys working a big cattle roundup up the Pecos to halt their work as their wagons bogged down. Among those who took advantage of the break in routine to ride into Roswell and raise a little hell was a hard case named George Griffin. According to Judge Smith Lea of Roswell, who told the story in later years, Griffin "had been making the brag all up the Pecos that when he got to Roswell, he was going to kill Charley Perry, the city marshal. News of the threat had reached Perry before Griffin arrived on the scene, but he did not let it disturb the even tenor of his way."[19]

On the night of August 27, Griffin, well tanked up in a Roswell brothel, boasted loudly of his intentions regarding the city marshal while a crowd of raucous cowboys, including his brother James, cheered him on. One of the girls summoned Perry, who came to the back door of the house just as the Griffin brothers and their pals were leaving by the front. The cowboys mounted up and started back to their camp. As they rode past the corner of the building, one of them spotted the marshal at the rear and called out, "There's Charley Perry now."

"Well, I will kill him right now," shouted George Griffin. Raising his pistol, he pointed it in Perry's direction and squinted through the sights with booze-bleared eyes. One of his cooler-headed companions grabbed his arm, preventing him from shooting. Perry jumped back out of the light from the doorway and, according to Judge Lea, "dropped prone on the ground to await developments."[20]

Whooping, the cowboys thundered out of town. Perry rounded up two deputies, Jim Manning and a man named Johnson, and headed for the cow camp on South Spring River to arrest George Griffin. At the narrow bridge over the Rio Hondo the officers slowed their horses to cross single-file. Suddenly shots rang out. The Griffin brothers,[21] anticipating Perry's pursuit, had dropped back to set up in ambush under the bridge.

"It was a full moon, but the sky was so filled with floating clouds that it was alternately dark or light for a short spell," recalled Judge Lea. Fortunately for the officers, it was dark as they crossed the bridge and the shots missed them. Perry could not see his attackers either, but he ripped off a few blind shots in the direction of the muzzle flashes and spurred his horse across the bridge. Simultaneously reaching a decision that Charley Perry's problems with the Griffins were not their own, Manning and Johnson wheeled their horses and returned to Roswell at a gallop.

On the other side of the Hondo, Perry jerked his rifle from the scabbard, slid off his horse, and concealed himself in the bushes. After several moments the Griffins emerged from below the bridge, secured their horses, and attempted to mount. One of Perry's blind shots had torn three fingers from George Griffin's hand and he had difficulty controlling his animal, now badly frightened by the gunshots and the smell of blood. Griffin finally managed to get in the saddle, but the horse bucked as he spurred it up to the road. Silently, Perry watched from the dark.

The moon came out from behind a cloud as Griffin reached the road, and Perry from his lower position in the brush "skylighted him and fired, the ball striking square in the back of his head." The exiting bullet "made a big hole in Griffin's forehead."[22]

As the lifeless body of George Griffin slid to the ground, Jim Griffin's horse bucked free and ran off, leaving its rider afoot in the darkness with Perry. The two men exchanged several ineffective shots before Perry broke off the engagement and slipped away to look for his own horse. "Finding him," Judge Lea continued, "he mounted and rode out half way across the big flat between Rio Hondo and South Spring.

There he dismounted, tied his horse to a little bush, and lay down on the ground."[23]

After some time a figure emerged from the darkness. Perry was sure it was his quarry, "because there was no one else who would be splashing along in the mud on foot at that time of night." James Griffin saw Perry's horse and, thinking it was his own runaway, trudged through the mud toward it. When he was exactly a hundred and twenty-six steps away—they measured the distance the next day—Perry fired. The bullet struck Griffin "in the corner of the forehead, tearing the skull open and exposing the brain for about four inches."[24]

Perry left his victim where he fell and headed back. At the Rio Hondo bridge he met a large posse. His defecting deputies had spread the word in town that the marshal had been killed, and the possemen were looking for his body when Perry rode up. He led them to the bodies of the Griffin brothers, both shot in the head. George was very dead, but James, even with his horrible wound, clung to life until the next day, when he joined his brother in death.[25]

For Charley Perry, this gunfight with the Griffins did much to restore a reputation somewhat tarnished by the Jeff Kent affair. He was now known as a formidable mankiller as well as a mancatcher. From that time on, folks in Roswell and environs would think of him as he was remembered by Judge Smith Lea: "Perry was a quick and accurate shot with either a gun or a pistol . . . , a brave and efficient officer who was neither ashamed nor afraid to go after the worst of them."[26]

In January 1891 the New Mexico territorial legislature created Chaves County from an eastern section of Lincoln. Campbell C. Fountain took office as the first sheriff of the new county, and Charley Perry added a Chaves County deputy sheriff's badge to his collection.[27]

When Frank Lesnet, a Chaves County trustee and receiver of the U.S. Land Office at Roswell, disappeared under mysterious circumstances in late January 1893, Perry, acting in a dual capacity as deputy sheriff and deputy U.S. marshal, set out to find him. He followed Lesnet's trail to Las Cruces and El Paso, but lost it at Pecos. He returned to Roswell and reported that after being seen at Pecos in the company of some unsavory-looking characters, Lesnet had simply vanished. It seemed that the man had been robbed and murdered and his body hidden.[28] When a $9,000 shortage was discovered in Lesnet's accounts, many believed he had absconded with the funds.

Lesnet was never found, dead or alive, and the mystery remained unsolved.[29] But for Charley Perry the incident may have sown the seed of an idea that would bear fruit in the future.

In the spring of 1894 Perry was lauded in the press for preventing an already violent affair from becoming even worse. He was in the Alexander & Smith saloon in Roswell on the night of April 28 when a man named T. J. Thomas, who had previously been warned to stay out of the establishment on pain of death, wandered in. H. P. Alexander, one of the proprietors, immediately pulled a six-shooter from under the bar and shot Thomas three times. Perry leaped up, wrestled the pistol from the saloonman, and placed him under arrest.[30]

Becoming increasingly active in county politics, Perry served on the Central Committee of the Democratic Party and in November 1894 ran for sheriff on the Democratic ticket. With the help of his relatives, the influential Ballard family, he was elected.[31]

A highly publicized search for an outlaw gang leader on the run from Indian Territory in January 1895 gave Perry the opportunity for reward money and widespread fame he had so long sought. In 1894 an outlaw gang led by twenty-year-old, baby-faced William Tuttle "Bill" Cook went on a murderous crime spree, robbing trains, banks, stores, and post offices. When officers made it too hot for them, the gang members split up. Cook headed west.

Lawmen across the southwest, learning of high rewards offered for Cook's capture, kept a sharp lookout for the fugitive. Texas sheriffs Jeff Harkey of Dickens County, Tom D. Love of Borden County, and Y. D. McMurray of Mitchell County, and Texas Ranger W. J. L. Sullivan tracked him into New Mexico where Perry got in the hunt. On January 8 Texas Ranger Sergeant Sullivan rode into Roswell and enlisted Perry's aid. Since he was out of his jurisdiction, he needed a New Mexico officer or a federal marshal to make the official arrest if Cook could be apprehended. Perry's interest grew apace when he heard of the rewards on Bill Cook's head.

While Sullivan followed some leads in town, Perry did some investigating of his own and learned that a man calling himself "John Williams" who answered Cook's description had been in Roswell and had recently left for White Oaks. That night, while Sullivan slept, Perry saddled up, and accompanied by Tom Love, set out after the suspect. Y. D. McMurray later joined them on the trail that led into Lincoln County. If Cook

Christopher Columbus "Charley" Perry, sheriff of Chaves County, New Mexico. From the author's collection.

could be found, Perry would have to make the arrest as a deputy U.S. marshal. He swore in the two Texas sheriffs as federal possemen. On January 12, 1895, the officers ran the outlaw to ground at Farrell's ranch near Fort Sumner and effected his capture without incident.

"Me and my deputies . . . recognized Cook at first glance," Perry later told reporters. Quicker than a flash we had our Winchesters out and Cook was so thoroughly surprised that he lost his nerve, and although he had two sixshooters about his waist his hands went up at my command."[32] Perry proceeded to Fort Stanton, the nearest telegraph office, where he wired his superior, U.S. Marshal Edward L. Hall at Santa Fe, that he had Cook in custody and requested instructions. Hall told him to come to Santa Fe to obtain the necessary papers for the return of the prisoner to Indian Territory.[33]

After getting the legal papers at Santa Fe, Perry, Love, and McMurray started on the long journey to take Bill Cook back to face Judge I. C. Parker in the federal court at Fort Smith, Arkansas. At the change of trains at El Paso, newspapermen surrounded Perry, who reveled in the attention and responded to their questions with alacrity. Wire services disseminated the interviews, and soon papers across the country were extolling the heroics of Charley Perry, "one of the most fearless officers in New Mexico." A Santa Fe correspondent said that "no arrest in the southwest since the days of Billy the Kid and Kit Joy has stirred up as much interest as the capture of Bill Cook."[34]

The El Paso stop was not entirely enjoyable for Perry, however. Ranger Sergeant Sullivan, furious at Perry for finagling him out of a share of the reward money, braced him at the depot. "That was a dirty game you played on me, Perry," he stormed. "You have treated me worse than any honorable officer would treat another." Looking up at the big ranger, six feet, three inches tall, Perry made no reply, but turned on his heel and boarded the train.[35] When he published his memoirs thirteen years later, Sullivan still had not received a penny of the reward and was still bitter over the affair.[36]

The officers delivered Cook to the federal lockup at Fort Smith, where he subsequently was convicted in Judge Parker's court and sentenced to forty-five years in prison.[37] Perry returned to New Mexico, but he was back again two months later. He had arrested James Turner, another member of the Cook gang who had eluded the Indian Nation marshals and the Texas Rangers. He delivered his catch to the authorities at Fort Smith and on his return trip again granted frequent interviews to admiring journalists. A New York reporter, long on hyperbole and flights of imagination, described Perry as "a short man, spare of figure though very broad of shoulders, with a keen razor-like face and light blue eyes, which when he was engaged in peaceful conversation round the stove of the corner grocery, were as mild as an antelope's but when roused by anger or to action, flashed like the rays of a revolving light." In a particularly ludicrous addition, the writer explained to his Eastern readers that Perry "carries his revolver in front of his belt instead of behind, so that by a quick muscular movement of the stomach he can toss the pistol into his hand before his adversary has time to draw on him."[38]

It is unclear whether Perry or any of the other officers actually collected any of the $8,000 rewards offered for Cook's arrest and conviction. Perry strongly argued his claim to at least a share in the press, saying that he had expended $1,500 of his own funds in the pursuit of the outlaws. Although the *Kansas City Times* opined that "whenever a man undertakes to arrest such desperadoes as Cook, he risks his life and should be paid without quibbling," an Indian Territory paper noted that "if any reward is ever paid for the capture of Bill, it will be done grudgingly."[39]

If Perry did not gain financially by the Cook gang affair, he certainly achieved his other goal: celebrity. Newspapers were now comparing him favorably with Pat Garrett, the most famous lawman in the southwest. He was said to have been the constant companion of the legendary sheriff, who had given him "many a lesson" in manhunting. As "Garrett's lieutenant," he had ridden in the pursuit of Billy the Kid. When Garrett "summoned a posse the first man to respond was C. C. Perry." Garrett was aging, and "the people came to look upon Perry as his natural successor."[40]

As much as Perry enjoyed his newfound acclaim, he still brooded over the delays in payment of the reward money. In the following months he drank more heavily, and his behavior became increasingly unpredictable and violent. Dee Harkey, a deputy U.S. marshal who worked with him in New Mexico, wrote in his autobiography that Perry "had a mania to kill people that posed as bad men and killers."[41] Interviewed in 1947, Harkey said that "Charley was mean as hell and . . . he liked to kill fellers. He was just one of these fellers that liked to kill. . . . But he wasn't brave. . . . He and I got to be good friends when he first got out here. . . . We got to be damn good cronies. He was United States deputy marshal . . . and I was [too], so we worked together on a good many cases. [But it got so] the only thing he wanted [was] to kill. He didn't want to arrest. Hell, he wanted to kill."[42]

In April 1895, according to an account published in a Santa Fe paper, Perry so angered one of his own deputies that the man pulled a gun and fired three shots at the sheriff, missing all three. Perry vehemently denied the story, and it may not have happened, but the credence given it is an indication of the tension surrounding the Chaves County sheriff's office during this period.[43] Another story went the rounds that Perry "tried to boss" the Albuquerque to El Paso train one day. An unidentified man told a newsman he was on that train. "I saw the little dried up conductor make him go and apologize to the Pullman porter. Perry didn't like the job, but he was looking down a .41 Colt's when he did the humility act. . . . Charley Perry was an arrant coward."[44]

In May Perry set out with the express purpose, he said, of killing John Wesley Hardin, the legendary Texas gunfighter, recently released from prison, who had come to El Paso and whose antics were getting much coverage in the local papers. On the evening of May 23, Perry, well fortified with alcohol, entered El Paso's Wigwam Saloon, one of the gunman's hangouts. When he loudly demanded to see Hardin, George Gladden politely told him Hardin was not there at the moment, but that he was a friend and asked if he might be of help. Perry fixed Gladden with a bleary-eyed stare. "Mr. Hardin has sought an introduction to me on several occasions," he said, and I want nothing to do with him or you, for you and Hardin have murdered my friends."

"I desire no row," said Gladden quickly. "I am unarmed."

"Here are two pistols. Take your choice," Perry said, placing two six-guns on the bar. When Gladden refused the challenge, Perry slapped his face and called him a coward. Promising to return the next morning to fight both Gladden and Hardin, he gathered up his artillery and stalked out.

There can be little doubt that in the old days Wes Hardin would have cheerfully accepted Perry's challenge, but his gunfighting days were over. He was a lawyer now, and his battlefields were the courts.

When he heard the story from Gladden, he swore out a warrant and had Perry arrested on charges of carrying a gun, "rudely displaying" a pistol, threatening to take life, and assault and battery." The next morning in the city court, Perry, sober and chastened, entered a plea of guilty to two of the charges. The magistrate fined him five dollars on each count.[45]

An El Paso paper later carried a story that Perry had been put up to challenging Hardin by Constable John Selman, another deadly gunman, who three months later would put out Hardin's light. "[Perry] tanked up on whiskey and allowed John Selman to persuade him to go to the Wigwam after Hardin. When Perry called for Hardin at the bar that morning John Selman was standing on the stairs with a gun in his hand," a habitue of the Wigwam Saloon told a newsman. "After taking a nap Perry realized that he had run a big risk, so he sent word to Hardin that he would be around to apologize in a few minutes; and I heard him make the apology."[46]

Dee Harkey thought that Perry "made a very good criminal officer," despite his drunken binges and irrational behavior. "He and I were deputy United States marshals at the same time and became friends, working together in a number of arrests," wrote Harkey.[47] That friendship was strained only a month after the debacle at El Paso when Harkey rode into Chaves County, Perry's bailiwick, and captured a man named Malcolm Campbell, wanted for a double murder in Texas. There was a reward offered for Campbell, and Harkey claimed it. Perry was furious. Texas Ranger Sergeant Sullivan, if he heard of the incident, must have smiled broadly.[48]

For some time Perry's eyes had been bothering him. This was a particularly worrisome problem for one in his profession. In August 1895 he had an operation for removal of cataracts and was out of action for most of the balance of the year.[49]

In February 1896 he was one of thirteen federal marshals sent to El Paso to prevent a scheduled prizefight between heavyweight title contenders Bob Fitzsimmons and Peter Maher. Three Texas Ranger companies, totaling some forty men, including Sergeant W. J. L. Sullivan, were also on hand to see that the fight did not come off. Gamblers, pickpockets, thugs, all the flotsam and jetsam of the Western underworld, flocked to El Paso for the big fight, but, as the local papers noted, the only threats of violence were "occasioned by outside people who are commissioned to carry guns," and "visiting officials [made] all the sensational gun plays."[50]

One of those "sensational gun plays," according to Ranger Sergeant Sullivan, was an attempt by Deputy U.S. Marshal Charley Perry to shoot him in the back. As Sullivan related the story, he and several officers were quieting a saloon row when Special Ranger Gene Miller shouted a warning that a man in the crowd had a pistol trained on Sullivan's back. "I glanced quickly around," said Sullivan, "and there, standing behind me, was [Perry,] the man who stole Bill Cook away from me in Roswell, N. M. I could see the handle of his sixshooter, which he held in his hand behind him. . . . [He] left before anything else was said about the incident. . . . Miller then told me that the man had his pistol cocked and pointed at my spine. . . . It seems that [he] was about to take advantage of the moment, while confusion reigned, and murder me from behind, because of his grudge against me. I told Miller that if I had caught the man pointing his gun at me, I would have killed him on the spot."[51] No one will ever know if Charley Perry really intended to murder the ranger that night, but it is clear Sullivan thought him capable of such an act.

That same month Las Cruces lawyer Albert J. Fountain, one of New Mexico's most prominent and controversial figures, disappeared with his eight-year-old son, setting off a mystery that baffled investigators at the time and remains unsolved to this day. Governor W. T. Thornton appointed Doña Ana County sheriff Pat Garrett to head up the investigation. Garrett, in turn, enlisted Charley Perry to help him. It is clear from the reports of John C. Fraser of the Pinkerton National Detective Agency, also assigned to the case, that Garrett placed great confidence in Perry, whom he regarded "as quite a detective." Garrett, said Fraser, relied on Perry's "word and advice for the truth or falsity of statements and rumors which [came] to them." Fraser, however, distrusted Perry and felt he had a negative influence on Garrett. Perry, in turn, made no effort to hide his disdain for the Pinkerton man. "Perry treated my investigation . . . in a very light manner," Fraser reported. U.S. Marshal Hall shared his deputy's low opinion of the Pinkertons. He told Fraser that "if Pat Garrett and Mr. Perry could not find the evidence it was utter folly for anyone else to try."[52]

Charley Perry worked on the Fountain case sporadically during the spring of 1896, but, as later events revealed, he was preoccupied during these months with dark plans for his own future. As sheriff, Perry was also responsible for tax collections in Chaves County. He made those collections that spring and in June deposited the proceeds in an account he opened in a Santa Fe bank. He also transferred his personal funds from his Roswell bank to the Santa Fe account.

He was still in the territorial capital, contemplating his next move, when Marshal Hall called him into his office. Bandits had robbed a store in Liberty, New Mexico, and killed two men who pursued them. The robbers, later identified as brothers Tom and Sam Ketchum, had taken postal funds in the holdup, making it a federal case. John Legg, a deputy sheriff under Perry and also a deputy U.S. marshal, had joined officers Dee Harkey and Cal Carpenter in pursuit of the outlaws. The trail led out of New Mexico into Texas. When the lawmen located the outlaw camp on Toyah Creek and wired Santa Fe for help, Marshal Hall dispatched Perry with warrants.

The assignment did not fit into Perry's plans, but he made quick adjustments. He withdrew the money in his account, some $9,000, taking the full amount in twenty-dollar gold pieces, and entrained for Texas. On June 7 he met Harkey, Legg, and Carpenter at Pecos, and the four officers went out to the outlaw camp, but found that their quarry had flown. The lawmen followed the trail, making camp that night near Fort Stockton.[53]

Dee Harkey was in for a surprise when he bedded down with Perry that night. When Perry rolled over, "a big handful of twenty dollar gold pieces rolled out of his pocket," Harkey recalled.

"I said, 'My God, what are you doing with so much money?'"

"Perry said, 'I have nine thousand dollars in my pocket and am going to settle up with Cahoon, the crooked-eyed son-of-a-bitch and tell him to go to hell.'"[54]

The reference was to Edward A. Cahoon, president of the First National Bank of Roswell, and a man with a crossed eye, but the reason for Perry's angry eruption is not known.

On June 24 Perry wired Marshal Hall from Fort Davis that "the murderers are heading for the Mexican line [but] I shall overtake and capture them."[55] He was overly optimistic, however; the Ketchum brothers escaped across the border before the pursuing posse caught up with them. When Mexican authorities at Ojinaga, a village across the Rio Grande from Presidio, on July 1 sent word that they had one of the fugitives in custody, Perry told the other officers he would go to Santa Fe to obtain extradition papers. He left and disappeared.

Within days Chaves County officials awoke to the realization that their sheriff had absconded with more than $7,600 in tax money. The revelation did not come as a surprise to some. Chaves County pioneer Joseph C. Lea wrote Governor Thornton on July 15 that Perry's outrageous escapades and association with criminal types had long been a concern. Good citizens acknowledged that the sheriff's conduct had been "very bad," he said, but "not any worse than we expected."[56]

Rumors flew regarding Perry's whereabouts. A recurring story had him joining the "Black Jack" gang of the Ketchum brothers, and a year later federal marshals were still pursuing these reports.[57] Another account had him appearing in El Paso with "a good looking woman" shortly before his theft was discovered and then going on alone to Mexico. This woman later misled some searchers with a tearful tale that Perry had been killed in Mexico. "She even went so far," said one officer, "as to describe to me how he was shot in the abdomen while making an arrest and before dying wrote to her. That's a slick girl and she is now in the City of Mexico in the employment of a very slick man."[58]

It was later learned that Charley Perry, the "very slick man," had taken a steamer, bound for South Africa, from the Mexican port of Tampico. The "good looking woman" and Harry Thompson, a close friend, accompanied him.[59] In November a man named D. W. Shoemaker reported seeing the absconding sheriff in Cape Town.[60] Later J. H. Bradstreet, recently returned from South Africa, delivered a gold watch to Roswell resident C. R. Carr. Perry had borrowed the watch from Carr shortly before his disappearance and had returned it.[61]

Charley Perry left a wife and daughter in Roswell.[62] He was never seen in New Mexico again. A number of stories concerning his eventual fate appeared over the following years; he had been killed in a fight with Kaffirs;[63] he had fallen in a battle with Bantu tribesmen;[64] he had joined the British army with Thompson and had been killed by the Boers;[65] he had been mortally wounded leading a command of foreign mercenaries for the Boers at the Battle of Elandslaagte;[66] and he had been killed in a Johannesburg gambling house.[67]

None of the reports was ever substantiated, but it is significant that they all had Charley Perry dying violently; no one ever believed such a man could die peacefully in bed.

— 9 —

BARNEY RIGGS
(1856–1902)

"I was still a friend of law and order."

Barney Riggs often bragged that he was the only man ever sent to prison for killing one man and released for killing two. Although the claim was exaggerated and not exactly accurate, it came very near the truth. Riggs could also boast of having served one of the shortest life sentences on record—one year to the day. Lying on his deathbed he may have ruminated on the strange irony that he, a man who lived by the gun his entire life and whose notoriety as an expert gunfighter was widespread, would be armed only with a walking stick in his last deadly encounter.

Barney Kemp Riggs was born in Arkansas on December 18, 1856, the second of seven children born to Thomas and Hannah Felton Riggs. Shortly after Barney's birth his parents moved to Texas, where began a history of violence that would plague the Riggs family through two generations.[1] In March 1859 Indians killed Barney's uncle, John Riggs, in Coryell County. His older brother, Brannick, got into a shooting scrape in Kimble County in October 1885, stood trial for murder and assault, and came off clear. Dick, a younger brother, also was tried for murder at El Paso in 1909 and acquitted.[2]

Barney, however, outdid all his clan in violent encounters. He killed at least four men—perhaps many more—before falling victim himself to the deadly six-shooter. At the age of eighteen he may have killed his first man in what was described in sketchy reports as an accidental shooting.

On August 30, 1875, at Salado, in Bell County, Texas, according to the *Austin Democratic Statesman*, Hugh Armstrong received a wound, believed to be fatal, from a gun in the hands of his friend Barney Riggs. "The pistol was empty and Barney was only 'fooling with it.' Empty guns and pistols kill almost as many people as non-explosive coal oil lamps."[3]

Five years later Riggs left Texas, bound for Arizona. According to family tradition, the departure was hurried and rather farcical. "He got into a little trouble, nothing serious, in Texas," said a family member. "The sheriff came and told him he would have to go to the office with him as he wanted to ask him some questions. . . . Barney asked if he could clean up and change his clothes. Sheriff said O.K., so Barney went in the house and carried on a conversation with his sister, only his sister was not home. He dressed up in his sister's clothes and walked out past the sheriff and left."[4]

Two Riggs brothers, uncles of Barney, had settled in Cochise County, Arizona, and were well established. Brannick Riggs, "Uncle Billy," had the Sycamore ranch on Pine Creek in the Sulphur Springs Valley, where Barney found employment as a cowboy. "Uncle Jim," James Munroe Riggs, lived with his second wife and her children in the nearby town of Dos Cabezas, where he ran a grocery store and was the postmaster.[5] Another prominent entrepreneur of Dos Cabezas was a Mrs. Hicklin, who owned the Central Hotel, the Alhambra Saloon, and a meat market.[6] Of more interest to Barney Riggs than Mrs. Hicklin's business enterprises was her attractive daughter Vennie. Soon Barney and Vennie announced their engagement. On February 21, 1882, Justice of the Peace A. E. Fay conducted the wedding ceremony at the J. M. Riggs home in Dos Cabezas.[7]

These were turbulent times in Cochise County. Only four months before, national attention had been drawn to the celebrated street fight in Tombstone when, on October 26, 1881, three men were shot dead by the three Earp brothers and Doc Holliday. A hearing into this event went on throughout the month of November, and then on December 28 hidden assassins shotgunned Tombstone city marshal Virgil Earp, crippling him for life. On March 18, 1882, less than a month after the Riggs marriage, gunmen shot and killed Morgan Earp in Tombstone. Two nights later Wyatt Earp and Doc Holliday killed Frank Stilwell, believed to be one of Morgan's murderers, in Tucson.

Wyatt then led a pack of gunmen on his famous "Vendetta Ride" after other enemies he accused of the shooting of his brothers. Cochise County sheriff John Behan deputized a number of possemen to assist in the hunt for the Earp party, including Barney Riggs.[8]

Although he did not play a prominent role in these memorable events, Riggs, according to stories that circulated within the Riggs family, was personally involved in unpublicized criminality and murder at this time. He and others were stealing horses in Arizona, driving them into Mexico, and returning with stolen horses for sale north of the border. On one expedition with his cousin he got into a dispute with two Mexican men and three women at a watering hole and shot and killed the two men. Later he said to his cousin: "You know, those women will go into town and tell on me." So, said the cousin, "he went back and shot the three women."[9]

Riggs's first recorded murder, however, took place on September 29, 1886, and his victim was a stepson of Uncle Jim, twenty-six-year-old Richmond L. Hudson, whom Barney accused of having more than a familial interest in his wife, Vennie. Returning from Texas, where he had gone on a lengthy cattle-buying trip, Riggs was told by friends that Hudson and Vennie had carried on an affair in his absence. When he confronted his stepcousin about it, Hudson denied the story. Riggs let the matter pass for the moment but made it clear that he would kill anyone making advances toward his wife. A few days later Hudson was heard to brag that he had seduced Vennie and was not a bit afraid of Barney Riggs.

At dusk on the evening of September 29, Richmond Hudson, William "Deadshot" Moss, and several other cowboys were driving cattle into a pen at the Osborne ranch, seven miles east of Dos Cabezas. Hudson was standing at the corral gate when suddenly an unseen gunman opened fire. Bullets struck Hudson in the head, the neck, and the hand. As Moss and the other startled cowboys rushed to the dying Hudson, his assailant slipped off into the gathering darkness.[10]

The wrangle between Riggs and Hudson over Vennie had been the juiciest item of gossip in the county, and Riggs was the obvious prime suspect in the murder. Suspicion hardened into certainty when it was learned that he had stopped at the house of his cousin, Thomas J. Riggs, and admitted the shooting before riding off into the mountains on the best horse on the ranch.[11] Officials offered a $250 reward for his capture.[12]

The story of that capture was related later by Fred Dodge, a Tombstone gambler and sometime lawman. Suspecting that Riggs was hiding out near the Brannick Riggs ranch and that his wife was providing him supplies, Dodge enlisted the aid of Deputy Sheriff Charley Smith and set up what lawmen called a "still hunt." In order to avoid alerting Riggs's friends, he and Smith slipped separately out of Tombstone at night. They met secretly at a rendezvous in the Dragoon Mountains and continued on to a site overlooking the Riggs ranch in the Sulphur Springs Valley. There they set up a round-the-clock watch.

They were quickly rewarded. Dawn's first light disclosed a rider on the opposite hill signaling to a woman at the ranch house. With his field glasses Dodge was able to identify the two figures as Barney Riggs and his wife. The officers waited all day. As dusk descended they saw Vennie load provisions on a horse and ride out to meet her husband. Smith and Dodge circled the hill, approached from the opposite direction in the darkness, and surprised the couple. Smith placed both under arrest, and he and Dodge took them to Tombstone, where Riggs was held for the murder of Hudson and Vennie was released.[13]

County residents were divided on the merits of the case. Many felt that by killing a man who had made sexual advances to his wife after giving him fair warning Riggs was acting in the best Southern tradition. Others could not condone a murder from ambush. The case came to trial in Tombstone on November 11, 1886. Heading the prosecution was Marcus A. Smith, who later represented Arizona Territory in Washington for many years. William Herring represented Riggs. The division in public sentiment regarding the case was reflected in the jury, which could not reach agreement on a verdict. Judge Webster Street declared a mistrial and scheduled a new trial for the following month.

Before the second trial began, Attorney Herring withdrew from the case. Allen R. English, considered the most adept attorney in Arizona in swaying juries, agreed to defend Riggs, but demanded $500, a whopping legal fee for the time and place. "Blood being thicker than water, Uncle Billy came up with the money."[14]

Tension had gripped Tombstone all during the first trial, and it did not ease as the second opened. Sheriff Robert Hatch hired special deputies, including Fred Dodge, to protect jury members, Judge Street, and other court officials. One morning Dodge and another deputy were escorting the twelve jurors up Allen Street when shooting broke out. Everyone scurried for cover, but no one was injured. It was later disclosed that Brannick Riggs and another man (probably a family member) had fired their pistols in an unsuccessful attempt to frighten and scatter the jury and force another mistrial.[15]

The testimony of Tom Hannon, another cowboy from Sulphur Springs Valley, provided a brief moment of comic relief in the tense court drama. English had called Hannon as a defense witness, but probably regretted it. After being sworn, Hannon was asked his occupation.

"Horse stealing," he replied.

When the resulting uproar in the courtroom subsided, Hannon explained that he had been stealing horses from the Indians and hiding them in the canyons for later sale. He was doing pretty well, too, he said, until someone found out about this business and threatened to turn him in to the law unless he split the profits with him.

"And who was that?" asked the incredulous English.

"Old Man Brannick Riggs, and he got the lion's share," Hannon responded, and the courtroom erupted in laughter.[16]

Brannick Riggs did not think Hannon funny at all. Although it was a bitterly cold day in Tombstone that December 23 and he was wearing two overcoats, he was aflame with anger and indignation as he left the courtroom and walked toward the OK Corral. Spotting Hannon, he pulled a gun, snapped off a hasty shot, and missed. Hannon leaped behind a cottonwood tree and returned the fire. "Uncle Billy went down like a 'poled ox'" when a bullet struck him in the chest, but after passing through the heavy overcoats, the slug lodged in a leather wallet he had in a breast pocket. "It knocked him out and turned his side blue but never broke the skin."[17]

There was a moment of high drama as the trial neared its completion. In his closing argument the district attorney compared Barney Riggs to an Apache renegade, sneaking up on an unsuspecting Richmond Hudson and murdering him without a chance to defend himself. Riggs, who had listened with mounting fury, suddenly grasped a large inkstand from a table and lunged at the prosecutor. "Yes, you son-of-a-bitch, and I'll murder you!" he shouted.

Fred Dodge, seated near the judge with a cutoff double-barreled shotgun at his knee, was keeping a sharp eye on the defendant. When

Riggs moved, Dodge jumped. Bounding over the prosecutor's table, he landed on Riggs, driving him to the floor. As Dodge later related the tale, Mark Smith, always imperturbable, murmured "Thank you, Fred," and continued his summation.[18]

On the last day of the year 1886 the jury brought in a verdict of guilty of murder in the first degree, and Judge Street sentenced Barney Riggs to prison for life. Sheriff Bob Hatch immediately conveyed him to the Arizona Territorial Prison at Yuma, where he was given a striped suit and became Convict Number 426. He was described in the prison records as literate, five feet, six and a half inches tall, with "sandy" complexion, brown hair, and gray eyes.[19]

At the age of thirty, Barney Riggs faced a bleak future. He could expect to spend what life remained for him in the dismal confines of the notorious "Hell-Hole of Yuma." Up to this point he had done nothing to place him in the ranks of the storied gunfighters of the West. He was simply a killer, a back-shooting, cold-blooded murderer of defenseless men and women. Like many before and after him, he would live out his days behind bars, die, and be buried, unmourned and forgotten.

But even as Riggs sweltered in the heat of the Yuma prison in the summer of 1887, events were taking place in Pima County that would ultimately have a profound effect upon his future. Six Mexican desperadoes, led by Librado Puebla, crossed the border and staged a drunken revel in Tucson, terrorizing the citizenry. Later they tortured an old man they believed had money hidden, burning his hands and feet in an effort to make him talk. Pima County Sheriff Matthew F. Shaw ran down and captured the Mexicans, and convictions and sentences of thirty years at Yuma for each of the gang quickly followed. Within weeks of his incarceration Librado Puebla led his followers in a desperate breakout attempt.

On the morning of October 27, 1887, inmate Jose Lopez, who spoke English and was often used as an interpreter by the prison administration, approached Superintendent Thomas Gates as he walked through the prison yard. When Gates stopped to talk with Lopez, convicts Puebla, Fernando Vasquez, and Esequiel Bustamente suddenly surrounded him. Puebla pinned Gates's arms behind his back and held a knife to his throat. He shouted for the inmate gatekeeper to open up. When the barrier swung wide, three other convicts, Tiopelo Baca, Ricardo Padilla, and Albino Villa, ran through the opening to the superintendent's house to look for weapons. Padilla attacked Fred Fredley, the yardmaster, with a pick before Assistant Superintendent John H. Behan rescued Fredley at the point of a rifle.[20] Guard W. H. Reynolds cut loose on the other two with a rifle, hitting Villa in the arm and shoulder. Meanwhile, Lopez and Vasquez broke open a desk in Gates's office and obtained a pistol.

Riggs was at work in the carpenter shop when the excitement began. "I saw [Lopez and Bustamente] run by the door of the shop as if excited," he later wrote.[21] "Thinking it was a fight between the prisoners, I went to the door and through the shoe and tailor shop before I could see what was the matter." When he saw Gates struggling with the two Mexicans, Riggs went into action. "As soon as I saw what was the matter I ran to his assistance. . . . As I reached the gate, Pueblo [sic], who was holding him, made a lunge at me with his knife. I jumped back."

Superintendent Gates, still in Puebla's grasp and threatened by the convict's knife, yelled at Guard Frank Hartley in the main watchtower to open fire. Just as Hartley cut loose with his rifle, Lopez emerged from Gates's office, pistol in hand. At the same moment Prison Secretary Richard Rule appeared on the scene, also waving a six-shooter.

Lopez took deliberate aim at Gates's head and fired, but at that instant the superintendent twisted away and the bullet struck Puebla in the arm. Rule clubbed Puebla on the head with his pistol, stunning him, but the embattled Mexican stubbornly maintained his grip on Gates. Rule and Lopez exchanged shots, both missing. Rule then ran for cover.

Guard Hartley in the watchtower now found the range, and his rifle began to wreak deadly effect.[22] In turn he shot Lopez, Bustamente, and Vasquez. "Just as Lopes [sic] fired his second shot," Riggs said, "Hartley shot him and he fell on his face and rolled over on his side and fired one shot at me."[23] Hartley pumped a second round into Lopez, and Dick Rule gave him another.

Librado Puebla, bleeding from head and arm wounds, still managed to keep Gates's body between himself and Hartley's deadly rifle. With his accomplices dropping on all sides, he viciously plunged his knife into the superintendent's back. Said Thomas Gates: "[He] drove his butcher knife . . . into my body near the neck, on the right side of the backbone, making a wound about five inches long and touching the lung. So badly was I cut that when I tried to breathe the air would pass from the lung through the orifice of the wound. Puebla also turned the knife in the wound, still grasping me, the knife still in my body."[24]

"Just at that time," Riggs remembered, "the superintendent called to me: 'Barney, the fellow is stabbing me to death!' I started toward him and he said: 'Get my pistol. Lopes has it.' I ran and jumped astride of Lopes and wrenched the pistol from his hand, and, turning on Pueblo, I shot him in the right breast."[25]

"The shot," said Gates, "caused [Puebla] to pull the knife from the wound with such force that it flew over his head more than ten feet and caused him to break loose from me."[26]

"He threw up the knife and turned to run," Riggs went on. "I shot him again . . . in the small of the back. He ran a little further, when Hartley fired and broke his thigh. I whirled and caught the super-intendent before he fell, put my hand over the wound in his back and held him until another prisoner came and we carried him into the house."[27]

Hartley told Gates later that he very nearly shot Riggs, believing him to be one of the escapees. "Had he killed Riggs, Puebla would certainly have killed me," Gates said.[28]

When the smoke cleared and order was restored, four prisoners, Puebla, Lopez, Bustamente, and Vasquez, were dead or dying. Convict Villa, with two gunshot wounds, eventually recovered. Superintendent Thomas Gates also survived, but never completely regained his health. The following April he was forced to resign because of his injuries and remained an invalid the rest of his life. A few years later he reportedly committed suicide.[29]

For his part in the bloody affair Barney Riggs found himself suddenly lionized. He had "proved himself to be a hero," said the Yuma newspaper. "Barney Riggs has earned his freedom and we are sure the press of the Territory will join us in asking Governor [C. Meyer] Zulick to send the brave fellow an unconditional pardon."[30]

Soon a petition requesting a full pardon for Riggs appeared on the governor's desk. Gates, Behan, members of the board of prison commissioners, all the prison guards, and several leading Arizona citizens signed it. Many citizens of Dos Cabezas and Sulphur Springs Valley, fearful that the return of Riggs would trigger a wave of violence, submitted another petition to the governor, entreating him to keep Riggs locked up.[31] Confronted with conflicting demands from two constituencies, Zulick, a shrewd politician, took a middle course. On December 21, 1887, he granted Riggs a pardon, in recognition of his "prompt and courageous action" during the riot two months earlier. There was one condition: Riggs must "leave the territory forthwith and never return thereto."[32]

Riggs was informed of the pardon on the 24th of December as a kind of Christmas gift. He walked out of the Yuma prison a free man one week later, on December 31, 1887, the first anniversary of his incarceration. In conformance with the provisions of his pardon, he left Arizona immediately and went to nearby California.

One child had been born to the marriage of Barney and Vennie Riggs, a son, William Earl, who was then living in a foster home in Los Angeles. Riggs went to Los Angeles, collected his son, and met his wife in San Diego. However, tragedies past made it impossible for Barney and Vennie to resume a normal life together. Soon Riggs took his son and headed for Texas, leaving Vennie behind.

Back in Texas Riggs formed a partnership with his younger brother Tom in the operation of a horse ranch about thirty miles west of Fort Stockton in Pecos County. For several years he avoided trouble. When the *Albuquerque Citizen* reported in the spring of 1889 that he had been arrested for killing a cowboy, the story was picked up and reprinted in a number of Western papers. Riggs wrote a letter to the *Los Angeles Herald*, denying that anything of the kind had happened. "I am in trouble of no kind, and prospering as well as I desire, being engaged in horse raising and have about 200 of as good horses as can be found in West Texas," he said. The current newspaper reports had been falsely spread, he believed, as a "sneer at Governor Zulick" who had pardoned him. It was true that back in 1886 he had killed a man, but he still felt justified in the act. "I think I demonstrated during the revolt of the convicts at Yuma that I was still a friend of law and order, for I had not the slightest hope of pardon, and the assistance I rendered the authorities speaks for itself."[33]

Although no record has been found that Riggs and his wife Vennie were ever divorced, and Vennie was still alive as late as 1902,[34] Riggs entered into another marriage, apparently bigamous, on September 23, 1891 in Pecos County. The new Mrs. Riggs was Annie Stella

Frazer Johnson, divorced wife of James Johnson, former Pecos County sheriff and treasurer. The union produced four children, three sons and a daughter,[35] but was torn by strife during its ten-year duration and eventually led to Riggs's untimely death.

Annie's family, the Frazers, had a history of violence rivaling that of the Riggs clan, with which they were connected by at least three marriages. On the night of June 29, 1885, at Fort Stockton, George A. "Bud" Frazer, Annie's brother, shot and killed neighbor Crispin Sosa after Sosa slashed the throat of Jim Frazer, another brother. Jim bled to death as Pablo Sosa, a participant in the affair, fled the scene. Ernest Riggs, Barney's son, told a researcher that when the Frazers learned Pablo was hiding in Presidio, they "sent someone down there" after him. This unnamed avenger "killed Sosa, hacked his body to pieces, fed the remainder to the hogs, and brought back evidence of his death in the form of a small pocket-change purse made from the scrotum of the victim."[36]

Bud Frazer, elected sheriff of adjoining Reeves County in 1890, became involved in a bitter and bloody feud with James B. "Deacon Jim" Miller, notorious killer-for-hire. His brother-in-law, Barney Riggs, was destined to play a major role in this feud, one of the worst in a state known for the ferocity of its family wars.

But even as the Frazer-Miller troubles were developing, Riggs was having his own difficulties. He was arrested on several occasions in both Pecos and Reeves Counties for public drunkenness, unlawfully carrying a pistol, and assault. In March 1893 a Reeves County grand jury indicted him for assault with intent to murder a man named Augustin Palanco. Testifying at the trial a year later, Palanco claimed that when he went to the Riggs home to recover a strayed burro, Riggs shot at him and beat him over the head. The jury listened to Palanco's story, but evidently concluded that it was unconvincing. If Barney Riggs had intended to murder the man, they reasoned, he would have done so. It took them only fifteen minutes to bring in a verdict of "not guilty."[37]

Only four days after his indictment on Palanco's charge, Riggs was arrested by Sheriff Bud Frazer on a gun-toting charge and brought before County Judge George M. Frazer, Bud's father and Barney's father-in-law. Because of the judge-defendant relationship, the case was transferred to the district court, where it was dismissed eighteen months later.[38]

Barney Riggs, feeling undressed without a pistol close at hand, decided to pin on a badge to make his gun carrying legal. On August 29, 1893, he accepted appointment as a deputy under Pecos County sheriff Andrew Jackson Royal. The badge apparently gave him an increased sense of power, and he took on four men in a battle. Details are lacking, but it is known that within a few days Texas Ranger J. W. Fulgham arrested him on a charge of "assault with intent to murder Florentine Tercero, Tainas Tercero, Ramon Tercero and Victoriano Rodriquez." This case, too, came to trial at the March 1894 term of district court and was dismissed on the grounds of "insufficient evidence to warrant a conviction."[39]

Riggs's boss, Sheriff A. J. Royal, was, by all accounts, cantankerous, overbearing, bullheaded, intemperate, and fearless, qualities shared in full by Barney Riggs, and the two Pecos County officers got along handsomely. Royal and Riggs, however, managed to alienate most of the influential citizens of Pecos County, as well as both state and federal authorities. In November 1894 Texas Rangers and Deputy U.S. Marshal George Scarborough arrested both the sheriff and his deputy and held them on a charge of complicity in the escape of a prisoner. A justice of the peace released them on their own recognizance.[40] Less than a week later, on November 6, Royal was soundly defeated in his bid for re-election. It had been a bitterly contested election battle, as evidenced by a number of criminal charges and countercharges arising out of it. Two days after the balloting Riggs charged two political opponents with assault, and the following day a man named George Miller charged Royal with assault and battery. The deposed sheriff paid a five-dollar fine after pleading guilty. When county court convened on November 19, on the docket were three cases in which Royal was under indictment for assault and five cases in which he was the complaining witness.[41]

The new county officers, including newly elected Sheriff R. B. Neighbors, were sworn in on November 12, but nine days later A. J. Royal had still not vacated his office. He was sitting at his desk in the Pecos County courthouse in Fort Stockton on November 21 when someone blasted the life out of him with a shotgun. No one was ever convicted or even charged with this murder. Riggs had remained loyal to Royal to the end, and it was rumored that he was also marked for death, but no attempt was made on his life at this time.[42]

For almost two years Riggs stayed close to his horse ranch and avoided trouble, but events in the Frazer-Miller feud in Reeves County again put him on the warpath.

Sheriff Bud Frazer had originally hired the sinister Jim Miller as a deputy, but the two had a falling-out that soon developed into a violent feud. On April 12, 1894, Frazer had out-dueled Miller in a gunfight on a Pecos street. He did not kill him, but sent him to his bed for a long period of recovery.

Then had come November 6, 1894, a dark day for the lawmen friends of Barney Riggs. Not only was A. J. Royal defeated for re-election, but Barney's brother-in-law Bud Frazer lost his job as sheriff. So Frazer no longer wore a badge on December 26 when he tangled again with Miller, who had returned to the streets. The second six-gun battle was almost a replay of the first. Frazer dropped Miller with bullets in his arm and leg, but again failed to kill his man. Shaken by his inability to dispose of his enemy and his defeat at the polls, Frazer left Pecos and went to Eddy, New Mexico, where he opened a livery stable.

Jim Miller then became top dog in Pecos, but this stone-cold killer could not rest until Bud Frazer was dead. It took him a year and a half, but in September 1896 Bill Earhart, one of his lieutenants, informed him that Frazer could be found in Toyah, Texas. Bud was quietly engaged in a game of seven-up in a Toyah saloon when Miller thrust the twin barrels of a shotgun through a swinging door and blew most of his head away. Miller was tried twice for this brutal murder. His first trial ended with a hung jury; at the second he was finally acquitted in January 1899 on the grounds that "he had done no worse than Frazer."[43]

By that time Barney Riggs was deeply embroiled in the Reeves County feud. When he learned of the murder of Bud Frazer, he packed up his family and moved to Pecos, clearly intent on evening the score with the killer of his brother-in-law. He was not deterred by Miller's apparent invincibility, for he had learned the secret of Deacon Jim's miraculous gunfight survival; under his black frock coat Miller wore a steel breastplate that had twice stopped bullets from Frazer's six-gun accurately aimed at his heart. Miller's cohorts also were believed to be wearing bulletproof vests.

Jim Miller had made the rules, but Barney Riggs could play the game. As he approached Pecos in a buggy with his wife and small children,

Riggs reined in his team and made preparations. "Dad got out of the buggy," one of his sons recalled. "[He] went into the brush and put on a bulletproof vest. After that, with his pistol in his hand, he walked into Pecos ahead of the team, while Mama with a shotgun across her lap held the lines."[44]

Jim Miller was not in Pecos at the time, and he made it a point to stay out of town while Barney Riggs remained there. Some who knew him well believed the deadly killer feared Riggs above all others.[45] Instead of facing Riggs himself, he sent two of his closest and most dangerous associates from Eddy, New Mexico, to Pecos. One was Bill Earhart, considered a topflight gunman since his active participation in the Cooper-Good feud in New Mexico eight years before, and the man who had fingered Bud Frazer for Miller. The other was John Denson, a cousin of Miller by marriage and the slayer of Con Gibson, an early casualty in the Frazer-Miller war.

The two gunmen made no secret of their purpose in coming to town. "I heard Denson and Earhart say that they were going to kill old Barney Riggs while they were in Pecos," recalled Dee Harkey, a deputy U.S. marshal at Eddy. "Barney was an old friend of mine, so I wired him and told him what they had said and told him to watch out for them."[46]

On the afternoon of October 3, 1896, less than three weeks after the murder of Bud Frazer, Barney Riggs and Miller's gunmen met in the Number Eleven Saloon in the Orient Hotel in Pecos. Riggs exchanged a few words with Earhart at the bar. When Denson walked over and joined the two, Riggs backed off a step or two. Jesse Heard, co-owner of the saloon, was behind the bar. He later testified that Denson "took Earhart by the arm and they moved back from the bar. [Suddenly] a pistol came out of Earhart's pants. I then heard the report of a pistol and raised my eyes and saw it was in Riggs' hand and aimed at Earhart's head."[47]

Riggs's first shot struck Earhart in the left cheekbone below the eye, killing him instantly. Riggs then turned his gun on Denson and snapped off a shot that missed. Denson ran backward in an awkward effort to escape and stumbled out the door. Riggs ran after him and at the doorway took careful aim and fired again. The bullet passed through the head of Denson, who pitched forward on the plank sidewalk, gasping out his last breaths.

Having dealt with Miller's gunmen and their reliance on body armor with two fatal head shots, Riggs strode back to the bar and reloaded his six-shooter. Calling to his brother Tom, who was present, to bring him "the best horse in town," he retreated to the darkened back room of the saloon. Sheriff Dan Murphy and Texas Ranger Ed Aten appeared moments later and surveyed the bodies littering the premises. The officers were reluctant to approach the embattled Riggs in the back room. After Tom Riggs talked to his brother, conveying Sheriff Murphy's assurance that he would be protected from any retaliatory action by other Miller henchmen, Barney emerged and submitted to arrest.[48]

At a trial held in El Paso eight months later, Riggs, charged with two counts of first-degree murder, was acquitted by a jury on May 18, 1897, It was, said the *El Paso Daily Times*, "a clear case of self-defense. Earhart drew first. The jury which brought in the verdict of 'not guilty' was out only long enough to write the two words down."[49] The *El Paso Daily Herald* commented that the jury members "were fully satisfied that the dead men only got their just desserts and returned verdicts accordingly."[50]

Jim Miller, meanwhile, had moved to Eastland County where his first trial for the Frazer killing was scheduled for the June 1897 term of court. His decision to move to Eastland seven months earlier may have been prompted by a desire to put several hundred miles between himself and Bud Frazer's deadly avenger. But if he hoped to avoid Riggs forever, he would be disappointed. Riggs, fresh from his exoneration at El Paso, was on hand at Eastland in June for the Miller trial.

According to one newspaper report, Miller's gunmen stalked him there. Riggs was attending an ice cream social at the Christian church when some of the ladies present "spied two men slipping along outside the church, each of whom had a six-shooter in his hand." When the women screamed, "the men sneaked off. The belief is that they intended to assassinate Riggs." Noting that "suspicious plays" had been made on previous occasions by "the many tough characters" Miller had in town, the paper predicted "that if Riggs gets away alive he will be a lucky man."[51]

Barney Riggs was not killed, nor was Jim Miller convicted of the Frazer murder. The murderous "Deacon Jim" survived, adding more killings to his sanguinary record until a lynch mob at Ada, Oklahoma, ended his career at the end of a rope in April 1909. Even at that, he would outlive his nemesis, Barney Riggs, by seven years.

After the 1897 trials Riggs moved back to his ranch in Pecos County. He was a living legend now, his name high in the ranks of the storied gunfighters whose exploits were discussed and debated around saloon tables, cowboy campfires, and the potbellied stoves in general stores. In the telling and retelling even the physical stature of the legendary gunfighter became exaggerated, as evidenced by the recollection of William A. Preist, who was a twenty-year-old horse wrangler on the W Ranch in the Pecos country in the 1890s. "I reckon Burney [*sic*] Riggs was the quickest on the draw and the most true shot in the section," Preist told an interviewer in 1938. "He was a wizard with the gun. . . . He was six foot six tall and rawboned. A man that was cool as a cucumber at all times, and one may as well try to excite a hippopotamus as to fluster Burney Riggs."[52] The legendary Riggs was a full foot taller than the flesh-and-blood man whose actual height had been recorded at the Yuma penitentiary.

Despite the "cool as a cucumber" description of the legend, Riggs became increasingly unstable and erratic in his later years. Perhaps tormented by the ghosts of his violent past, perhaps obsessed by dread of Miller and his assassins, he drank to greater and greater excess and became more quarrelsome and abusive.

He could suddenly explode in a fit of temper. Seated one day in the front of the Koehler Hotel in Fort Stockton holding a small child in his lap, he saw Newt Teel, son-in-law of the late A. J. Royal, approaching. Teel had recently disagreed with Riggs over some matter, and when Riggs caught sight of the young man it seemed to trigger an instant rage. "Barney dropped the child on the floor and rushed out, saying, 'I'll kill the son of a bitch!'" an eyewitness remembered. Bystanders intervened and pushed Riggs into the kitchen until he cooled down. Teel said he "was not afraid of Barney, but hated to be in town at any time Barney was [there]."[53]

By June 1900 Annie Riggs had all she could stand and filed for divorce, charging that her husband had a violent and ungovernable temper and was abusive and dangerous to her and the children. He was, she said, "addicted to habits of dissipation and improper associations."[54]

To support herself and her children Annie managed the Koehler Hotel. At the time Barney Riggs was having divorce problems with his wife," recalled a Fort Stockton old-timer, "Mrs. Riggs was running the hotel and would have nothing to do with Barney." One day, while intoxicated, Riggs "drove his team across the creek, picked up the dehydrated carcass of a long-dead cow and loaded it in his buggy. He then drove his team with the cow's carcass in the seat beside him along in front of the hotel, shouting to Mrs. Riggs that he had at last got something to ride with him."[55]

Despite such outrageous behavior by Riggs, the couple reconciled for a time and Annie dropped the divorce proceedings. Then, on February 14, 1901, she filed a second divorce petition, stating that the previous day Riggs, intoxicated and "wild with rage," went on a rampage, tearing up the furnishings of their home. When she protested, he threw her down and "attempted to pour coal oil . . . upon her and to set fire to her clothing." He would have succeeded, she said, but for the timely "assistance of other persons."[56] Annie grabbed her children and ran screaming from the house.

She was granted a divorce on March 27. A provision of the settlement was an order that Riggs make periodic child-support payments totaling $2,000. Named as the trustee to handle these payments was Daniel J. "Buck" Chadborn, the twenty-one-year-old husband of Annie's daughter by her previous marriage.[57]

Riggs resented Chadborn's involvement in the family dispute and told him so in strong language. In an effort to extricate himself from his mother-in-law's legal difficulties, Chadborn in March 1902 petitioned the court to relieve him from the responsibility. But Barney Riggs, unmollified, berated the young man profanely in public and on April 6, 1902, reportedly beat him with a cane.

While drinking in Mart Adams's saloon the next day, Riggs looked out the window at Chadborn's house and spotted Chadborn loading Annie's belongings into a buggy. He headed in that direction, but Sheriff Bob Neighbors, fearing trouble, intercepted him and demanded that he leave his pistol in the saloon. Riggs complied and stalked across the street, yelling at Chadborn and brandishing a cane.

As he neared the buggy, Riggs made a move that Chadborn saw as threatening. Some witnesses claimed he raised his walking stick to strike the young man; others said he reached for his hip pocket as if to draw a gun. In any event, Chadborn reacted swiftly. Picking up a pistol from the buggy seat, he shot Riggs in the chest. With a finger jammed

Barney Riggs, surrounded by friends, in 1902. Standing are his brother Tom (*left*) and Lon "Stump" Robbins. Seated are (*left to right*) Moye Grinder, Barney Riggs, and John Chalk. From the author's collection.

in the bullet hole, Riggs staggered blindly more than a hundred feet before collapsing. He was carried to the Koehler Hotel where he died the following day, cursing Buck Chadborn with his final breath.[58]

Indicted for second-degree murder, Chadborn stood trial at Alpine, Brewster County, in October 1903. The jury deliberated less than fifteen minutes before finding him "not guilty." Chadborn moved to New Mexico where he had a long career in law enforcement, serving for many years as a deputy sheriff and U.S. customs agent. He died at the age of eighty-six at Deming, New Mexico.

In 1904 Annie Riggs purchased the hotel where Barney died, changed the name to the Riggs Hotel, and operated it successfully for many years. She died on May 17, 1931.

Without doubt Barney Riggs was a violent, vindictive man, a brutal, probably psychopathic, killer. But he was respected by many for his fearlessness in standing up to and trading lead with gunmen considered as bad or worse than himself. When Riggs died, James Gibson, county clerk at Pecos during the Frazer-Miller feud and a brother of Con Gibson, one of the casualties of that conflict, wrote an obituary that made the point. "We believe," he said, "that Barney Riggs was an instrument in the hands of a just God to rid Reeves County of one of the hardest gangs of criminals that ever infested any land, that he did it and did it well. No one who is familiar with the history of the county and has any regard for the truth will deny [this]. . . . Who can say that he will not receive a just reward?"[59]

— 10 —

DAN BOGAN
(1860–?)

"Are you heeled?"

For seven years in the 1880s some of the most famous lawmen in the West were kept busy dogging the trail of a young gunman from Hamilton County, Texas. At one time or another renowned lawmen Pat Garrett, Jim East, Frank Canton, N. K. Boswell, Malcolm Campbell, John Owens, T. J. Carr, and Charles A. Siringo tracked the cowboy-turned-outlaw. Two of the officers, Garrett and Owens, managed to apprehend the slippery desperado, only to have him escape the clutches of the law later. Difficult as he was to catch, he proved even more difficult to hold; on at least four occasions he escaped custody after arrest, finally disappearing with a death sentence and a $1,000 reward on his head.

Dan Bogan, alias Bill Gatlin, alias Bill McCoy, was born in Alabama in 1860, but moved with his family to Hamilton County, Texas, sometime before reaching maturity. During those years his mother was widowed or divorced three times.[1] Bogan was twenty-one when he had his first recorded serious brush with the law, but if a story in a Wyoming newspaper can be credited, he had two older brothers who preceded him in a life of crime. One was said to have been killed by a sheriff while resisting arrest for horse stealing, and the other went to the Texas penitentiary for the same offense.[2]

Dan Bogan began his long criminal career on Monday, May 2, 1881, when he and a younger pal, Dave Kemp, got into an altercation in the town of Hamilton that resulted in gunfire and sudden death. Bogan and Kemp had spent several hours touring the Hamilton saloons, and, as he drank, Bogan became increasingly belligerent. They were preparing to leave when Bogan loudly announced that he could lick any man in town and defied anyone to dispute the claim. No one took up the challenge, and Kemp, more sober than Bogan, led the way to their horses at the hitchrack in front of W. T. Cropper's store. He mounted up and urged his friend to do the same.

Bogan still was spoiling for a fight, however. As a wagon pulled up in front of the store, he chose the driver, F. A. "Doll" Smith, as a target for a foul-mouthed diatribe. Smith, a farmer in town to purchase supplies, was not acquainted with either of the young men and was surprised and offended by the unprovoked verbal assault. Finally he told Bogan that he did not whip dogs or he would get down off his wagon and whip him.[3]

At this, Bogan seized a chair from the wagon, beat it once on the ground, and seemed about to attack Smith with it. Abruptly changing his mind, he tossed the chair back into the wagon and unloaded a new flood of invective at the farmer.

Smith had taken enough. Described as "a tolerably stout, active man," about fifteen years older and twenty-five pounds heavier than Bogan,[4] he climbed down from his wagon and started after his youthful tormenter.

As Bogan backed off, his right hand slid under his coat.

"Draw your God damned pistol and I'll knock you down," warned Smith, still advancing.[5]

Bogan's hand, holding a revolver, came into view. A blow from Smith struck him full on the chin and he reeled backward. Smith hit him again and Bogan went down, one arm outstretched, the hand still clutching the pistol. Smith planted a foot on the arm and wrested the gun from Bogan's grasp.

Dave Kemp then got into the action. Dismounting, he drew his own weapon, ran up behind Smith, and struck at him with the six-shooter. The gun discharged as the barrel glanced off the side of Smith's head. Smith spun around, Bogan's revolver in his hand, and started after his new adversary. Retreating, Kemp thumbed back the hammer of his pistol and pulled the trigger. The hammer clicked on a defective round, or "squib" as it was called by witnesses.[6]

Smith kept coming. Kemp backed away, frantically cocking and triggering his single-action six-shooter and getting nothing but "squibs." Smith made no effort to fire the pistol he held, but swung it at Kemp's gun hand in an effort to knock it away.

Meanwhile, Bogan got up off the ground. Seizing a large rock from the roadway, he ran up behind Smith and struck him two heavy blows on the head and neck with the stone. Smith staggered. At that moment Kemp's gun began to work. He shot Smith once and then, stepping closer, shot him again. With a final desperate effort, Smith raised his arm and threw Bogan's gun at Kemp. The weapon struck him in the neck, glanced off, and flew across the street almost to the courthouse steps.[7] Smith then pitched forward on his face, mortally wounded. He would die within moments.[8]

Sheriff G. N. Gentry came running from the courthouse. Kemp turned his pistol on the officer, but the hammer fell on another defective shell. Backing away, Kemp fell into the muscular arms of bystander Tom Moss, a big man who picked him up and "shook him as a dog does a chicken" until he dropped the six-gun.[9]

Sheriff Gentry arrested Bogan and Kemp and held them for an inquest held by Coroner S. Loyd. There a jury found that "Smith was murdered by Dan Bogan and David Kemp" and that both had been "actively engaged" in the commission of the murder. A grand jury later in the month handed down indictments against the two men, charging them with "murder with malice," a crime calling for the death penalty.[10]

The law firm of Eidson and Miller of Hamilton represented the defendants. "Doll" Smith had been very popular and, as it became evident an impartial jury could not be impaneled in Hamilton County, the defense attorneys were granted a change of venue to neighboring Coryell County. The trial opened at Gatesville on June 11, 1881, only five weeks after the shooting. A jury found both defendants guilty. As Judge T. L. Nugent pronounced the sentence of death, Bogan suddenly made a desperate break for freedom. Jerking the six-shooter from the holster of a careless guard, he began firing. Taking advantage of the wild confusion as court officials, jurors, and spectators made a rush for the door, Bogan and Kemp ran to an open window and jumped two floors to the street below. Kemp broke a leg in the fall and was quickly recaptured, but Bogan jumped on a horse, and made good the

Dan Bogan, alias Bill Gatlin, alias Bill McCoy, around 1880.
Courtesy of the Nita Stewart Haley Memorial Library, Midland,
Texas.

first of his daring escapes.[11] After long legal wrangling and two trials, Kemp was convicted and sentenced to twenty-five years in Huntsville prison.[12]

Bogan became a fugitive from Texas justice and appeared on the state's wanted lists for the next two decades. He was described as a white man, five feet, ten inches tall, weighing 175 pounds, with dark complexion, dark eyes, and brown hair.[13]

Like many young Texas men who had run afoul of the law during this period, Bogan took a new name—he now called himself Bill Gatlin—and became a drover on the northbound cattle trails. At the end of one drive he and two other rampaging cowboys are said to have hurrahed the cattle town. Riding their horses the length of a dance hall, they ventilated the ceiling with their six-shooters and scattered everyone inside. This was so much fun they rode around to the front of the building to repeat their antics. The dance hall proprietor met them at the doorway, rifle in hand.

"You can't pass except over my dead body," he told them.

"That's easy," laughed Bogan, alias Gatlin, shooting him down and spurring his mount across the man's body.[14]

"Bill Gatlin" next turned up in the remote Canadian River Valley ranges around Tascosa in the Texas Panhandle. Many of the cowpunchers working the ranches of the district had dark and unsavory pasts, and few questions were asked of a newcomer. Even the general manager of the big LX Ranch, W. C. Moore, was known as "Outlaw Bill," and it was common knowledge around the campfires that he was wanted for murder in California and Wyoming.[15] Gatlin fit in well with these tough cowmen. Charlie Siringo, who was cowboying for the LX at the time and later as a Pinkerton detective would stalk the trail of the Hamilton County desperado, recalled that Gatlin "was well liked by all the cowboys around Tascosa, including myself."[16]

Panhandle cowboys during this period were earning only twenty-five dollars a month. In March 1883 a group of disgruntled range riders under the leadership of Tom Harris, foreman of the LS Ranch, issued a written ultimatum to the owners demanding an increase in wages to fifty dollars a month for cowhands and seventy-five dollars for crew bosses. One of the signers of this document was Bill Gatlin. Some two hundred cowboys agreed to strike against the ranch owners on April 1, but soon some started to defect and the only cowboy strike in history ended in failure after only a month.[17]

Gatlin had been a ringleader of the strike. Now blacklisted and unable to find work on any of the Panhandle ranches, he rode down to Wilbarger County and signed on as a drover with a trail herd from the Stephens and Worsham R2 Ranch. T. J. Burkett, who also made that drive, recalled Gatlin as a valuable addition to the crew. When a thunderstorm struck one night, spooking the herd, Gatlin alone managed to hold 600 head and prevented them from joining the general stampede. After they reached Dodge City, Kansas, and set up camp, some of the boys rode into town, took on a load of bad whiskey, and attempted to hurrah the place. City Marshal Jack Bridges and other officers got after them, chased them out of town, and in a running gun battle killed herder John Briley. Burkett was one of those detailed the next day to go into Dodge and arrange for Briley's burial on Boot Hill.[18] Given his proclivity for rowdiness and gunplay, Bill Gatlin was probably one of those involved in this escapade.

Returning to Tascosa, Gatlin found that animosity between the big ranchers and the strike ringleaders still rankled. Tom Harris and other blacklisted cowboys had organized what was called the Get Even Cattle Company and were burning calves with their own brands in defiance of the range law that a calf was to be marked with the same brand as the mother it followed. Gatlin enthusiastically entered into this practice. He registered two brands, the K-Triangle, under the name W. A. Gatlin, and the Tabletop in partnership with Wade Woods. Both were designed to facilitate the altering of existing Canadian River Valley brands. The tabletop, a rectangle with four extended legs, was considered a classic "maverick" brand. Almost all the established brands of the district could be converted into a Tabletop.[19]

The large ranch owners took action against the rustlers. They commissioned Pat Garrett, the former sheriff of Lincoln County, New Mexico, who was nationally renowned for having broken up the Billy the Kid outlaw gang, to organize a force of rangers to rid the Panhandle country of the maverickers. Garrett came to believe that he had been hired to kill the worst offenders (probably including Bill Gatlin), rather than bringing them in for trial.[20] During the summer of 1884 Garrett and his "Home Rangers," assisted by loyal cowboys from the LS, LIT, and other large ranches, confiscated cattle with "outlaw" brands wherever they could be found. On one occasion they rounded up thirty-three cows with the Gatlin-Woods Tabletop brand and threw them in with other mavericks held at Tascosa, where many of them were butchered and sold in a meat market.[21]

Gatlin went to H. H. Wallace, a Tascosa lawyer, and demanded reparations. Wallace threatened Oldham County officials with a $25,000 suit for damages. Unless Gatlin was satisfied, he said, criminal action would be started against the county commissioners for illegal seizure. Frightened, the county officials settled the claim for $800.[22]

A grand jury, meanwhile, was hearing charges brought by the ranchers against the outlaw cowboys, and in the fall of 1884 handed down 159 bills of indictment, mostly for theft of cattle.[23] Armed with the indictments, Garrett and his Home Rangers began a sweep of the Canadian River Valley. They made no secret of their movements, as Garrett wanted to avoid confrontation and possible bloodshed. A general rustler exodus began, but Bill Gatlin, Wade Woods, and Charlie Thompson, three of those named in the warrants, sent word that they would not be driven out.

In February 1885 Garrett learned that the three defiant cowboys were holed up at the Howry Cattle Company headquarters, about forty miles west of Tascosa. Garrett's rangers and Oldham County sheriff Jim East started for the site, a rock house at Red River Springs, just over the state line in New Mexico Territory. They rode all night through a snowstorm guided by Home Ranger G. H. "Kid" Dobbs, who had hunted buffalo throughout the section and whose father-in-law had built the rock house.

In a bitterly cold dawn they reached their destination. They were cautiously approaching the house when Bob Bassett, who had been out gathering firewood, spotted them and ran back, shouting a warning. Tom Harris emerged and angrily demanded to know why the posse-men were skulking about. Garrett told him he had warrants for Gatlin, Woods, and Thompson, but wanted no trouble with anyone else. Harris said that Gatlin and Thompson were inside, but Woods was not there. Upon Garrett's assurance that they would not be molested, nine cowboys filed from the building, leaving only Gatlin and Thompson inside.

Garrett called for them to come out quietly. Thompson stepped out of the doorway in his shirtsleeves and, shivering in the cold, conversed for several minutes with Jim East. The sheriff had cowboyed with both Thompson and Gatlin and believed they would trust him. Saying he was going to get his coat, Thompson went back inside, but then slammed shut the door and shouted that he would stand and fight beside Bill Gatlin. Over a howling wind East pleaded with the two men within to submit to arrest. At a trial they might come clear, he said, but if they insisted on fighting, they would surely die. His arguments finally persuaded Thompson and he came out with his hands up, but Gatlin stubbornly refused to surrender. He taunted the officers, challenging them to try and take him. East and Garrett took turns threatening and cajoling without success.

Cold and out of patience, Garrett finally directed his possemen to start removing the poles from the lean-to roof of the house so that they could shoot down on the obstinate outlaw. Several had been stripped away when Gatlin yelled that he would talk terms if one of them would come inside. Jim East volunteered, telling Garrett that he didn't believe Gatlin would shoot an old saddle pal, but if Garrett went in he would kill him for sure.

Warily, his Winchester at the ready, East stepped into the building. Bill Gatlin was crouched against the opposite wall with two six-shooters in his hands. With weapons trained on each other and trigger fingers tense, the two men conferred. Upon East's sworn assurance that Gatlin would be protected from any mob action, the outlaw finally agreed to give up his guns and surrender.[24]

The officers took Gatlin and Thompson to Tascosa and, since the town had no jail, chained them to the floor of an old adobe building, guarded by Constable Jim Moore. Their incarceration was of short duration, however, for that night confederates slipped them a file and they freed themselves from the irons and escaped out a window. Moore fired several shots in their direction, but the prisoners reached horses and disappeared in the darkness.[25]

Dan Bogan, alias Billy Gatlin, again went north with a trail herd. Using a new name, Bill McCoy, he next came to public attention in distant Wyoming, where he is believed to have joined for a time the Teton Jackson gang of horse thieves operating out of Jackson Hole.[26] He is known to have punched cattle for Quint Pennick, foreman of

Luke Voorhees' LZ Ranch at Rawhide Buttes, Wyoming, in 1886, before being drawn to the booming new town of Lusk in Laramie County.[27]

"Lusk is on the line of the new railway [the Fremont, Elkhorn & Missouri Valley] pushing into this territory from the east," J. K. Calkins, editor of the *Lusk Herald*, announced in the first issue of his paper on May 20, 1886. "The town is only two months old and [already] has 40 business houses." When the railroad reached Lusk, Bogan, under his new name "Bill McCoy," went into partnership with a man named John Hogle in the operation of a saloon and livery stable at the new railhead. In Lusk he also found a mistress, a woman named Emma Rigs.[28]

The cattle trail from Texas to the expanding ranches of Wyoming, Montana, and Dakota Territories crossed the Cheyenne to Deadwood road at Lusk, and Texas drovers were frequent visitors to the town. It was inevitable that some of them would recognize the man calling himself Bill McCoy as the fugitive wanted back in the Lone Star State under two other names. One or more of them conveyed this information to Editor Calkins of the *Herald*, who printed it in his paper.[29]

Infuriated, Bogan, accompanied by another Texan, Sterling Ballou, hurrahed the town. The two went looking for Calkins in the saloon of the Cleveland brothers, Larkin and Harper, the favorite resort of the *Herald* editor. Calkins was not there, but Bogan waved a pistol around and challenged any of the newspaperman's friends or supporters to step forward and defend him. One of the Cleveland brothers eased a sawed-off shotgun from under the bar, brought it to bear on the two Texans, and ordered them out. At this point Charles S. Gunn, who held papers as both constable at Lusk and deputy sheriff of Laramie County,[30] came on the scene and, with drawn gun, backed the saloonkeeper's play. Bogan and Ballou made an ignominious exit.[31]

The incident seems to have been the basis of personal animus between Bogan and Gunn that would end in tragedy. On another occasion Bogan went on a rampage while Gunn was out of town. When the officer returned, he warned Bogan to cease his riotous behavior or he would lock him up. Bogan sneered that he would do as he liked.[32]

But Charlie Gunn was not a man to be intimidated. About thirty-two years old, tall and powerfully built, he was very popular in Lusk. The few women and children of the town especially liked him. He had a small ranch near town where he ran a few cattle. Like many Wyoming cattlemen, he had come up the trail from Texas, where he was said to have served in the rangers and seen his share of hard cases like Bogan.[33] Editor Calkins of the *Herald* was a great admirer of the lawman, once referring to him in his paper as a "terror to evildoers."[34] In his Christmas Eve issue of 1886, Calkins said: "Charlie Gunn is enjoying the reputation of being able to 'hold a town down.'"[35] His remarks only further inflamed Bogan's hatred of the officer.

On January 14, 1887, Bogan created another disturbance in a dance hall and again Constable Gunn stepped in to control him. The next morning Bogan was waiting in Jim Waters's saloon for Gunn to stop in on his usual rounds. When the officer entered, Bogan walked over to him and asked, "Charlie, are you heeled?"

"I'm always heeled," Gunn replied.[36]

Bogan, who had been holding a pistol behind his back, immediately whipped it around and fired, hitting Gunn in the stomach. Gunn fell to his knees with his forehead on the floor. Clutching his midsection with one hand, he drew his revolver with the other. He was trying to pull himself up when Bogan stepped closer, put the muzzle of his six-shooter close to Gunn's head, and fired "a second shot which splattered his brains over the floor and set fire to his hair."[37] Bogan was so close to his victim, witnesses said, that he had to jump out of way when Gunn toppled over.[38]

Brandishing his pistol at the horrified spectators, Bogan ran from the building and around to the back of his own saloon, where he mounted a horse belonging to Jack Andrews and started out of town. Suddenly, Deputy Sheriff John Owens was in the street, a double-barreled shotgun in his hands, blocking his way. Owens ordered Bogan to stop and fired a shot into the air by way of encouragement. Bogan hesitated only a second before spurring his horse forward.

John Owens turned his shotgun loose again. The charge struck Bogan in the shoulder and sent him tumbling out of the saddle. The fall knocked the revolver from his hand. With the weapon lying only inches from his fingers, Bogan watched Owens approach with the shotgun trained on him. In his excitement he forgot that Owens had fired both barrels and the shotgun was now empty. Seconds later Owens reached him, picked up the pistol, and Bogan's opportunity to escape had passed.[39]

"I guess you've got me, boys, but I sure would like to fight it out with you on even chances," a newspaper reported Bogan as saying as others joined Owens in the street.[40] John Owens, who had been ill for several days and confined to a sickbed, asked the young desperado why he killed Charlie Gunn. "Well,' Bogan replied with a crooked grin, "I would not have done it if I hadn't supposed that you were at home and abed."[41]

Justice of the Peace Roe Kingman held an immediate hearing and bound Bogan over without bail to be tried before the district court at Cheyenne at the spring session. Like Tascosa and many other raw frontier towns, Lusk had no jail. Deputy Sheriff Owens shackled Bogan and held him in the back room of a saloon. All day long rumors spread that a lynch mob was forming to deal with the killer of popular Charlie Gunn. John Owens let it be known, however, that he would fight to protect his prisoner. Few wanted to take on the tough lawman who had a formidable reputation as a fast and deadly gunman and whose violent history extended back twenty years to Confederate army service with Frank James, Cole Younger, and William Clarke Quantrill.[42] The story went around town that Sterling Ballou was making threats against Owens after the arrest of his pal. Owens called Ballou out of a saloon and told him:

> "There has been enough killing, Ballou—or else there hasn't. I don't like your talk. If you are in town two hours from now I'll shoot you on sight."
> "Well, I'll go if you say so, Johnny," Ballou told him.
> "I say so," replied Owens.
> Ballou left on the first stage.[43]

Since Bogan was wounded and a snowstorm was moving into the area, Owens was less concerned about his prisoner's escape as he was of possible mob action against him. Several of Bogan's friends, including Tuck Jester, foreman of the Node ranch, and Quint Pennick, Voorhees ranch ramrod, volunteered to help guard and protect him. Owens swore them in as special deputies, and some time after midnight, after having arisen from a sickbed to spend a hectic day, he retired, leaving Bogan in the care of his friends.[44]

He was awakened at 3:30 to learn that Bogan, with assistance from his guards, had flown, disappearing on horseback into the teeth of the swirling blizzard that quickly obliterated his tracks. Owens knew that Bogan, suffering from his gunshot wounds, could not go far through roads deeply covered with snow, and was probably hiding out in one of the nearby cattle company line camps. Owens watched the roads and waited.

Two weeks later he was proved correct. Bogan, burning with fever and badly in need of medical attention, sent word to Owens that he wanted to surrender. On Saturday, January 29, Owens met the outlaw by arrangement at a point some sixteen miles from Lusk. Another storm was moving in and they could not return to town. They spent that night and all day Sunday at the LZ Ranch. Bogan, still in deathly fear of a lynch mob, did not want to enter Lusk during daylight. He agreed to wait at the LZ while Owens made arrangements for an after-dark return. That night Bogan met Owens and four deputies at the railroad water tank outside of town. All the officers were armed with two pistols and a shotgun. Owens gave Bogan a pistol to use in his own defense if they were faced with a mob. The entry into town proved uneventful, and once again Owens placed Bogan in irons in a back room of Peter Sweeney's saloon. The next day Owens started for Cheyenne with his prisoner and finally lodged him in the Laramie County jail on Friday, February 4.[45]

Bogan became an immediate newspaper celebrity and the darling of the Cheyenne underworld. His exploits were reviewed at length in the papers, and a steady stream of visitors, both male and female, descended on his jail cell.[46] A Cheyenne paper described him as an average-sized man of about twenty-eight years, with close-cropped dark hair and a small dark mustache. He walked slightly stooped and had thin lips, bluish-grey eyes, and a scar on the back of his neck. He had a high instep and wore a number six boot.[47]

With his likable, ingratiating personality, Bogan had managed to develop during his few years in Wyoming many friends, including ranch foremen Jester and Pennick and other members of the powerful Wyoming Stock Growers Association. These people came forward now to aid him in his difficulty. They employed a defense team that included some of the ablest legal minds in the territory: William W. Corlett, former delegate to the U.S. Congress; John A. Riner, former city attorney and U.S. district attorney; and John W. Lacy, former chief justice of the Wyoming Supreme Court and a lead attorney for the cattlemen's association. Walter R. Stoll led the prosecution; A. C. Campbell assisted.[48]

The Laramie County grand jury indicted "Dan Bogan, otherwise called William McCoy," for premeditated murder on May 23, 1887, with June 16 set as the trial date. The defense attorneys managed to get a series of postponements and a change of judges. Trial was finally scheduled to begin on August 29 before Judge Samuel T. Corn of Evanston.[49]

Three visitors from Texas with a particular interest in the case appeared in Cheyenne that summer. Charles K. Bell, who had prosecuted Bogan and Kemp for the murder of "Doll" Smith back in 1881, was there. Accompanying him were Hamilton County sheriff J. W. Massie and W. T. Cropper, the storekeeper who had been one of the chief witnesses against Smith's killers at their trial. Bell wanted Cropper to confirm positively that McCoy was Bogan. In the event that the defendant gained an acquittal in the Gunn slaying, Bell also directed Sheriff Massie to claim him as a fugitive from Texas and return him to be tried again for the Smith murder. Bogan was visibly shaken when he saw the three Texans in the courtroom at one of the legal wranglings.[50]

This development apparently convinced Bogan that he could not wait around for a trial. On August 7 he made an attempt to break out of jail. Using the spring from a watch to pick the cell locks and the steel from a truss to saw the corridor bars, he was prepared to make his escape when discovered by Sheriff Seth K. Sharpless and his deputies. Bogan and other prisoners eager to join in the breakout had prepared lengths of rope and "villainous-looking gags made of wire and towels" for binding and gagging their guards.[51]

When Bogan's trial opened on August 29, the state presented a strong case. To make their plea of self-defense, Bogan's lawyers had to put their client on the stand to testify in his own behalf. Bogan said that the altercation at the dance hall the night previous led to the shooting. After that incident Waters and Gunn had attempted to bushwhack him. The next morning Waters was agreeable to patching up the differences, but when Gunn came into the saloon, Bogan thought he was coming to fight. He asked Gunn if he was heeled and when he answered that he was, both went for their guns at the same moment. Bogan was simply faster, he said. Afterward, he escaped from custody at Lusk because he was afraid of being lynched.[52]

The jury was unconvinced. On September 7, after nineteen hours of deliberation, they found Bogan guilty of murder in the first degree. Conviction carried an automatic death sentence, and Bogan heard Judge Corn intone the solemn words that he would be hanged by the neck until he was "dead, dead, dead." Throughout the proceedings, reported the *Cheyenne Daily Leader*, Bogan remained stoic: "Without provocation or pity he ruthlessly murdered a man far superior to himself in every way—and has murdered two other men. Since this 'infamous reptile' has previously escaped merited punishment, it is not surprising that he would hear himself condemned to death without a change in his outward demeanor. He appeared completely unconcerned." The paper acknowledged that Bogan still had many friends who would work on his behalf "until the executioner's noose is placed around his worthless neck."[53]

Some of those devoted friends would do more than merely remain faithful. One was a man known as Tom Hall, the foreman of the Keeline Ranch on the Platte River near Fort Laramie, who was also a fugitive from Texas. Charlie Siringo, who knew him on the cattle ranges of the Panhandle, said his name was really Tom Nichols and characterized him as a "mankiller."[54] Like Bogan, Hall had taken a new range and a new name, but he did not forget his Panhandle pal. He visited the Cheyenne jail and hatched a plan to spring his friend from jail before the hangman could do his business.

Hall paid James Jones, a professional safecracker, to commit a minor crime in Cheyenne in order to get locked up in the jail. Concealed in the cracksman's shoes were saw blades with which Bogan and Jones sawed through the bars of the jail. On the night of October 4 Bogan and Jones, joined by accused horse thieves Charles H. LeRoy and William C. Steary, slipped out of their cells, went up through a ventilator to the roof of the building, and lowered themselves to the ground with the aid of an improvised rope. Tom Hall was waiting for Bogan with a saddled horse. Together the two rode out of Cheyenne, bound for a secret hideout on the Keeline range.[55]

Within hours officers mounted one of the biggest manhunts in Wyoming history. Territory and county officials posted a reward of $1,000 for Bogan, dead or alive. "Dan Bogan, alias Wm. McCoy, is a Texas desperado and a fugitive from that state, said the *Cheyenne Daily Leader* of October 5. "[He] is a reckless and blood thirsty character and the assertion is ventured that he will not be taken alive." More than fifty men rode in posses led by Laramie County sheriff Seth Sharpless; Albany County deputy sheriff Malcolm Campbell; Nathaniel K. Boswell, chief of detectives for the Wyoming Stock Growers Association; and Frank Canton, the cattlemen's association deputy chief of detectives for northern Wyoming.[56]

When these veteran manhunters came up empty, District Attorney Walter R. Stoll, who had received information that Bogan was hidden out on the Keeline Ranch, contacted Dave Cook of the Rocky Mountain Detective Agency in Denver and employed undercover agents to infiltrate the ranks of the Keeline cowboys and seek him out. But the riders for the Keeline, many of whom were themselves ex-convicts and fugitives from the law, soon exposed the detectives and sent them packing.[57] Stoll then sought help from the famous Pinkerton's National Detective Agency. The Denver office assigned Charlie Siringo, the former Texas cowboy turned detective, to the case.

Posing as an outlaw on the dodge, Siringo was successful in gaining the confidence of Hall and his cohorts and learned for the first time that the fugitive he was hunting was the man he had known as Bill Gatlin back in Texas. He also learned that just two days prior to his arrival on the Keeline range, Bogan had ridden out toward Utah, mounted on Tom Hall's roan racehorse and trailing as a pack animal a big bay stolen from one of the posses. By the time Siringo acquired this information, the trail was cold and he did not continue pursuit of the killer. He did provide information implicating Hall and other Keeline riders in Bogan's escape. They were later apprehended and indicted in Cheyenne, but the cases were dropped before trial.[58]

Thirty years later, A. C. Campbell, who had assisted Walter Stoll in the prosecution of Bogan, ran into "an early client, one H. [Tom Hall]," who admitted that he had secreted the condemned man after his escape. "Even the thousand dollar reward was no temptation to H. While Bogan was there H. entertained the officers who were in search of Bogan."[59]

According to information Siringo was later able to piece together, after leaving the Keeline, Bogan rode into Utah where he picked up a traveling companion, a twelve-year-old boy, who, riding the bay pack horse, continued on with him. Taking a circular route, Bogan swung south toward New Mexico and then east again. He stopped to rest several days at the camp of Lem Woodruff at Los Portales Lake near the Texas line. Woodruff, an old Panhandle friend with whom he had maintained contact, had been badly wounded in the big shootout at Tascosa on March 21, 1886, in which four men died.[60] Bogan told Woodruff that he was tired of running from the law and was heading for New Orleans and a ship that would take him to South America.

The boy, who had become attached to the personable outlaw, wanted to go with him. Bogan, fearing the lad would somehow give him away to the authorities, refused to take him along. The boy was insistent, but Bogan made it clear that he was going alone, and if the boy followed, he would kill him. Woodruff agreed to keep the youngster and also warned him not to try and follow Bogan. But shortly after the outlaw left, the boy slipped out of the cabin, saddled one of Woodruff's cow ponies, and took off on a gallop on his trail. Two days later, the horse, saddled and bridled, showed up in the Woodruff pasture. Dried blood covering the saddle provided mute evidence, Woodruff was convinced, that somewhere along the trail the boy had overtaken Bogan and had met the fate the desperado had promised.

Bogan made his way to New Orleans where he wrote a letter to Tom Hall, back in Wyoming. Hall had given him a letter of introduction to an expatriated fugitive from Texas law who was then practicing dentistry in Buenos Aires, Argentina. The dentist, Hall said, could put him in touch with a band of American outlaws on the pampas.[61]

The later history of Dan Bogan, alias Bill Gatlin, alias Bill McCoy, is not known, but stories abound. Charlie Siringo believed that after several years as an outlaw in South America Bogan returned, settled down in southwestern New Mexico under yet another name, raised a family, and became a prosperous cattleman. When he published his reminiscences, *A Lone Star Cowboy*, in 1919, Siringo believed Bogan was still living. "The chances are Bill Gatlin, alias Bill McCoy, would sweat blood did he know that I knew his present name and address, for the hangman's noose would stare him in the face," he wrote, adding, "If he really did kill that boy he should be hanged more than once."[62]

But newspapers had announced Bogan's demise several times. The *Laramie Sentinel* reported in December 1889 "that William McCoy, less than a month ago, near El Paso del Norte in old Mexico, 'died with his boots on'; he had gotten in a quarrel with a Mexican who drew and shot him first."[63]

Calvin Morse, who provided William MacLeod Raine with much of his information about Bogan's activities in Wyoming, remembered a newspaper story with a New Mexico dateline about 1907 that said Bogan had been bucked from a horse and died from a broken neck.[64]

In 1931 A. C. Campbell said the last he heard of Bogan, "he had married, owned a ranch some place in Texas, and was branding mavericks and raising Hoover Democrats."[65]

— II —

DAVE KEMP
(1862–1935)

*"It is hoped that he will quit chewing gum,
which is the only bad habit he has."*

"Justice is blind," goes the expression, and Justice is depicted as a woman holding a balance scale and blindfolded to show she is not influenced by what the eyes, subject to illusions, show her. However, in the early West, as now, Dame Justice could still be capricious.

The story of Dave Kemp, the man convicted with Dan Bogan of the murder of "Doll" Smith at Hamilton, Texas, in 1881 (see chapter 10), is a case in point. Twice Kemp was brought before the bar of justice, charged with the shooting death of another man. In the Hamilton case he had killed Smith, with whom he had had no previous difficulty, as the man advanced threateningly toward him with a gun in his hand. For this he was convicted of murder with malice and sentenced to hang. In the other case he assassinated a sworn enemy, cold-bloodedly shooting him down without warning. For this he was acquitted and freed.

Dave Kemp and Dan Bogan had been friends through boyhood, but when they leaped together out of that courthouse window at Gatesville in June 1881 and Kemp's leg snapped, their lives took separate paths. But wherever they went, each would become known and feared as desperate and dangerous gunmen.

David Lyle Kemp was born March 1, 1862, in Hamilton County, where his father, William Alexander Kemp, and mother, Jane Bush

Kemp, had settled after leaving Alabama in 1854.[1] Hamilton County was still wild country when young Dave was growing up. Indian war parties were a constant threat. The teacher at the one-room school he attended bore arrow scars from a Comanche raid in 1867.[2]

It is apparent from the first that the Kemps, their relatives, and neighbors were a rough crowd. Walker Bush, half brother to Dave and seven years older, was a wild one and no doubt had an influence on the direction of the young man's life. When the federal census was taken in Hamilton in 1880, both Dave's father and Walker Bush were being held on criminal charges and were enumerated in the jail.[3] The Bogan family lived nearby. Dan Bogan, two years older than Dave, would take to outlawry after the Smith killing. Newspapers reported that two of Bogan's brothers also ran afoul of the law, one being killed by lawmen as a horse thief, and another sent to prison for the same offense.[4]

According to other sketchy reports, Dave Kemp killed a man a year before the "Doll" Smith shooting. About 1880 he is said to have ambushed and murdered William Snell, a forty-year-old neighboring farmer, and reportedly got off because of alibi testimony provided by the Bogans, Dan, his mother, and four of his sisters.[5] Perhaps influenced by gratitude, Kemp in early 1881 became engaged to marry one of the Bogan girls, probably sixteen-year-old Emma.[6]

Following his trial with Bogan at Gatesville and his abortive escape attempt after being sentenced to death for the murder of Smith,[7] Dave Kemp remained in jail, waiting for his broken leg to mend and his lawyers to pursue the appeals process. The legal team of J. A. Eidson and G. P. Miller argued the case before Texas State Court of Appeals at Tyler and were successful in getting the verdict reversed and remanded on the ground that there was an insufficient basis for the showing of malice.[8]

At Erath County in November 1882 Kemp stood trial again on the lesser charge of murder in the second degree. Another jury convicted him, but sentencing was delayed until the April 1883 term of court, pending appeals. On April 3, 1883, his appeals denied, a judge sentenced him to twenty-five years in the state penitentiary. Three days later he went behind the forbidding walls of the prison at Huntsville as Convict Number 959.[9]

On September 7, 1885, he made an escape attempt. Donning civilian clothes that had evidently been smuggled in to him, he tried to pass through the gates posing as a workman. Discovered, he was punished by a forty-eight-hour lockup in a "dark cell" and cancellation of two months and twenty-one days he had earned toward sentence reduction.[10]

In January 1887 J. A. Eidson filed a petition with the office of Governor John Ireland for Kemp's release. Signed by sixty-five citizens of Hamilton County, the petition requested executive clemency based on Kemp's youth at the time of the crime and a belief that he had been "punished sufficiently" and would "make a good, quiet and law-abiding citizen" if pardoned. Thomas J. Goree, superintendent of the prison at Huntsville, reported to the governor that the failed escape attempt was the only black mark on Kemp's record. His conduct in prison was otherwise described as excellent. A note added that he had "given authorities here much valuable information," a comment implying that Kemp had perhaps been acting as an informer for the guards. Governor Ireland granted Kemp a conditional pardon, and he walked out of the gates at Huntsville on January 15, 1887.[11]

Kemp returned to Hamilton County, where he worked as a cowboy for about a year. In 1888 and early 1889 he worked cattle in Nolan and Fisher Counties with Walker W. Bush, his half brother. During this period Kemp drove a herd of horses to western Louisiana to sell to cotton farmers. There he met Elizabeth King, daughter of a prominent landowner of Mansfield, and married her a few months later.[12]

In 1889 Kemp, his new wife, and Bessie, Elizabeth's daughter from a previous marriage, settled down in Eddy, a boomtown on the Rio Pecos in the southwest corner of New Mexico. Later that year a son, Joseph Clyde Kemp, was born to the couple, and later still W. A. Kemp, Dave's father, and Josie Kemp, his unmarried sister, came from Texas to live with them.[13] Kemp's brother Yancy and half brother Walker Bush also joined them in Eddy.

Promoters Charles B. Eddy and W. W. Hagerman had organized the town of Eddy (later to be called Carlsbad) on the site of the old John Chisum roundup and branding grounds. It was established as a business and trading center for a huge irrigation project underway in the Pecos Valley. Following the pattern of boomtowns throughout the West, Eddy was quickly flooded with an army of saloonkeepers, gamblers, pimps, and harlots, the ubiquitous quick-buck artists who flocked to each new excitement. They soon learned, however, that Charles Eddy, a prohibitionist and sworn foe of vice in its various forms, was determined to keep them out of his new town. He added a stipulation to the deed of each new town lot sold that if liquor were manufactured or sold on the premises the property would revert back to the seller. Dave Kemp, who quickly became a leading figure of the sporting crowd, circumvented Eddy's ban in 1889 by opening a saloon on the road leading north just beyond the city limits. Kemp and his partner, Tom Gray, called their establishment The Wolf in recognition of a large stuffed wolf they kept on display. The Wolf was simply a tent framed with rough wood, but it quickly became the mecca for the sports of the town. Other shacks and tents sprouted up around it, and the little saloon community came to be called Lone Wolf, or Wolftown.[14]

Everyone knew The Wolf was a booze joint, but in order to get some advertising in the Eddy papers, the owners euphemistically called the place a "drug store." However, it was clear what goods they offered:

> The nearest place to buy wines and liquors for medicinal purposes is at Kemp & Gray's, Wolftown.[15]

> Kemp & Gray of Wolftown have just received a big supply of "Belle of Bourbon," the liquor so highly esteemed by invalids.[16]

> If you feel debilitated and all out of sorts, remember at the palatial drug store of Kemp and Gray, Wolftown, you can get any kind of stimulant from Anhouser beer to the highest of high wines.[17]

> Kemp & Gray. Of Wolftown, have added old Dublin stout and London "alf-and-alf" to their stock of medicines. Remember them when you get sick.[18]

> The afflicted will be pleased to learn that Kemp & Gray, the Wolftown druggists, have received thirty barrels of Anhouser beer.[19]

The Wolf was just the first of many business enterprises for Dave Kemp in Eddy and environs. In August 1890 he bought out Tom Gray's interest,[20] and three weeks later sold the business to William Graham.[21] Over the next decade he would invest in several saloons and other commercial properties, including stationery and cigar stores, a newspaper, a pool hall, a meat market, and a theater. He would become a partner in a well-drilling concern and the Pecos Orchard Company. Always he would remain close to the ranching business, ranging cattle in New Mexico, Texas, and as far away as Indian Territory.

Eddy County was organized in 1890, and elections for the first county officers were scheduled for November 4. Kemp saw in the office of sheriff another opportunity to make money. As official tax collectors, frontier sheriffs were authorized by law to withhold a percentage of tax receipts, and in a booming community like Eddy that percentage could be huge. Kemp also knew that as chief law enforcement officer in the county he would be in position to control the lucrative vice trade and reap its financial benefits. As early as April 1890 he had announced his candidacy for sheriff.[22]

But there was a problem. He was still under conditional pardon from the state of Texas. In order to run for sheriff he needed the restoration of his rights as a citizen. Once again he called on Hamilton attorney J. A. Eidson for assistance. Eidson circulated a petition in Hamilton, Nolan, and Fisher Counties of Texas, requesting a full pardon for Kemp. The petition again emphasized Kemp's youth at the time of the "Doll" Smith shooting. Since his release from prison, his petitioners contended, he had demonstrated that he was "a sober, industrious, quiet and peaceable man." On September 8, 1890, Eidson filed his petitions with an application for executive clemency. That same day Governor L. S. Ross granted Kemp a full pardon, restoring his citizenship.[23]

Kemp's opponent in the contest for election as the first sheriff of Eddy County was fifty-one-year-old Charles Holmes Slaughter, elder brother of John H. Slaughter, celebrated sheriff of Cochise County, Arizona. C. H. Slaughter had a long and distinguished record. The son of a Texas pioneer, he had fought Indians in Texas and Yankees in the War between the States. After the war he drove cattle from south Texas as far north as Wyoming and Montana. He was no recent arrival to the Rio Pecos country as was Kemp; he had established a ranch near Seven Rivers in 1879 and served in the New Mexico Territorial Legislature as an assemblyman in 1887.[24]

Perhaps Slaughter did not campaign too vigorously for the sheriff's job. The *Eddy Argus*[25] commented in early August: "Dave Kemp seems to be the only candidate really looking after his chances."[26] At any rate, when the ballots were counted after the November 4 election,

Kemp and Slaughter were tied. Later Kemp claimed that, as a gentleman, he had voted for his opponent. The *Argus* thought "this bit of political courtesy" rather foolish, for if he had voted for himself he would have been elected by one vote.[27] The paper's editors had no preference in the runoff election campaign, characterizing both candidates as "good men" and the campaign "an honorable struggle . . . without any trumped-up charges."[28]

At the special election held in December Kemp defeated Slaughter by twenty votes, 214 to 194. "Now that Dave Kemp has been elected sheriff," said the *Argus*, "it is hoped that he will quit chewing gum, which is the only bad habit he has. He is perhaps the only sheriff-elect in New Mexico who does not use tobacco, drink liquor or indulge in profanity."[29] Kemp may not have practiced any of the common vices, but some lawmen considered him dangerous and untrustworthy. Deputy Sheriff W. L. Goodlett had publicly stated back in July that he would "pull out without waiting for his washing if a certain man" was elected sheriff. His meaning was clear, because Dave Kemp was the only announced candidate for the office at the time.[30] And Deputy U.S. Marshal Dee Harkey was outspoken in his contempt for Kemp. "A majority of the first county officers elected were crooks and criminals," he said, "especially the sheriff."[31]

Harkey was a Texan, like most of the New Mexico lawmen. A tough, fearless little man, he has been described as "thin and wiry, [with] enormous ears which stuck straight out from his head, blue eyes, a long nose, and a quiet, matter-of-fact manner."[32] He and Kemp would become bitter enemies.

For a time it appeared that, having attained the highest law enforcement post in the county, Dave Kemp, convicted murderer and former convict, was well on his way to a life of respectability and honor. He moved his wife and two children from Texas and began construction of a "commodious" five-room house at the corner of Halagueno and Tansill Streets. When the building was completed in March 1891 and the family moved in, neighbors and friends surprised them "with a string band and any number of pretty girls and smiling gallants. . . . Everyone had a jolly time and a pleasant dance."[33] By the following September Elizabeth, Kemp's wife, and Josie, his sister, had passed county examinations, received teaching certificates, and were instructing children in the public school.[34] Elizabeth, or "Lizzie" as

In a violence-marked career, Dave Kemp went from convicted murderer, condemned to hang, in Texas, to county sheriff and political power in New Mexico. Courtesy of Bill O'Neal.

she was called, moved easily into the women's social activities of the town and was active in sponsoring dances at the courthouse.[35] A few years later she and her daughter Bessie joined the Methodist Episcopal Church South during a large revival.[36] Dave's father, W. A. Kemp, remained a staunch member of the local Baptist church.[37] There is no evidence that Dave attended either church.

Dave Kemp served two terms as sheriff of Eddy County, and during those four years he made few notable arrests and participated in no gunfights. His only reported violent altercation took place in 1893 when he and "red-headed carpenter W. H. Johnson" tussled. Kemp said he was trying to collect $125 (whether this was a personal or a county obligation was unclear), when Johnson refused payment and Kemp was forced "to compel him by administering a beating." Johnson had a knife and cut Kemp's thumb badly before bystanders separated the two. A constable arrested both men for "public affray," but the charges were later dismissed.[38]

Sheriff Kemp seems to have left most of the fieldwork to a coterie of gunmen deputies: William Graham, Tom Fennessey, W. H. "Bill" Smith, Lon Bass, Tom Williamson, Dick Wilson, and Walker Bush. Graham, to whom Kemp sold The Wolf, was his chief deputy until half brother Walker Bush came to Eddy and assumed the title. Fennessey was clerk of the probate court, but accompanied Sheriff Kemp on some of his infrequent manhunts.[39] "Tom Fennessey has been with Sheriff Kemp so long," commented the *Argus* in December 1891, "that he, also, has learned to chew gum."[40] The man known as Bill Smith in Eddy was a relative of the notorious Texas gunfighter John Wesley Hardin, and a cousin of John Denson, the gunman dispatched by Barney Riggs at Pecos in 1896.[41] A fugitive from Texas, Smith was wanted there under his true name on larceny charges.[42] He tended the county jail for Kemp and later served as a constable.

Richard Alonzo "Lon" Bass was a gambler and sometime law officer who was never far from trouble. In April 1893 he defeated one Jeff Kirkendall in a no-holds-barred saloon brawl.[43] Later that year Kemp arrested him for striking John Waldie, the jailer, with a brick from behind in an attack the *Eddy Current* called "one of the most brutal and bare-faced pieces of cold-blooded treachery ever known."[44] In 1894 Bass traded shots with the desperado Denson and managed to wound him slightly.[45] The redoubtable Wes Hardin, who had studied law during sixteen years in the Texas penitentiary, came to town in March 1895 to defend his cousin Denson, charged with shooting at Bass. He arranged for bail, and Denson promptly skipped town.[46] The following August, Hardin was back in town and attempted a trick he had accomplished successfully in El Paso. Relying on the fear his reputation as a mankiller engendered in most men, he simply helped himself to a stack of silver dollars on Lon Bass's gambling table, money that did not belong to him. But Bass stuck the muzzle of a pistol in his face and forced him to return the coins.[47]

(Dee Harkey claimed that the incident almost precipitated a shooting match between Hardin and John Denson on one side and Lon Bass, Ed Lyell, and Dave Kemp on the other. He said he intervened, arrested all five men on assault charges, and took them before a justice in Eddy. They made bond and went their separate ways.[48] This story is suspect, however, as it never appeared in the Eddy papers, although it would have made sensational copy. The *Current* told how Bass called Hardin's bluff and the gunfighter turned lawyer left town on the next train. John Denson was not in Eddy in August 1895, having jumped bail and fled town five months earlier after his row with Bass.)

W. T. "Tom" Williamson was involved in several violent episodes as a sheriff's deputy assigned to patrol Phenix, the saloon suburb of Eddy. In January 1893 three patrons of Seay's saloon were "horribly beaten up by about seven men with sixshooters," according to the *Eddy Current*. Williamson was accused of participating in the beating.[49] In another altercation the following April he shot and killed Francisco Tarango and wounded Amando Gutieros so badly in the leg that the limb had to be amputated.[50]

That same month Kemp had another deputy, Dick Wilson, arrested in El Paso and held on a charge of murder. Wilson was soon released and told reporters it had all been a ploy on the part of Kemp to make him testify against another accused murderer.[51]

When Walker Bush came to Eddy in November 1892, Sheriff Kemp quickly appointed him chief county deputy and chief of police of the town.[52] Although he had a reputation as a killer (some said he had slain seven men),[53] Bush, with the help of Kemp, soon became a prominent figure in Eddy. "Bush has only been in Eddy for a few months, but is already well liked," noted the *Eddy Current* of January 13, 1893. While they served together in the sheriff's office, Kemp and Bush were partners in a meat market and a billiard hall.[54] In 1894 Kemp completed his second term as sheriff. Prohibited by territorial law from seeking a third term, he threw his support to his half brother, but in a bitterly contested primary election Bush failed to win the endorsement of the Democratic Party.[55] After Kemp left office and Bush no longer wore a star, Bush demonstrated his lethal propensities by killing former employee Joe Gunderliach, alias Joe Watson. Reports conflict as to how he inflicted the fatal wound—a newspaper reported that he struck his victim over the head,[56] but Dee Harkey, who was there and followed the case closely, insisted Bush shot the man in the head. Bush ran off and hid for about ten days, Harkey said, before surrendering to Sheriff J. D. Walker, Kemp's successor.[57] Dave Kemp was one of four bondsmen who put up $15,000 to effect Bush's release.[58] Defended by noted New Mexico attorney A. B. Fall, Bush won acquittal on the familiar plea of self-defense.[59]

Sheriff Dave Kemp's most newsworthy arrest was his pursuit and capture of Augustine Cejes in May 1894. Cejes was wanted for the robbery and murder of two peddlers, characterized in the press as "Arabian Jews." Notified that the bodies of the peddlers had been found thirty-five miles south of Eddy, near the Texas line, Kemp led a posse to the scene and followed a trail to Sierra Blanca, where he apprehended the suspect.[60]

Four months later he presided over the execution of James Barrett, convicted of the murders of John Holohan and James Barnes, two fellow laborers at a dam site of the Pecos Valley irrigation project. Barrett, a self-proclaimed "bad man from Texas," had shotgunned the victims to death while they slept. His only motive, apparently, was a desire to prove himself dangerous.[61] Barrett fled, but Kemp easily collared him the next day and jailed him at Eddy. When a mob threatened to remove him from the calaboose and administer Judge Lynch justice, Kemp spirited his prisoner, disguised in a linen duster, out of the jail and hid him in a nearby field until passions cooled.[62] After a jury convicted Barrett, District Judge A. A. Freeman sentenced him to be hanged. Kemp had a scaffold built near the city cemetery and with the assistance of Deputy Bush carried out the sentence of the court on September 15, 1894. An Eddy paper said the affair "drew better than a circus," and lauded Sheriff Kemp and Deputy Bush for their fine work.[63] According to local legend, the hanging was botched. When Barrett dropped, his feet reached the ground. Kemp is said to have rushed forward with a shovel and dug out the soil beneath Barrett's feet until the condemned man was hanging and slowly strangling to death.[64] However, the newspapers made no mention of this extraordinary sight, and Lance D. Smith, who, as a boy of eight, witnessed the execution, denied its validity.[65]

Sometimes the sheriff's work was not so deadly serious, as the embarrassment Kemp suffered following the 1891 Fourth of July celebration in Eddy. As the train pulled out of the station that evening, "a boy fired a 75 cent pistol from it." Kemp, who was on the depot platform at the time, deemed this behavior criminal and jumped on the train to arrest the culprit. He pulled the emergency cord to stop the engine, but the thing did not work, and he ended up riding the cars all the way to Pecos, Texas, where he found he could not arrest the boy because he had no Texas warrant. The *Argus* reported that Kemp returned empty-handed and seven dollars out of pocket in train fares.[66]

Eddy County did not have a permanent courthouse or jail until 1892, and for the first year and a half of his term as sheriff, Kemp had to house his prisoners in a temporary lockup constructed of leftover railroad ties on South Main near the depot.[67] This rough structure was difficult to keep clean, and several grand juries berated Kemp for the "very filthy and lousy" conditions in the jail. He was ordered to white-wash the place monthly and maintain its cleanliness.[68] Kemp also came under criticism for his prisoner feeding procedures. The county allowed him 75 cents a day to feed each jail inmate three meals a day, but he reportedly fed his charges only twice and pocketed the difference in expenses. The editors of the *Argus* found this outrageous. "The law giving the sheriffs 75 cents per day for feeding of prisoners is nothing less than legal robbery," it said. "It costs no more than 25 cents, and in Eddy it costs only 15 cents."[69]

In June 1892 a new courthouse and jail were opened in Eddy.[70] Sheriff Kemp chained a large bulldog, believed to have "great fighting qualities," outside the main entrance to the jail.[71] It was not clear if the vicious-looking bulldog was there to help keep inmates inside or discourage unwelcome visitors. The sheriff and his deputies obviously kept busy nabbing miscreants; the *Eddy Current* noted on May 26, 1893, that there were twenty-three inmates locked up in the county jail, the largest number ever. The same paper complained a few months later that the zealousness of the officers in making arrests for "trivial" offenses was bankrupting the county, already $12,000 in debt. When an offender, usually a Mexican, was arrested for drunkenness, assault, or disorderly conduct, the county got stuck for the trial costs and the additional expense of keeping the convicted in jail, as invariably he could not pay the fine. The system was nothing but a cash machine for the county officers, said the *Argus*: "The arresting officer gets a fee. The JP gets a fee, and the sheriff gets 75 cents to feed the prisoner—when he lives on much less."[72] The editors of the *Current* predicted that "the time will come when Mexicans can fight as much and as long among themselves as they desire."[73]

Eddy's saloon suburb of Wolftown, never more than a cluster of tents and shacks, was soon outstripped by a larger and bawdier sin town on the other side of town. The sporting men of Eddy acquired land just south of the city limits and established a town devoted to the vice trade. With great optimism they called the place "Phenix" after the mythical bird that was said to have risen from the ashes to attain great beauty and live for hundreds of years. The change in spelling from that of the Arizona city may have been deliberate, but more likely was due to ignorance. The town's first building housed a combination saloon and gambling house that opened for business on May 3, 1892. Proprietor Harry A. Bennett called it the Legal Tender. Other establishments quickly followed.

Prominent in the vice crowd were Edward S. Lyell, who ran the Silver King, an ornate theater, saloon, and gambling hall in Phenix, and his wife, Ellen "Nellie" Nelson Lyell, who operated the biggest bordello in town, with more than a dozen prostitutes in her employ. The Lyells had a close friend and backer in Sheriff Dave Kemp, who was a silent partner in the Silver King. Kemp and Lyell also had ranching investments together.[74] Other leading sports of Phenix included the Legal Tender proprietor, thirty-one-year-old, 250-pound Harry Bennett;[75] the King brothers, Ed and George (the latter was an unsuccessful candidate to unseat Dave Kemp for sheriff in the 1892 elections);[76] Argyle Rhodes, at 283 pounds even more corpulent than Bennett, who, when he was shot to death with two others in a Phenix gunfight in November 1896, was described by a paper as "a kindly, big-hearted whole-souled fellow without an enemy in the world;"[77] George Fee, who downed one of the men in the big shootout in which Rhodes died;[78] H. Philbrick; James B. Seay; Bill Barfield; and, of course, the redoubtable Lon Bass.

Violence was commonplace in Phenix. The vexatious John Denson constantly stirred up trouble when he was in town. In one of the deadly clashes in the bloody Frazer-Miller feud of Pecos, Texas, Denson shot and killed gunman Con Gibson in Ed Lyell's Phenix saloon on June 1, 1894.[79] When he didn't like the way the affair was written up in the *Eddy Current*, he attacked editor William H. Mullane with a club, an offense for which he was fined five dollars.[80] In September 1894 Juan Aureloa and his wife accused Denson of invading their home near Phenix, attempting to rape the woman, and of firing four shots at Aureloa when he went to her defense. He was arrested and bound over on $300 bail. "Were he a Mexican and made an assault upon a white woman, what would have been the result?" snorted *Eddy Current* editor Mullane.[81] Denson was arrested and charged with "flourishing a pistol" in a Phenix dance hall on the first of October.[82] In December Denson had the shooting scrape with Lon Bass in front of the saloon of Rhodes and Philbrick. With the help of his lawyer cousin, Wes Hardin, he managed to avoid facing the court on any of these charges. He jumped his bond and returned to Texas, where Barney Riggs put out his light on October 3, 1896.

There were so many instances of violence in Phenix that the editors of the Eddy papers at times treated a story with levity. "Last Saturday night a Mexican at Phenix opened up the bowels of William Evans to empty a cargo of beer that he was carrying," reported the *Argus* of June 23, 1893. "It was a mean trick to treat him that way, after Evans had gone to so much expense to load up. Dr. Kinsinger sewed up the opening, and thinks the injured man will again be able to beer up."

Throughout his residence in Eddy County, Dave Kemp remained a leader in the local Democratic Party. He allied himself with Tom Fennessey, probate clerk, and William K. Stalcup, deputy clerk. In the elections of 1892 Kemp easily defeated his shrievalty challenger, Phenix saloonman George King, and Fennessey and Stalcup also continued in office. Not satisfied with control of the county and its finances, this combine, through Kemp's appointment of cronies Walker Bush, Bill Smith, and others to municipal law enforcement posts, attempted to exert power over the city administration as well. But in the municipal elections of April 1894 a Progressive Party slate, headed by S. I. Roberts, mayoral candidate, and supported by Editor Richard Rule of the *Eddy Argus*, soundly defeated the Democratic ticket.[83] Kemp didn't realize it at the time, but this setback spelled the beginning of the end for him as a popular figure of power in Eddy. His second term as sheriff was coming to an end, and he could not run again. He hoped to maintain control by recapturing the sheriff's office with Walker Bush, but when Bush lost to J. D. Walker in the Democratic primary, that plan was blown. In November Walker defeated Les Dow, the Republican nominee, in an election that has been called "more than slightly irregular," with stolen ballot boxes and candidates' names erased and changed.[84]

It should have been clear to Kemp that he had lost all political clout when, despite his best efforts to help them, his pals, Bush and Smith, were soundly thrashed in an election the following January. Bush lost his bid to become justice of the peace. His opponent, S. I. Roberts, defeated him by almost 100 votes out of less than 500 cast. Smith took an even worse thumping from Dee Harkey in a contest for constable; he received fewer than 100 votes and lost by more than 300.[85] If Kemp needed any further proof that his own popularity in Eddy had evaporated, it was provided in April 1895 when he was defeated for a seat on the school board.[86]

Much of the public's displeasure with him could be attributed to problems with his handling of county funds, problems that were frequently publicized in the pages of the *Argus*. As early as October 1891 the paper had denounced the "Democratic Ring" of which he was a leading member, and had cited extensive expenditures by Kemp and Fennessey.[87] In February 1892 the first grand jury to sit in Eddy was reported as "unhappy with the sheriff's bookkeeping system,"[88] but, other than this mild rebuke, did not pursue the issue at the time. In October of that year the *Eddy County Citizen* published a listing of Sheriff Kemp's billings to the county for 1891, provided by an anonymous reader.[89] In a letter to the *Citizen* Kemp attacked the author of the listing, calling him a liar and slanderer, but did not explicitly deny the accuracy of the data.[90] In July 1893 the *Argus* reported that an independent auditor had found the sheriff owed the county $5,362 for taxes and penalties he had collected but not turned in. In addition, he had been paid $2,702 in unauthorized expenses.[91] Kemp received some halfhearted defense in the pages of the *Eddy Current*, an opposition paper, which quoted him as saying he owed the county nothing. Editor Mullane suggested that if the sheriff had been allowed improper expenses by past county commissioners, they were at fault and not him.[92]

Much of the problem seemed to stem from confusion over taxing authority between the city and county governments, especially during the period before the first municipal elections. Kemp continued to contest the auditor's charges and adamantly refused to refund any money as the controversy raged on into 1894. But he lost much of his support among taxpayers and voters when they learned through the pages of the *Argus* in March of that year the extent of the financial bonanza their sheriff was enjoying. By law, Kemp was entitled to retain 5 percent of all county taxes collected; his report for the previous four months showed that had meant a $4,000 windfall for him.[93] Angry public reaction to this news prompted Kemp to attempt a compromise with the commissioners. In April he offered to pay back $1,860, and by June he actually had returned $2,610 to the county treasury.[94] The dispute was not helped in the least when Harry P. Brown, county treasurer and cashier of the First National Bank of Eddy, absconded in August with $8,168 in county funds. Rumors later spread that Kemp had been implicated in Brown's disappearance.[95]

Kemp still withheld $3,200, claiming the amount was to reimburse him for legitimate expenses. The *Argus* called this "an official grab, not according to law, and a bluff that should be called at once."[96] In September the town trustees laid claim to the disputed $3,200 and directed their attorney to take legal action against Kemp.[97] Finally, in January 1895, after he had left office, Kemp, the county commissioners, and the town trustees came to a compromise. The contested amount had now grown to $9,747. Kemp agreed to a total liability of $5,466, and the balance was allowed him for his claimed expenses.[98]

Other personal difficulties assailed Kemp during this period. Just before Christmas 1892 his wife Lizzie gave birth to a child, but the infant lived only a few hours.[99] When an epidemic of diphtheria swept Eddy in 1893, many families were struck, including the Walker Bush and Dave Kemp households. Theodosa, Bush's wife, succumbed to the disease, leaving him with seven surviving children, ranging in age from fourteen months to sixteen years.[100] Kemp's four-year-old son, Joe, also became seriously ill, but survived.[101] In the summer of 1894

Kemp got caught in a flash flood while crossing Dark Canyon in a wagon. He lost his wagon and almost his life.[102] Lizzie Kemp delivered another blow, filing for divorce from her husband in November 1895.[103] She returned to Louisiana where, within a year, she married a man named Norman E. Young.[104]

Several new developments in 1895 endangered the continued prosperity of the sin city of Phenix, in which Kemp was heavily invested. The new sheriff, J. D. Walker, seemed more committed to controlling the rowdy element than Kemp had been. Dee Harkey, newly appointed special deputy U.S. marshal, began a vigorous campaign to enforce the Edmunds Act, a convenient tool for harassment of the notoriously libidinous sporting crowd. Originally passed by Congress in 1882 as a measure to curtail polygamous practices in Mormon Utah, the law made it a misdemeanor for a man to cohabitate with women to whom he was not legally married. In April 1895 Harkey rounded up several Phenix sports and charged them with violation of the law. Lon Bass was one of those arrested. Harkey accused him of living in adultery with a woman known as Jessie Cross. An angry Bass, in retaliation, filed a complaint against Harkey for violating the same statute. The cases were later dropped.[105]

That spring fire destroyed Nellie Lyell's big twelve-room parlor house and threatened her husband's nearby Silver King Theater. Arsonists were believed responsible for the losses, estimated at $1,800.[106] The next year Walker Bush's house and barn also went up in flames, and arsonists were again blamed.[107] In addition to these disasters, Kemp and his pals were suffering losses as cronies they had supported financially suddenly sought healthier climes. The *Eddy Current* reported that within a two-month period in 1893 a man named Cy Davidson had suddenly decamped owing Kemp $100; and Bob and A. E. Murrell, in debt to Kemp and Fennessey to the tune of $2,000, had also left town between suns.[108] In March 1895 a Phenix rounder, gunman, and rustler named Martin Mroz, rather than face cattle theft charges, liquidated his holdings, and fled to Mexico. Although he took with him several thousand dollars, Ed Lyell was left holding his IOU for $100.[109] Lyell would never recover his money, for lawmen shot Mroz dead three months later.[110]

When, in the spring of 1895, "a petition containing the signatures of nearly all the people of Eddy" condemned the evils of their suburb to the south and demanded that Constable Dee Harkey suppress those evils, the Phenix sporting crowd realized it was time to move on.[111] It took all summer to make preparations, but on September 19 the *Current* announced that "next Monday a large party from Phenix will leave for Globe, Arizona, where Lyell & Kemp have erected a building and purchased a large saloon. The group totals fifteen." Two weeks later the paper described the grand exodus:

> Three six-mule teams, each hitched to a big wagon and another wagon behind called a trail wagon, passed through town last Saturday from the saloon suburb—Phenix—en route to Globe, Arizona. They are the outfits of Lyell & Kemp, who have located in Arizona and intend as soon as possible to close out business here entirely. The outfits were in charge of Lon Bass as captain with W. W. Anderson and E. H. Asbury as lieutenants. Those who left Eddy with the outfits were: Lon Bass, Tom Crooks, Joe Morgan, W. W. Anderson, W. K. Stalcup, H. L. Swift, Herve Buchanon, E. H. Asbury, Jasper Evans, Dan Kinkle, Joe Goodinson, Jack Bonham, George Dines, George Shieks, W. D. Robinson, R. R. Stringfellow, Antonio Holquin, wife and child, and Charlie Gonzales, twenty in all. While passing through town Dan Kinkle perched away up on one of the big loads, played Bonapart's Retreat in his inimitable way. Dan is a good violinist and the band this outfit can muster is probably the best in the west. All are jolly boys and will no doubt make fortunes in Arizona. To the people of Globe we can say they have acquired a rare lot of good fellows, who, if they deport themselves in Arizona as while in New Mexico, can be said to be first class citizens.[112]

One of those "first class citizens," W. K. Stalcup, neglected to turn in all the receipts of fines he had collected while acting as justice of the peace. Officers received warrants for him the day of the exodus, caught up with the wagons near Seven Rivers, and brought Kemp's crony back under arrest.[113]

A few weeks later the *Current* reported that Nellie Lyell left Phenix for Globe at the head of a flock of some sixteen soiled doves. Only six or seven "fallen women" remained in the saloon suburb.[114]

Dave Kemp did not join the parade of sports to Arizona, but stayed on to manage the local business affairs of Lyell and Kemp while his partner handled the Globe enterprise. Ten months later a disastrous flood destroyed the Kemp & Lyell saloon and gambling house at Globe, and the partners suffered a $3,000 loss.[115] At Eddy, Kemp had devoted most of his energies to expanding his cattle holdings, and this expansion soon caught the attention of James Leslie Dow, the unsuccessful candidate for sheriff the previous year.

Dow, a rancher and saloonkeeper from Seven Rivers, now working as a detective for the New Mexico Cattlemen's Association, was widely feared and respected as a gunfighter after killing a notorious gunman named Zack Light in April 1891. Dow had personal reasons for targeting Kemp and his crowd. In 1893 he and Kemp cohort Bill Smith had what the *Argus* called "a little racket with revolvers" at Dow's Seven Rivers saloon. "Each [claimed] that the other attempted to draw first. Dow, however, made Smith leave the house and 'hit the road.'"[116] In addition, Dow was a Republican while Kemp and his friends were staunch Democrats—this in a day when folks took their political differences very seriously.

In October 1895 Dow charged Dave Kemp and Walker Bush with cattle theft, and Sheriff Walker arrested them. The case against Kemp was weak, and he quickly got a dismissal. A few days later Bush went to trial before Justice of the Peace S. I. Roberts, the man who had defeated him in the previous year's election, and won an acquittal.[117] Kemp retaliated against Dow in May 1896, bringing charges against the stock detective for stealing twenty-three head of Kemp's cattle. Justice Roberts threw out the case.[118]

The previous month Walker Bush had been tried for the killing of Joe Gunderliach, alias Joe Watson. His attorney had been Albert B. Fall, one of the most successful lawyers in New Mexico, who quickly won an acquittal for Bush on the time-honored ground of self-defense.[119]

A tension-filled game of poker was held in an Eddy hotel room during that term of court. Sitting in the game were A. B. Fall, Sheriff Charley Perry of Chaves County, Dave Kemp, Les Dow, and Dee Harkey, court bailiff. Every player at the table, with the exception of attorney Fall, had killed at least one man and was considered a dangerous gunfighter. The situation was potentially explosive because several of the participants disliked each other intensely. Harkey had not hidden his contempt for Kemp, and the former sheriff, in turn, bore a grudge against Harkey for his part in the thrashing of Kemp cronies Walker Bush and Bill Smith in the previous year's elections.

The recent cow theft charges and countercharges had exacerbated the enmity Kemp and Dow felt for each other. Additionally, Fall and Dow were not on speaking terms. Harkey insisted that everyone be disarmed before the game could start. "They give me all their damn pistols," Harkey recalled. "I piled 'em up over on the bed . . . and put their cartridges—Goddamn!—I guess there was a hatful of 'em—piled 'em down over there. . . . They got some whiskey . . . and so they got a little bit high. And Harry Christian he came up there. Came to the room and saw all those pistols piled up there, you know, and Goddamn! his eyes opened up like that."[120]

Despite Harkey's apprehensions, the poker game ended late that night without trouble. But within a year Charley Perry would disappear with $9,000 of Chaves County funds,[121] and Dave Kemp would shoot Les Dow dead. Albert Fall would survive a turbulent career in New Mexico to become interior secretary in the administration of President Warren G. Harding and attain ignominy as a central figure in the Teapot Dome scandal of the 1920s.

Dee Harkey later claimed that Dave Kemp tried to assassinate him on several occasions. A final showdown came as Harkey was working up additional cattle theft cases against Kemp and Bush. As Harkey tells the story, he was tipped off that Kemp had been overheard saying he was going to ambush and kill the little lawman, naming the time and place. Harkey said he sneaked up on Kemp as he waited and got the drop on him. Then followed an incredible account: "I unarmed him and told him I was going to kill him. He begged me not to kill him, for he was unarmed, but I insisted I had to kill him to keep him from killing me. But, of course, I could not kill him after I had unarmed him. After an hour or two of deliberation [!] I decided not to kill him if he would sign an affidavit that he would leave the country and never come back. Dave agreed to do this, and I took him over to U. S. Bateman's law office, and Mr. Bateman prepared the affidavit and took Dave's oath on it. I gave Dave back his pistol and we separated. Dave complied with his agreement for some years until he came back to kill Les Dow."[122]

Although attorney Bateman confirmed this extraordinary tale in an interview many years later,[123] it is still difficult to swallow. Kemp was indeed absent from Eddy for several months in 1896; his name was strangely absent from the local papers. He was in Globe, Arizona, working with his partner Ed Lyell to get back in business after the destruction of their saloon and gambling house in the August flood. But Kemp still retained many other business interests in Eddy, and it is very doubtful that he would agree to depart with no intention of returning. Whether he returned for the express purpose of killing Les Dow, as Harkey asserted, is also questionable, but he did come back and he did kill Dow.

In June of 1896 Les Dow announced his candidacy for sheriff of Eddy County. He switched parties, challenging incumbent J. D. Walker for the Democratic nomination. He won the Democratic Party endorsement and prepared to face M. Cicero Stewart in the November election. His fame as a nemesis of stock thieves stood him in good stead in the contest. "Les Dow is the democratic nominee for sheriff of Eddy County. Cattle rustlers will be sorry to hear this," commented the *El Paso Daily Herald*.[124] Even as he campaigned, Dow took on other law enforcement responsibilities, accepting appointment as a deputy U.S. marshal on July 21.[125] In November he defeated Stewart, and on January 1, 1897, took office as Eddy County sheriff, a position he would hold for only forty-nine days.[126]

About this time Dee Harkey and Dow had what Harkey called "a mix-up." Harkey had been former sheriff Walker's chief deputy, and the race for sheriff, always bitterly contested, may have triggered the difficulty. As Harkey told the story, Kemp, out in Arizona, heard of the Harkey-Dow "mix-up" and saw an opportunity to eliminate a man he hated—Les Dow—and at the same time get back in the good graces of the man who had outlawed him from Eddy County—Dee Harkey. Kemp returned to Eddy in disguise, so goes the story, and admitted to Harkey that he intended to kill Dow. Harkey said he warned Dow of Kemp's presence and intention, but did not explain why he did not immediately demand that Kemp get out of town and stay out as stipulated in the affidavit he had supposedly signed.[127]

Shortly before seven o'clock on the evening of Thursday, February 18, 1897, Dow walked from the post office, reading a letter. Suddenly Dave Kemp stepped out of the darkened doorway of the *Eddy Argus* building, stuck a pistol in the sheriff's face, and pulled the trigger. The bullet, entering the left side of Dow's mouth, smashed the jawbone and exited the neck, just under the left ear. Dow jerked out his revolver, but the flash had powder-burned his face and blinded him. He staggered about in the street as Kemp and another man, later identified as Will Kennon, disappeared into the evening shadows.

Men rushed to the scene, assisted Dow to Blackmore's Drug Store, and attempted to staunch the blood flowing from his wound. Doctors Walsmith and Whicher then removed him to his home and treated him as he lay on a table in the front room. He was chloroformed and pieces of teeth and bone were picked out of his wound. The doctors believed at first that the injury would not be fatal, but Dow died about eight the next morning without regaining consciousness.[128]

The ubiquitous Dee Harkey claimed to have pursued Kemp and Kennon to Dark Canyon where he placed them under arrest. "Dave admitted to me that he shot Les and said he tried to shoot him between the eyes because he wanted to be certain to kill him," Harkey wrote. "He said Les wore a steel jacket all the time, and it was foolish to try to shoot him any place but the head." Harkey said he feared that Dow's brothers and friends would kill his prisoners if he placed them in the Eddy jail, so he kept Kemp and Kennon in his own house until passions cooled somewhat.[129]

The assassination of Les Dow caused great public indignation and outrage. Hours after the sheriff's death, territorial rewards, augmented by public subscription, reached $2,500 for the arrest and conviction of the killer or killers. Kemp and Kennon were locked up in the Eddy jail under heavy guard on February 19. "What evidence can be secured against them is not known to many at present," said the *Current* in its edition of the 20th. "It is the general opinion that the men were enemies. Were the assassin known, he would no doubt be lynched at once for Mr. Dow had a host of friends. He was a man who feared nothing except assassination. None were so quick with a revolver as Les Dow. His air was perfect and his nerve always steady."

Kemp and Kennon were charged with the murder, but it took eight months before they were indicted. On October 14 a grand jury finally brought in murder indictments against both of them. Prosecuting attorney John Franklin then brought charges of witness tampering and intimidation against Kemp, who, he alleged, threatened the life of a prosecution witness named Bruce Jones if he did not leave town before the trial. At a hearing a judge found Kemp guilty of contempt, fined him twenty-five dollars, and sentenced him to sixty days in the jail he had once overseen as sheriff. Kemp still had influential friends in Eddy County, however, and "well-signed" petitions secured his release after he had served only twenty-six of his sixty-day sentence.[130]

Because of the intense emotions still raging in Eddy, Kemp's defense attorneys, W. W. Gatewood and George Estes of Reeves County, Texas, succeeded in getting venue for the murder trial changed to Roswell, Chaves County, where proceedings in what the *Eddy Current* called "the most celebrated trial for murder ever to take place in the valley"[131] began in late March 1898. The defendants first entered a plea of not guilty. Kemp had lined up witnesses who were prepared to swear that he was not in Eddy at the time of the killing. But when his defense attorneys learned that C. W. Moore, compositor of the *Argus*, was ready to testify that he had seen and recognized Kemp and Kennon as they lurked in the doorway of the newspaper building, and that E. H. Asbury would say he had also recognized them as they ran from the scene of the shooting, they changed the plea to self-defense. Prosecution witnesses, including Dee Harkey, recounted how Kemp had frequently voiced threats against Dow. The defense produced a number of witnesses who testified that Dow was widely feared as a deadly gunman and that he wore a steel breastplate. They said he had threatened Kemp on several occasions, and once had thrown down on him with a Winchester rifle. Kemp, testifying in his own defense, said he and Kennon had just been passing the *Argus* office when Dow saw them, unloosed a torrent of curses, and reached for his gun. Kemp said he beat him to the draw, and aware of Dow's body armor, shot him in the head in defense of his own life. Bill Smith, former constable at Eddy, was a surprise witness for the defense. He corroborated Kemp's testimony, saying he was with the defendants when Dow approached, spotted Kemp, cursed him, and went for his gun, only to be beaten by Kemp's quicker hand. Cross-examination disclosing that Smith was using an alias and was a fugitive from Texas apparently did not detract from the effect of this testimony on the members of the jury. After only three hours of deliberation on March 30, 1898, they brought in a verdict of not guilty.[132]

The Dow family was convinced that the acquittal had been obtained by perjured testimony. Many substantial Eddy County residents, including Judge Charles R. Brice and attorneys U. S. Bateman, E. P. Bujac, and S. I. Roberts, shared that view.[133] Dee Harkey stated flatly that the self-defense plea was "framed." He said Kemp paid Smith, who was nowhere near the scene of the shooting, fifty dollars to commit this perjury, and then chased him out of town after the verdict. Harkey did admit, however, that Dow's fighting reputation helped the defense, as the jury considered the killing a clash between dangerous gunfighters who were expected to protect themselves.[134]

It has been suggested that the mysterious Will Kennon, who was not known around Eddy before the shooting and seems to have disappeared soon thereafter, was the latest incarnation of Dan Bogan, alias Bill Gatlin, alias Bill McCoy, the man who had been convicted with Kemp of the Doll Smith murder back in 1881.[135] Apparently Bogan was in Eddy at the time; Kemp later told A. C. Campbell, who had assisted in the murder prosecution of Bogan in Wyoming, that he had been in the court room from the beginning to the end of the trial. "I did him a good turn once, and I needed his assistance in case I was convicted," Kemp told Campbell,[136] hinting that he and Bogan were prepared to attempt the same sort of desperate escape from the courtroom they had engineered back in Gatesville, Texas. According to Campbell, Cicero Stewart, who replaced Les Dow as sheriff, suspected Bogan was in town and wanted a crack at the reward offered back in 1887 for his capture. He contacted Campbell and asked if he could identify the fugitive and if the Wyoming authorities would still pay the reward for his apprehension. "I did not lose Bogan," replied Campbell, who was deathly afraid of the desperado, adding that he would only identify him if he saw him in a coffin and Campbell could be absolutely certain he was dead and not in a trance. Campbell did contact Walter Stoll, who had prosecuted Bogan in Wyoming and was told the rewards were no longer outstanding as the state was no longer interested in the eleven-year-old case. When he received this information, Sheriff Stewart lost all interest in Bogan also.[137]

Sporting man E. H. Asbury had joined the great exodus from Phenix in the fall of 1895, but he was back in Eddy the following year and was one of the chief witnesses against Kemp at his trial. In December 1896, prior to the Dow shooting and the trial, he and Kemp had "an altercation" on an Eddy street. Kemp evidently was the aggressor and received a one-dollar fine.[138] The trouble between the two may have stemmed from Asbury's marital problems. Asbury and his wife were divorced shortly thereafter, and Kemp, within a week of his acquittal, married the former Mrs. Asbury.[139]

It was a joyous time for Dave Kemp, as he celebrated his victory in court and wedding, but soon he was to be hit with adversity. A little more than two months later the body of Denton Robertson, Kemp's former brother-in-law, was found in the ashes of his burnt-out home a few miles from Eddy.[140] It was suspected, but never proven, that Robertson had been murdered in retaliation for Kemp's killing of Dow. Eddy County sheriff Cicero Stewart appointed Dee Harkey as his chief deputy, and Harkey, bitter enemy of Kemp, harassed him at every opportunity. In July Harkey arrested Kemp for carrying a six-shooter. A grand jury later true-billed him on the charge, and he was fined.[141] In August a horse threw him and he broke his arm.[142] His mother passed away at San Angelo, Texas, in February 1900, and his father followed her in death three years later.[143]

By this time Walker Bush, Kemp's half brother and business partner, had left New Mexico to join his former Phenix pal, Lon Bass, in Douglas, Arizona. Douglas was a tough town, reminiscent of Phenix in its heyday. There Bush opened his Coney Island Saloon No. 1 on Sixth Street and partnered Bass and Tom Hudspeth in the operation of the nearby Cowboy's Home Saloon.[144] On February 8, 1903, Arizona Ranger Bill Webb shot and killed Bass in the Cowboy's Home.[145] Dee Harkey said Bush was killed in Arizona,[146] but he may have confused him with Bass. Veteran southwestern lawman Jeff Milton said Walker Bush later got religion and became a preacher.[147]

In 1900 Dave Kemp moved to Lipscomb County in the extreme northeastern corner of the Texas Panhandle. At Higgins he speculated in real estate and served as a deputy sheriff. He is remembered for having "the first house in the area to have running water . . . , a sink with a pitcher pump and a tin bathtub, luxuries for a pioneer home."[148] In 1908 he founded a town he called Kemp City just across the border in Oklahoma Territory. Later this name was changed to La Kemp, and later still the entire town was moved to a site adjacent to a new railroad and became Booker, Texas.[149]

Kemp was never punished for what appeared to be the premeditated, cold-blooded murder of Les Dow, but he must have lived out his days in constant fear of revengeful Dow supporters. At least three men who were close to him died suddenly and violently: Denton Robertson in 1898, Dave's brother Yancy thirty years later, and his son, Leon, five years after that. Yancy's bullet-riddled body was found near his ranch in the Pine Lodge area, west of Roswell, about 1928.[150] On December 22, 1933, a man named Robert L. Pounds shot Leon Kemp to death on his own front porch.[151]

Dee Harkey wrote that Dave Kemp also died violently, shot and killed at Higgins by his sister,[152] but this assertion was based on an unfounded rumor that circulated in Eddy and Chaves Counties. Kemp died on his ranch near Booker of a massive heart attack on January 4, 1935.[153]

— 12 —

JEFF KIDDER
(1875–1908)

"Big man with the big gun"

"The only trouble with Jeff Kidder," Jefferson David Milton used to say, "was that he wanted to be a bad man and didn't know how."[1]

Milton, who in his time had been a Texas Ranger, city marshal of El Paso, express messenger for Wells Fargo, border patrolman, and gunfighter with few peers, never liked the young man who shared his first name. That was probably because Kidder was an Arizona Ranger and Milton had a bias against Arizona Rangers. The antipathy dated back to the formation of the elite territorial law enforcement in 1901, when Milton, although well qualified, for political reasons was not chosen to head up the organization.

Actually, Jeff Kidder never wanted to be a "bad man"; he just wanted to be a top-notch gunfighter. Folks back in Vermillion, South Dakota, where he grew up, remembered that he packed a six-shooter from the time he was big enough to hold one in his hand. When he worked at the post office where his father was postmaster, most of his wages went to buy ammunition. He practiced the draw-and-shoot by the hour.[2]

The Kidders were a prominent family in Vermillion. Young Jeff was the namesake of lawyer Jefferson Parrish Kidder, his grandfather, who had served as lieutenant governor of Vermont before moving west. In Dakota J. P. Kidder had a distinguished career as a jurist and legislator, accepting appointments to the supreme court of the territory from

Presidents Lincoln, Grant, Hayes, and Arthur. During the 1870s he served two terms as a delegate to Congress from the territory.[3]

The elder of Judge Kidder's two sons, Lieutenant Lyman S. Kidder of the Second U.S. Cavalry, died at the age of twenty-five in an Indian fight near the headwaters of the Solomon River in northwest Kansas in July 1867. His detachment of ten troopers and an Indian guide, detailed to carry dispatches to George Amstrong Custer of the Seventh Cavalry, was attacked and wiped out by a party of Sioux and Cheyenne. On July 12, 1867, Custer and his scout, Will Comstock, found the bodies, stripped, burned, and mutilated.[4]

Silas W. Kidder, the judge's other son, settled in Vermillion in 1868 and worked as a clerk in his father's court. Elected to the Territorial Council at the age of twenty-four, he was later mayor and postmaster at Vermillion. His farm home, four miles north of town, he called "Kidderminster." Kidder Island in the nearby Missouri River and Kidder Street in Vermillion were both named for the judge.[5]

When, on November 15, 1875, a son was born at Kidderminster, he too was named for the judge and christened Jefferson Parrish. Clay County, South Dakota, was agricultural country, inhabited by hard-working farmers, and while growing up young Jeff Kidder saw little of the violence that marked other areas of the West. But he read dozens of dime novels devoted to the exploits of Western frontier heroes, particularly masters of the six-gun, and dreamed of the day when he could be a great gunfighter. He worked on the farm at Kinderminster, the post office in town, and went through the public schools. Then he attended classes at the newly opened University of South Dakota at Vermillion, studying algebra, language, and composition.[6]

In 1901 Silas Kidder, in ill health, moved to southern California. His wife, Ada, and daughter, Lulu, went with him, but son Jeff, now twenty-five years old and still eager to display his gun prowess, did not, choosing instead to head for one of the last remnants of the wild western frontier, the southern counties of Arizona Territory. Perhaps not coincidentally, the Arizona Rangers were established that same year; Jeff Kidder may have gone to the southwest territory for that very reason, hoping to join the new law enforcement company. If that was his intention, he had to wait two years before his application was accepted. Meanwhile he took whatever employment he could find. He cowboyed, worked in the mines, served as a peace officer in Nogales, and even had a job at the Copper Queen Hospital.

The first captain of the Arizona Rangers was Burton C. Mossman, who had gained renown as an implacable foe of rustlers and outlaws during a stint as manager of the huge Hash Knife cattle ranch. To assist him in the awesome task of controlling outlawry in the vast reaches of the territory, the legislature authorized Mossman to select one sergeant and twelve privates, and he enlisted men he had known as law officers or cowboys previously. After a year of service, Mossman resigned and was succeeded by Thomas H. Rynning, an adventurer who had served with new Arizona governor A. O. Brodie in Theodore Roosevelt's Rough Riders during the Spanish-American War. When the territorial legislature a year later approved a bill doubling the Arizona Ranger force, one of those Rynning tapped to join the enlarged command was Jeff Kidder. On April 1, 1903, the "gun-crazy native of South Dakota who would prove to be the most notable of this group of recruits" as one Arizona Ranger historian characterized him,[7] signed his enlistment papers.

Kidder was a handsome young man, tall and slim, sandy-haired and clean-shaven, with very pale gray eyes. Western writer William MacLeod Raine, who met many of the old-time gunmen in their later years, remarked that most shared a common feature: "gray or blue eyes, often a faded blue, expressionless, hard as jade."[8] Jeff Kidder had such eyes—the eyes of a gunfighter.

As a private in the rangers, Kidder wore no uniform and generally dressed in worn cowboy attire, boots and denims. He was paid $100 a month ($55 salary and $45 for expenses) and given commission papers and a badge of solid silver. He was expected to furnish a suitable mount and a pack animal for his personal use, as well as clothing, camping gear, and a "six shooting pistol (army size)."[9] The territory provided the recruit a rifle and ammunition, but deducted the cost from his pay. Kidder may have been careless of his appearance, but that "six shooting pistol" in a holster at his waist was always cleaned and oiled, ready for action. He constantly practiced with his guns, and came to be "widely regarded as one of the fastest draws in the Southwest. There were many fine shots with the rangers, but only Harry Wheeler [later captain of the rangers] was considered Kidder's equal as a marksman."[10]

Handsome Jeff Kidder's burning ambition was to be the greatest gunfighter of them all. Courtesy of the Arizona Historical Society, AHS #45083.

Two months after Kidder's enlistment, Captain Rynning led the entire company to the strikebound Morenci mining district to quell threatened riots. At one point during this disturbance Graham County sheriff Jim Parks, sixty of his hastily commissioned deputies, and a couple dozen Arizona Rangers were surrounded by twelve hundred armed and angry miners. One shot from either side could have triggered a terrible battle, but leaders on both sides stayed calm, controlled their men, and bloodshed was averted. Shortly thereafter the Arizona National Guard, 230 men strong, and 280 federal cavalrymen from Forts Grant and Huachuca, arrived to maintain order, and the rangers were relieved.

On July 5, 1904, that pistol of which Kidder was so fond saw action in an incident that revealed an overbearing and belligerent side of the young man's nature. Before he was finished, three men lay sprawled outside Tony Downs' Turf Saloon in Bisbee. Remarkably, none of the three was shot. Kidder had cracked each over the head with the barrel of his revolver. In the parlance of the frontier lawmen, he had "buffaloed" them. He had apparently acted on little or no provocation, and a mob of miners, incensed by what they saw as an exhibition of unbridled brutality, began to form with intentions of lynching the ranger. But other officers responded quickly to the ugly situation, arrested Kidder, and hustled him away. Arraigned in court, he was charged with two counts of assault on men named Fagan and Graham, and one of assault with a deadly weapon on a man named Radebush.[11]

The *Bisbee Review* was scathing in its denunciation of the man it called "a thug, bully and butcher . . . , Mr. Kidder, the big man with the big gun." It asked: "Who sent this Ranger in here with his pistol to beat up men on the streets of Bisbee? Is the reputation of the Ranger force to be made and maintained by the muzzle end of a .45 in the hands of a hotheaded man wearing a star? Who gave this man Kidder, wearing an Arizona Ranger badge, the extraordinary powers warranting him to cut men's heads open with the butt end of a .45?" The editorial went on to accuse Kidder of having "a murderous mind, stimulated with the idea that he's the whole cheese, [eager to] demonstrate his ability of knocking out men and boys with his ever ready gatling," and called for his discharge. Captain Rynning, said the paper, should "take this man Kidder out of here, strip him of his star and badge which gives him the authority to 'pack a gun' and use it like a crazy man, unfitted to be an officer by every evidence in the world."[12]

Because of fulminations like this against Kidder, his lawyers requested and were granted a change of venue in the assault cases. At a trial in Tombstone two weeks later he was convicted on one count and fined fifty dollars. The prosecution dropped the other charge when important witnesses failed to appear. The more serious charge of assault with a deadly weapon dragged on for a year with a series of postponements and was finally transferred to Pima County in June 1905 when a judge ruled that "by reason of biased and prejudiced published reports of the case the defendant could not secure a fair and impartial trial" in Bisbee. After several additional delays, this charge was quietly dropped.[13]

Normally quiet-spoken and personable, Kidder soon developed a reputation as an obnoxious, belligerent young buck when under the influence of alcohol. "He did not have a bit of sense when he was drunk," as one friend put it.[14] A respected Western writer characterized him as "a good shot and a brave man but quarrelsome and overbearing when drunk."[15] Jeff Milton claimed in later years that he tangled with a drunken, obstreperous Kidder one night in Nogales and made him crawl. As Milton told the tale, he and the younger Jeff were having dinner together in Pete Cazobon's restaurant, and Kidder, in his cups, became increasingly loud and profane. Milton said he objected to this behavior as there were women and children present. Kidder jumped up from the table, six-gun in hand.

"I could have killed him then, dead easy," Milton told his biographer, "but I didn't want to do it there." He told Kidder to holster his gun and meet him outside. Once out on the sidewalk Milton dressed down the younger man in the strongest terms he could muster and tried to provoke him into drawing. But Kidder was thoroughly bulldozed, Milton said. He took the verbal abuse and slunk away.[16]

Border guard Arcus Reddoch's recollection of the confrontation between the two Jeffs was entirely different. In this version it was Kidder who ripped the other man in sulfurous language and he did it while looking into the muzzle of Milton's gun. "Jeff Kidder called Jeff Milton's hand and told him plenty," Reddoch said, adding that "it was a good thing Milton had Kidder covered, because in an even draw, Kidder would have beat him, everyone said."[17]

Another Nogales old-timer, Billy Bower, claimed that the trouble between Kidder and Milton ended in a shooting. "I saw Jeff Milton and Jeff Kidder shoot across the street, Jeff [Kidder] on the saloon side and Milton behind a pole—Castlebaum's store. You could see chips knocked off the post," he said.[18]

There can be little doubt that some kind of a Kidder-Milton confrontation did take place in Nogales, although Bower's assertion that the affair escalated into a shooting lacks any confirmation and probably never happened. Milton's claim that he made Kidder back down and hunt his hole is also not credible.

Both Arizona Ranger captains under whom Kidder served attested to the man's courage and coolness under fire. Tom Rynning adjudged him "a fearless young fellow, pleasant in his ways, and with plenty quiet good judgment . . . , a top hand among the Arizona Rangers."[19] Harry C. Wheeler, who followed Rynning as captain in 1907, wrote: "Whatever criticism may be made of him is only such as might be made of many another young man, but . . . the indiscreetness was far excelled and overshadowed by his manly qualities. . . . Jeff was a noble, manly fellow, brave and energetic, the best all-around man I had. . . . Jeff Kidder was one of the best officers who ever stepped foot in this section of the country. He did not know what fear was."[20]

W. A. "Billy" Old, a ranger lieutenant who sided Kidder in many a brush with outlaws, said they had ridden together into "places that try men's souls and Jeff was always found pure gold."[21] And ranger Fred Rankin called Kidder "one of those men who never knew fear."[22]

Other rangers were most impressed by Kidder's skill with a six-gun and his propensity to use it without hesitation. Joe Pearce remembered Kidder as "a gunman as well as a lawman [who] in a pinch would shoot first and ask the questions later on, if there was anybody left to answer them. . . . Kidder was a killer."[23] And John Clarke, the last surviving Arizona Ranger, in 1976 clearly recalled Kidder's revolver, a weapon, he said, that became legendary in the West. "Kidder had dug the grave of many a badman," Clarke told an interviewer.[24]

The "legendary" six-shooter was a silver-plated, single-action .45-caliber Colt's, serial number 246844, with factory engraving, pearl grips, and Kidder's name inscribed on the backstrap. He purchased this beautiful weapon shortly after his father died at San Jacinto, California, and left him a sizable inheritance. Kidder practiced constantly with this revolver as he had with other guns since his childhood back in South Dakota. A good share of his inheritance, possibly as much as three or four thousand dollars, went to buy ammunition.[25] He fired off so many rounds that within two years he had to return the pistol to the Colt's factory for repair and replating.[26] The constant practice produced results. Newspapers reported in 1908 that "Kidder was reputed to be the quickest man on the ranger force in drawing a gun. It was said of him that he could allow the average man to cover him with a gun, and then draw his own weapon and fire quicker than the other party. He was one of the best shots of the rangers. At thirty paces he demonstrated repeatedly that he could hit a playing card three times out of six on the average. He could shoot equally well with either hand."[27]

Captain Tom Rynning, who had seen many a gunslick in his time, was amazed at Kidder's pistol dexterity. "Jeff Kidder was the fastest—absolutely the quickest hand with a six-shooter I've ever met up with. [He] worked the hammer with the thumb of his pistol hand as fast as I could fan it with my other hand."[28]

As an Arizona Ranger, Kidder spent much of his time in the field chasing outlaws through the mountains and deserts of the sparsely settled territory. When the hounded criminals, in an effort to elude their pursuers, crossed the international line into old Mexico, Captain Rynning requested and received from General Luis E. Torres, commander of the northern district of Mexico and governor of Sonora, special commissions for himself and selected rangers Billy Old, John Foster, Tip Stanford, and Jeff Kidder, authorizing them to pursue their quarry across the border.[29] In Mexico the rangers worked in cooperation with the Sonora Rurales under their celebrated commander Colonel Emelio Kosterlitzky, who agreed that the apprehension of desperadoes was more important than international law.

For most of his ranger career Kidder patrolled that long stretch of borderland between Nogales and Douglas, ferreting out smugglers. He headquartered at Naco, a little town directly across the border from a village of the same name in Sonora, Mexico. Often he worked alone, but at times rangers Fred Rankin, Billy Old, or Bill Sparks joined him in this work. Rankin was with him on one occasion when they surprised a gang of gunrunners. In a fierce firefight Kidder "shot the arm off one of the outlaws" and Rankin killed the horse of another. The officers confiscated numerous weapons and 10,000 rounds of ammunition.[30]

Rankin thought that Kidder's energetic activity against the smugglers made him a target of the Mexican border officers who were in league with the criminals. "While Kidder and I were together at Naco," said Rankin, "we were warned several times that the Mexican officers would kill us the first chance they had." But Kidder scoffed at the reports, for, according to Rankin, he knew no fear.[31]

In 1906 Kidder almost lost his life in a melee that may have been staged to accomplish that very end. A gang of some fifteen tramps in a hobo jungle near the Naco railroad tracks began the disturbance. When Kidder and ranger Sergeant Bill Sparks arrived on the scene, the troublemakers turned on them, knocking both officers to the ground, kicking and pummeling them. As Kidder struggled to his feet, one of the gang pulled a knife and attempted to plunge it into his back. Fortunately, Sparks saw the flash of the blade and dropped the knife wielder with a shot from his pistol. The fight went out of the others, and the rangers managed to restore order and place all fifteen under arrest.[32]

On the last day of 1906 Kidder killed a man at Douglas. In spite of the fact that the town was the headquarters of the Arizona Rangers, it had become infested with holdup men, burglars, and street thugs. Captain Rynning decided to bring more rangers into town to help the local authorities control the rising wave of crime. Jeff Kidder was one of those transferred to Douglas in December 1906.[33]

It was raining on the evening of December 31 as Kidder and George Campbell, a local officer, made a routine check of the railroad yards. When a suspicious-looking character slipped out a rear door of the roundhouse and hurried across the tracks, Kidder called out to him: "Hold on there, Jack, we are officers and want to talk to you." Instead of complying, the man pulled out a pistol and snapped off an ineffectual shot in the officers' direction. Kidder whipped out his silver-plated six-shooter and fired three times. One bullet struck the suspect directly in the right eye. The man, later identified as an unemployed bartender named Tom T. Woods, was unconscious, but still alive. Taken to Calumet and Arizona Hospital, he died within a few hours.[34]

Kidder demanded a complete investigation to clear him of any suspicion of wrongdoing in the affair. At a hearing before Judge Ben Rice on January 10, 1907, all the evidence tended to vindicate the ranger's action. On motion of the prosecuting attorney, the court found that Kidder killed Tom T. Woods in the proper discharge of his duty.[35]

Captain Tom Rynning, before leaving the rangers in March 1907 to accept appointment as superintendent of the territorial prison at Yuma, elevated Jeff Kidder to sergeant, a promotion that carried an increase in pay to $110 a month. Rynning's successor as head of the rangers was Lieutenant Harry C. Wheeler, generally considered to be Kidder's only equal with handgun accuracy.

There was speculation in the Arizona papers that Kidder would be appointed to Wheeler's vacated position, making him second in command of the rangers. "Should the lieutenancy come to Sergeant Kidder it could not be given to a more deserving officer," opined the *Douglas Dispatch*. "He has been very active in the hunting down of criminals for the four years of his connection with the rangers. He has always been a careful, courageous and zealous officer and the people of Douglas would be pleased to hear of his promotion."[36] Captain Wheeler's choice, however, turned out to be Billy Old, Kidder's best friend.

Headquarters for Billy Old was first Prescott and later Flagstaff, where he directed ranger operations in the northern reaches of the territory. Old arranged for the assignment of his pal Jeff Kidder to Flagstaff for several months that year. According to one story, Kidder found it necessary soon after his arrival to prove to the local toughs that, despite his innocent, boyish appearance, he could handle himself very well in a fight. In a Flagstaff saloon a hulking cowboy heaped insults on the ranger he viewed as a baby-faced kid hiding behind a tin star and a fancy shooting iron. Instantly badge and gun were on the bar, and the big cowpuncher found himself in a knockdown, drag-out fight. After twenty minutes he had enough, acknowledged that Jeff Kidder was some tough hombre, and stood drinks for the house.[37]

By the fall of 1907 Kidder was back in his old haunts in southern Arizona. On the night of November 22 he and a Benson constable came upon four thieves, loaded down with stolen plunder, boarding a freight train. The officers charged, and a furious battle ensued. Showing considerable restraint, Kidder did not fire his pistol, even when one of the thieves jammed a gun into the constable's ribs, but clubbed the man over the head instead. Finally, two of the criminals broke off the fight and scurried away, disappearing in the dark, but the officers managed to collar the would-be gunman and one of his cohorts. A local policeman named Banta arrived on the scene in time to see the conclusion of the battle and later remarked that "Ranger Kidder showed the coolest judgment and best nerve combined of any officer he ever saw."[38]

Kidder's exemplary service did not go unnoticed. Early in 1908 Captain Wheeler promoted him to first sergeant, and a Nogales newspaper praised him. "Jeff is a mighty efficient, experienced officer," said the *Border Vidette*. "Where he is, there reigns peace and quiet."[39] When a month later "a number of undesirables" threatened to disrupt the peace and quiet of Nogales, the paper reported that Sergeant Kidder simply ran them out of town.[40]

He was still in Nogales on March 29 when he received word from Captain Wheeler reminding him that his year's enlistment was almost concluded. Wheeler, then on a long scout through the Chiricahua Mountains after horse thieves, directed Kidder to meet him in Naco where the captain could administer the oath for another year's service. Knowing that Wheeler could not reach Naco for several days, Kidder on April 1 began a leisurely ride, allowing himself two days for the sixty-mile trip across the Patagonia Mountains. His only companion was a tiny Chihuahua named Jip he carried on his saddle or inside his shirt. Kidder had found the little dog abandoned several years before, and since then the two had become inseparable.

After spending the night of April 2 at John Sutherland's Bootjack Ranch, Kidder rode into Naco the next afternoon, left his horse at the livery stable, cleaned up a bit at a barber shop, and checked in with Sergeant Tip Stanford at ranger headquarters. In the evening he told Stanford he was going over to Naco, Sonora, "to meet a friend coming out of Cananea." Stanford assumed the "friend" was one of the spies Kidder had enlisted to aid him in his campaign against border smugglers.[41]

Before leaving, he removed his heavy cartridge belt and gun holster and slipped the six-shooter behind the waistband of his pants. As an afterthought, he thumbed out a handful of .45 cartridges from the belt and dropped them in his pocket. Then, with little Jip at his heels, he sauntered over the international line into old Mexico.

For the next few hours he visited several cantinas, danced with a number of girls, and had some drinks. Whether he became intoxicated was later argued but never clearly determined. About midnight he retired to a back room of a cantina with a girl identified only as "Chia." After spending some time with Chia, "fooling around" as he later put it, Kidder started to leave, but noticed that a silver dollar was missing from his pocket and accused the girl of stealing the coin. Chia flew into a rage and struck at him. Throwing open the door, she began yelling for the police.

"I had not had a chance to move," Kidder told friends the next day, "when two Mexican police came through the doorway with their six-shooters drawn, and one fired, hitting me. I fell and was dazed, but knew that my only chance was to fight while I had cartridges left. I drew my own six-shooter while sitting on the floor and opened fire. I believe I wounded both of the men, and they went down helpless."[42]

The wounds suffered by Dolores Quias and Tomas Amador, the two Mexicans, were not life threatening. Quias had taken a bullet through the meat of his thigh; Amador's wound was just above the knee. Kidder, however, had been gut-shot. A bullet from Amador's gun had entered his abdomen just to the left of his navel and ranged downward, cutting through the intestines and emerging through the lower back.

Both Mexicans lay where they had fallen, but Kidder struggled to his feet and staggered out into the night, heading for the American line, several hundred yards away. "I was very weak," said Kidder. "Suddenly firing opened up in front of me, and I saw a number of men between me and the line armed with Winchesters. They were directing their fire directly at me." Kidder thumbed his single-action Colt's, but the hammer fell on empty cylinders. Rifle bullets cracking around him, he veered off to his left where he could see the boundary fence.

"When I got to the fence," he continued, "I put the last six cartridges I had into the gun. During all this time these men were firing at me, and as I was too far away to do any good with my six-shooter I saved my fire until one of their number came within range and I shot him. I then fired until my gun was empty. When my last cartridge was gone I yelled to them that I was all in and told them to come and get me."

They came, a dozen or more, led by Victoriano Amador, Naco chief of police and brother of the officer who shot Kidder. Chief Amador was wounded slightly in the side; he had been the third man winged by Kidder's fire. The enraged Mexicans began to beat the badly injured ranger. "If anybody had told me that one human could be as brutal to another as they were to me I would not have believed it," Kidder said. "I could scarcely stand, but one of this crowd . . . struck me over the head with his six-shooter and I fell. Between them they dragged me on the ground for about fifty yards, and then, seemingly tired by their exertions, stopped and beat me over the head with a six-shooter. They finally dragged me to the jail and threw me in there. I suffered terrible agony."[43]

Kidder spent the rest of the night in the jail cell without medical attention. In the morning American officials roused a Mexican judge and persuaded him to release the wounded prisoner to a private residence. Doctors F. E. Shine of Bisbee and Brandon of Naco ministered to him, but a bullet wound through the bowels in those days was almost always fatal and they held out little hope of recovery. In addition to his gunshot wound, Kidder had received severe injuries in his beating. Captain Wheeler later reported that "Kidder's skull was cut on top, a mark from a gun butt ran up and down his forehead, between the eyes and about three inches long and cut to the skull. His neck on the right side was swollen and bruised and looked clotted with blood. The back of his hands were torn and scratched and . . . his ribs were mashed in."[44]

Sergeant Stanford and former ranger Lieutenant John Foster, now a deputy U.S. marshal, visited Kidder on April 4, and to them he related the story of the fight. He did not fear death, he said, but wanted his friends to know that he had fought hard and would die honorably. "I did not precipitate this trouble," he said, "and never drew my gun until I was wounded and on the floor in that house. I had absolutely no chance for my life, except to keep fighting until I was helpless. It's too bad such an unfortunate thing occurred, but if I am fatally wounded, I can die with the knowledge that I did my best in a hard situation." Taking Foster's hand, he whispered, "You know, Jack, that I would have no object in telling what is untrue. They got me, but if my ammunition had not given out, I might have served them the same way."[45]

Jeff Kidder died at 6:30 on the morning of April 5, 1908. Initially Mexican officials refused to allow the removal of the body to American soil, but after a day of negotiations, General Luis Torres directed the local authorities to release Kidder's remains. It is fortunate for Mexican-American relations that he did, for the affair could have exploded into a major international incident. Captain Wheeler reported to the Arizona governor that "had they not yielded up the body, a thousand men were coming to take it."[46] The rangers took Kidder's remains to the Palace Undertaking Parlors in Bisbee.

On his scout in the Chiricahuas, Captain Wheeler learned of Kidder's death from passing cowboys. He hurried to Bisbee, arriving in time to serve as a pallbearer at the funeral,[47] and arranged for Kidder's remains to be sent by train to his mother in Los Angeles, California, for burial.[48]

Jip, Kidder's little Chihuahua, had been by his master's side throughout his ordeal. He had been with him at the cantina and in his desperate attempt to reach the American border after he had been shot. He had been at his side when he was dragged, battered and bleeding, to the jail and had cowered against his body as the stricken ranger's life slowly ebbed away. Shivering, he stood next to the casket at the Bisbee funeral, and, held in the arms of ranger Sam Hayhurst, watched with the sad, protruding eyes of his breed as the train carrying his master pulled away to the west. The rangers intended to keep the little dog as a company mascot, but it soon became evident that the poor animal was lost without Jeff. Finally Captain Wheeler passed a hat and collected enough money to send Jip by train to Mrs. Kidder in California. A year later the dog was bitten by a snake near San Jacinto and joined his master in death.[49]

Many Americans along the border, especially the Arizona Rangers, were angered by the circumstances surrounding Kidder's death. His brutal treatment at the hands of Mexican police they found inexcusable. Rumors abounded that police confederates of the smugglers Kidder had pursued so relentlessly plotted and carried out his assassination. Ranger Fred Rankin, who had assisted Kidder in his campaign against the smugglers, was particularly outspoken in voicing these charges.[50] In a report to Arizona governor Joseph H. Kibbey on April 8, Captain Wheeler said that he believed "honestly that poor Kidder was foully, cruelly and premeditatedly murdered."[51] At the insistence of Wheeler and others, Mexican authorities established a board of inquiry to look into the affair. After a two-week investigation, sufficient evidence was unearthed to conclude that there was some basis for the charges, although not enough to warrant indictments against individuals. All twenty officers and line riders headquartered at Naco, Sonora, were summarily dismissed on April 24 and new men appointed.[52]

None of this satisfied Billy Old. He and Jeff Kidder had been very close; Old had even named his son "William Kidder" to honor his friend. After the Arizona Rangers were disbanded in February 1909, Old disappeared into old Mexico where he remained for almost two years. Many, including Tom Rynning, were convinced he did not return until he had hunted down and killed each of the slayers of Jeff Kidder.[53]

Afterword

Why, beyond providing new material for the public's seemingly endless appetite for tales of frontier violence, are the histories of long-dead and forgotten gunfighters significant?

One could answer that, although they contributed to frontier violence, these gunfighting characters also played important roles in bringing law and order to emerging communities, either by enforcing what little law there was at the point of a pistol or, ironically, arousing peaceable citizens to action by brazenly flaunting that law and taking human life.

As the foregoing stories demonstrate, "grassroots gunfighters" in the early West stepped nimbly back and forth across the line separating outlaw from lawman. The color of their hats was usually gray and not the black or white so favored by producers of "horse opera" movies to distinguish the "good guys" from the "bad guys."

While ten of the twelve wore a badge at least for a time, only a few, most notably Jeff Kidder, could be considered career law officers. Gunfighters often drifted into law enforcement positions after having already established reputations for coolness under fire and a willingness to use firearms in deadly confrontations.

Barney Riggs and Dave Kemp had already been convicted of murder and served prison time when they first pinned on a badge. George Goodell would go to prison, and Milt Yarberry would swing at the end of a rope for using weapons too freely while serving the law.

Significantly, many of their gunfights were with other lawmen, characters of similar ilk. Pat Desmond twice engaged in shooting matches with fellow officers in Pueblo. Three of the four men George Goodell killed were lawmen. Dave Kemp's most memorable exploit was the murder of the newly elected county sheriff.

Some, like Milt Yarberry, were outlaws before they wore the badge, and some, like Charley Perry, were outlawed afterward, but only one whose story is recounted here, Dan Bogan, was a career outlaw.

As Clare V. McKanna, Jr., has pointed out in his recent study of Western frontier violence, the high incidence of police shootings "suggests a lack of professional standards among lawmen during the period 1880–1920. Virtually any male could become a deputy sheriff or town marshal, especially if he had connections with the sheriff or mayor."[1] Training in the law or law enforcement techniques was non-existent for prospective officers on the frontier, but few applied for the low-paying and highly dangerous jobs who had not already demonstrated ability with weapons and the nerve to use them.

When not fully employed in law-enforcement positions, these fellows worked as cattle inspectors and range detectives, and followed other economic pursuits: cattle herding, professional gambling, freight wagon and stagecoach driving, management of saloons, rooming houses, hotels, restaurants, livery stables, stores, private detective agencies, all manner of business activity. Most were family men, married, with children. (We know that at least eight, or two-thirds of the dozen, were married while actively engaged as gunfighters. Tucker and Bogan may have married after they disappeared from the frontier. Only Yarberry and Kidder are known to have been unmarried when they died.) The one thing differentiating most of these men from other Western settlers was their proficiency with a six-gun and the grit to use it. Were it not for their gunfighting notoriety, they would be indistinguishable from thousands of other frontier entrepreneurs.

In appearance and education the twelve gunmen examined here range from the gangling, coarse, and illiterate Milt Yarberry to the handsome, college-educated Jeff Kidder. Some turned heads when they walked in a room: gambler John Bull, with his neatly trimmed beard, his tailored suit, and his air of business prosperity, and Pat Desmond and Mart Duggan, who carried about them an almost visible aura of danger. But most were plain, unremarkable-looking men who would not stand out in a crowd.

Some were probably natural-born adventurers, attracted by danger and the excitement of deadly confrontation; others, like Barney Riggs, were no doubt psychopathic killers. But the twelve bravos whose lives are recounted here are representative of the many forgotten gun-fighters who lived and died by the gun during the latter half of the nineteenth century. Their stories provide additional threads in the vast, rich tapestry of the eternally fascinating history of the American frontier West.

Notes

INTRODUCTION

1. Among the best remembered are the good outlaw Ringo Kid of *Stagecoach* (1939), the tragic Jimmy Ringo of *The Gunfighter* (1950), the heroic Will Kane of *High Noon* (1952), and the almost saintly Shane of the 1953 film of that title. (The last name of the Western gunman John Ringo has held a strange fascination for screenwriters, but they have chosen to assign it to fictional characters who have no resemblance to the historical character.)

2. Rosa, *Gunfighter*, viii.

3. Roberts, "Gunfighters and Outlaws, Western," in Gottesman, ed., *Violence in America*, 2:72.

4. Brown, *No Duty to Retreat*, 39–40.

5. Ibid., 40–41.

6. McKanna, *Homicide, Race, and Justice*, 66–67.

7. Ibid.; Courtwright, *Violent Land*, 28–29.

8. None of the twelve is included in *The Album of Gunfighters*, by J. Marvin Hunter and Noah H. Rose, published in 1951. Only one, Barney Riggs, is sketched in Ed Bartholomew's *Biographical Album of Western Gunfighters* (1958). None appear in Leon Metz's *The Shooters* (1976). Only two, Riggs and Dave Kemp, are among the 265 pistoleers whose careers are covered in Bill O'Neal's *Encyclopedia of Western Gunfighters*. Jay Robert Nash features the same two, Riggs and Kemp, in his *Encyclopedia of Western Lawmen and Outlaws*, published in 1992. Only three of the gunfighters considered here, Jeff Kidder, Dan Tucker, and Milt Yarberry, are among the 5,530 biographical entries in Dan Thrapp's monumental four-volume *Encyclopedia of Frontier Biography*, published in 1988, with a supplemental edition in 1994. None of the dozen appears in the three-volume, nearly 2,000-page *Violence in America: An Encyclopedia*, edited by Ronald Gottesman and published in 1999. Only in the last two years have book-length treatments of two of the twelve appeared: Bob Alexander's *Dangerous Dan Tucker, New Mexico's Deadly Lawman*, published in 2001, and *Barney K. Riggs, the Yuma and Pecos Avenger*, by Ellis Lindsey and Gene Ripps, in 2002.

CHAPTER 1

1. James Stuart's journal is quoted in brother Granville Stuart's *Prospecting for Gold*, 218–21. The story is also recounted in Langford, *Vigilante Days and Ways*, 114–15.

2. Ibid.

3. Certificate of Death, John Edwin Bull.

4. O'Neal, *Fighting Men of the Indian Wars*, 181–82.

5. Langford, *Vigilante Days and Ways*, 432–33; Greenfield, "There Was Something about Him," 32.

6. Twain, *Roughing It*, 339.

7. Clark, *Journals of Alfred Doten*, 903–904. Bull's part in the affair is mentioned in Hoyt, *Frontier Doctor*, 24.

8. Twain, *Roughing It*, 569.

9. Greenfield, "There Was Something about Him," 50.

10. Sanders, *X. Beidler*, 144.

11. From an 1882 item in the *Helena Independent*, quoted in Sanders, *X. Beidler*, 144; Langford, *Vigilante Days and Ways*, 439.

12. Twain, *Roughing It*, 343–44.

13. Hoyt, *Frontier Doctor*, 23–24.

14. *Helena Independent* newspaper item quoted in Sanders, *X. Beidler*, 146.

15. Devol, *Forty Years a Gambler*.

16. Sorenson, *Story of Omaha*, 463–64.

17. *Omaha Daily Bee*, July 14, 1873.

18. Ibid., July 28, 29, 1873.

19. At the urgent telegraphic request of many prominent citizens, Iowa governor C. C. Carpenter had dispatched two companies of state militia to Council Bluffs to assist Sheriff George Doughty in stopping the fight. When promoters who had chartered the train informed the sheriff that he and his militiamen could accompany the entourage, but only upon payment of five dollars each for tickets, he watched helplessly as the train pulled out of the Council Bluffs station (Bristow, *Dirty, Wicked Town*, 121–23).

20. Sorensen, *Story of Omaha*, 467–68; Fleischer, *Flaming Ben Hogan*, 27; *Trinidad Daily News*, January 25, 1882. Bloodshed in the aftermath of the fight was not reported in the local press (Bristow, *Dirty, Wicked Town*, 126).

21. *Trinidad Daily News*, January 25, 1882; Sorenson, *Story of Omaha*, 465–66.

22. Devol, *Forty Years a Gambler*, 181.

23. Hoyt, *Frontier Doctor*, 27.

24. *Rocky Mountain News*, February 20, 1877.

25. Ibid., January 4, 1879. C. C. Joy was a notorious bully. He was elected alderman at Leadville and in May 1882 verbally and physically attacked volunteer firemen he deemed slow in response to a blaze (Blair, *Leadville*, 145–46). The following year he objected to newspaperman E. D. Cowan's criticism of him in the *Leadville Herald* and "knocked Cowan down, and while keeping the crowd at bay with a revolver, jumped up and down on Cowan's face and stamped him with heavy boots until he was almost unrecognizable." Cowan was so badly beaten he was expected to die, and his friend Eugene Field wrote his obituary for the *Denver Tribune* (Hicks, *Adventures of a Tramp Printer*, 97–98; *Colorado Chieftain*, October 11, 1883).

26. *Rocky Mountain News*, August 8, 1883.

27. Ibid., October 15, November 30, 1880.

28. Parkhill, *Wildest of the West*, 112.

29. *Denver Republican*, June 17, 1881; *Rocky Mountain News*, June 17, 1881; Cowan, "Memories of the Happy Bad Man of the West"; Guinn, "Timely End of Jim Moon." The killing of Jim Moon was obviously an act of self-defense, and Clay Wilson was not charged. A well-educated man who reportedly kept a diary in Sanskrit, Wilson later partnered con artists "Soapy" Smith and "Doc" Baggs for many years. In 1912 he was convicted of fleecing a man out of $15,000 and sent to prison. Released at the age of seventy, he died in San Francisco in June 1917 (*Denver Post*, February 2, 1912; June 6, 1917).

30. *Trinidad Daily News*, January 25, 1882.

31. *Denver Republican*, June 24, 1892.

32. Barnett had formerly managed the Comique, a notorious theater in Butte, Montana (*Anaconda Standard*, April 28, 1894; January 11, 1899).

33. *Spokane Daily Chronicle*, December 28, 1921.

34. *Vancouver Sun*, September 10, 1929; Certificate of Death, John Edwin Bull.

CHAPTER 2

1. Boessenecker, *Badge and Buckshot*, 108–109.

2. Miller and Snell, *Why the West Was Wild*, 472–506, 588–607.

3. Vickers, *History of the Arkansas Valley*, 793; *Ogden Standard*, June 25, 1890.

4. Vickers, *History of the Arkansas Valley*, 793; Callaghan, "Bold Fenian Men."

5. Vickers, *History of the Arkansas Valley*, 794.

6. Ibid., 845.

7. Ibid., 794. Billy Breakenridge, who later figured prominently in the dramatic history of Tombstone, Arizona, during the exciting days of the Earp brothers, was at Kit Carson in early 1870. He was much impressed by Tom Smith, "the bravest man I ever had the pleasure of meeting," but did not mention Desmond in his memoirs (Breakenridge, *Helldorado*, 58). Drawing on an item in the *Utah Desert News* of December 24, 1868, David Dary, in his *True Tales of the Old-Time Plains*, suggests that Tom Smith of Bear River notoriety and Tom Smith of Abilene were not the same man. However, T. C. Henry, the Abilene mayor who hired Smith and knew him well, asserted he was (Henry, *Conquering Our Great American Plains*, 159–60).

8. Otero, *My Life on the Frontier*, 35.

9. Desmond and his wife Annie had five children, two girls and three boys (*Colorado Chieftain*, April 8, 11, 22, 30, 1882).

10. Vickers, *History of the Arkansas Valley*, 794.

11. *Rocky Mountain News*, March 1, 1890.

12. *Denver Republican*, March 1, 1890.

13. General D. J. Cook, *Hands Up*, 216–21.

14. *Colorado Chieftain*, March 7, 1879.

15. Ibid., March 11, 1879.

16. Ibid., March 14, 1879.

17. Ibid., April 2, 1879. Desmond received 78 votes; a man named Tyler, his opponent, 26.

18. DeArment, *Bat Masterson*, 138.

19. Ibid., 153; *Colorado Chieftain*, June 12, 1879.

20. *Colorado Chieftain*, June 12, 1879.

21. Ibid., March 31, 1881.

22. Ibid., February 15, 1882.

23. Reprinted in the *Dodge City Times*, February 2, 1882.

24. Dugan, *Knight of the Road*, 44–47.

25. *Colorado Chieftain*, March 24, 1882.

26. Ibid., March 30, 1882.

27. Ibid., February 24, 1882.

28. Ibid., February 25, 1882.

29. Ibid., March 9, 1882.

30. Ibid., March 10, 1882.

31. Ibid.

32. Ibid., April 19, 1882.

33. Ibid., April 20, 1882.

34. Ibid.

35. Ibid., April 6, 7, 22, 25, 30, 1882. Another daughter, Nellie, had died several years earlier (ibid., April 11, 1882).

36. Ibid., July 7, 1882.

37. Ibid., August 17, September 13, October 10, November 29, 1882.

38. Ibid., March 20, 1882.

39. Ibid., November 18, 1882.

40. Ibid., May 25, 30; June 6, July 2, 4, 1882.

41. Ibid., January 24, 1884.

42. Ibid., February 10, 1883.

43. Ibid. The story was also carried in the February 10 and 11 issues of the *Santa Fe Daily New Mexican*.

44. *Colorado Chieftain*, March 1, 1883.

45. Ibid., January 7, 1884.

46. Ibid., June 4, 11, 1885.

47. Ibid., December 20, 1888.

48. Monaghan, *Last of the Bad Men*, 123.

49. *Rocky Mountain News*, March 1, 1890.

50. Quoted in the *Colorado Chieftain*, July 25, 1889.

51. Ibid.

52. *Denver Republican*, March 1, 1890.

53. *Colorado Chieftain*, March 6, 1890.

54. Ibid.; *Rocky Mountain News*, March 1, 1890.

55. *Ogden Standard*, June 26, 1890; *Rocky Mountain News*, March 1, 1890.

56. March 6, 1890.

57. *Rocky Mountain News*, March 1, 1890; *Colorado Chieftain*, March 6, 1890.

58. March 1, 1890.

59. March 1, 1890.

60. March 6, 1890.

61. March 2, 1890.

62. *Ogden Standard*, July 1, 1890.

63. *El Paso Daily Herald*, March 5, 1895; Record of Convicts Received in the Colorado State Penitentiary.

CHAPTER 3

1. Duggan, "Dictation Taken from Mr. Martin Duggan"; Blair, "Leadville's Marshal Who Knew No Fear."

2. Blair, *Leadville*, 106.

3. This story, taken from an early issue of the *Chicago News*, is told in Blair, "Leadville's Marshal Who Knew No Fear."

4. Willison, *Here They Dug the Gold*, 167.

5. Blair, *Leadville*, 40; Blair and Churchill, *Everybody Came to Leadville*, 3–4.

6. Duggan, "Dictation Taken from Mr. Martin Duggan."

7. Blair, *Leadville*, 105.

8. Duggan, "Dictation Taken from Mr. Martin Duggan."

9. Blair, "Leadville's Marshal Who Knew No Fear."

10. Wilson, *Out of the West*, 261.

11. Blair, "Leadville's Marshal Who Knew No Fear."

12. Duggan, "Dictation Taken from Mr. Martin Duggan."

13. Blair, *Leadville*, 106.

14. This was the same Jim Bush who fleeced suckers with the Canada Bill gang at Omaha earlier in the decade and later shot John Bull in Denver (see chapter 1).

15. Arbuckle also could claim notable family connections; he was reported to be the stepson of Judge George W. Miller of Denver (*Colorado Chieftain*, March 12, 1879).

16. Ibid.; Bancroft, *Tabor's Matchless Mine*, 16.

17. Quoted in Blair, "Leadville's Marshal Who Knew No Fear."

18. Bartlett, "Mart Duggan, Fighter."

19. Willison, *Here They Dug the Gold*, 167–68.

20. Quoted in ibid., 225.

21. Ibid., 224.

22. Quoted in ibid., 224.

23. Ibid., 230.

24. Ibid., 231.

25. Ibid., 232.

26. Frye, *Atlas of Wyoming Outlaws*, 31–32.

27. Blair, *Leadville*, 110. One Leadville historian has written that Mart Duggan, "as violently lawless as any desperado," participated with Frodsham in his criminal activities (Willison, *Here They Dug the Gold*, 228, 230). In view of the respect Duggan was accorded by many in Leadville and the fact that he was not even in the town during Frodsham's greatest period of criminal activity, this appears unlikely.

28. Quoted in Hunt, "Big Ed Burns."

29. Blair, *Leadville*, 110.

30. Duggan, "Dictation Taken from Mr. Martin Duggan."

31. Cowan, "Memories of the Happy Bad Man"; Hunt, "Big Ed Burns."

32. Collier and Westrate, *Dave Cook of the Rockies*, 196–98; Burke, *Legend of Baby Doe*, 92–93.

33. Blair, *Leadville*, 116–17.

34. Ibid.; Burke, *Legend of Baby Doe*, 72.

35. Blair, *Leadville*, 120–21.

36. The name is spelled both as "Youngson" and "Youngston" in contemporary sources.

37. Blair, *Leadville*, 121–22; Jessen, *Colorado Gunsmoke*, 129–31. A headstone erected at the site has since disappeared (Browning, *Violence Was No Stranger*, 76).

38. "George Evans"; "Duggan's Slayer."

CHAPTER 4

1. Yarberry was described in the *Albuquerque Morning Journal* of February 9, 1883, and the *Santa Fe Daily New Mexican* of February 10, 1883.

2. *Albuquerque Morning Journal*, February 10, 1883.

3. Ibid., February 9, 1883; *Santa Fe Daily New Mexican*, February 10, 1883.

4. An examination of the Arkansas court records has not confirmed this incident or any criminal activity involving John Armstrong, alias Milton Yarberry, Dave Mather, or Dave Rudabaugh in the area at that time (DeMattos, *Mysterious Gunfighter*, 23, 30).

5. McIntire, *Early Days in Texas*, 58–60.

6. Foy and Harlow, *Clowning Through Life*, 131–33.

7. Ibid.

8. *Colorado Chieftain*, March 7, 1879.

9. *Albuquerque Weekly Journal*, May 25, 1882; Bartholomew, *Wyatt Earp, The Man and the Myth*, 14.

10. Bartholomew, *Wyatt Earp, The Man and the Myth*, 14.

11. Buffum, *Smith of Bear City*, 216.

12. *Kinsley Valley Republican*, February 2, 1878; *Albuquerque Morning Journal*, February 9, 1883; *Santa Fe Daily New Mexican*, February 10, 1883.

13. *Albuquerque Morning Journal*, February 9, 1883; *Santa Fe Daily New Mexican*, February 10, 1883; Bryan, "Off the Beaten Path," *Albuquerque Tribune*, February 15, 1966.

14. *Santa Fe Weekly Democrat*, April 7, 1881.

15. *Las Vegas Gazette*, May 19, 1881; *Albuquerque Morning Journal*, February 9, 1883; *Santa Fe Daily New Mexican*, February 10, 1883; Bryan, "Off the Beaten Path," *Albuquerque Tribune*, February 15, 1966.

16. *Santa Fe Weekly Democrat*, June 23, 1881.

17. *Las Vegas Gazette*, June 21, 1881.

18. *Santa Fe Daily New Mexican*, June 22, 1881.

19. Ibid.

20. *Albuquerque Morning Journal*, February 9, 1883.

21. *Territory of New Mexico agt Milton J. Yarberry*, Cause No. 935, District Court, Bernalillo County; *Albuquerque Morning Journal*, February 9, 1883; *Santa Fe New Daily Mexican*, February 10, 1883.

22. *Santa Fe Daily New Mexican*, May 29, 1882.

23. Ibid., September 10, 1882; Lavash, *Wilson and the Kid*, 108, 119.

24. *Santa Fe Daily New Mexican*, September 12, 14, 1882. Billy Wilson eluded the posses and returned to his native Texas where he spent the rest of his life in law-abiding respectability under his true name, David L. Anderson (Lavash, *Wilson and the Kid*). The later history of Harris, the holdup man, is unknown.

25. *Territory of New Mexico agt Milton J. Yarberry*.

26. *Santa Fe Daily New Mexican*, February 9, 1883.

27. *Albuquerque Morning Journal*, February 8, 1883.

28. Ibid., February 10, 1883.

29. *Santa Fe Daily New Mexican*, February 10, 1883; *Albuquerque Morning Journal*, February 10, 11, 1883.

30. *Albuquerque Morning Journal*, February 10, 1883.

31. *Santa Fe Daily New Mexican*, February 10, 1883; *Albuquerque Morning Journal*, February 11, 1883.

32. *Santa Fe Daily New Mexican*, February 10, 1883.

33. Ibid.

CHAPTER 5

1. Otero, *My Life on the Frontier*, 240.

2. Lundwall, *Pioneering in Territorial Silver City*, 151.

3. Nelson and Nelson, *Silver City Book*, vol. 1, *Wild and Wooly Days* (unpaginated).

4. Rose, "Dan Tucker."

5. U.S. Census, Grant County, New Mexico, 1880. Alexander, *Dangerous Dan Tucker*, 8–11. The name is given as David Tucker in a listing of fees presented to the Silver City Council (*Grant County Herald*, October 11, 1879).

6. Rose, "Dan Tucker."

7. Chase, *Editor's Run*, 127.

8. *Silver City Enterprise*, December 14, 1882.

9. Blachly, "I'll Never Forget."

10. Ibid. Actually, Juan Garcia, the man shot by Tucker, survived for months before finally dying from the wound the following March (*Grant County Herald*, March 28, 1878, quoted in Alexander, *Dangerous Dan Tucker*, 29).

11. Rose, "Dan Tucker."

12. Ibid.

13. Blachly, "I'll Never Forget."

14. Rose, "Dan Tucker." Tucker's victim in this instance was evidently "Antanacio Bencomo, who died from being struck by a pistol ball from a pistol in the hands of Deputy Sheriff Daniel Tucker [while] the deceased was escaping from his custody" (*Grant County Herald*, August 18, 1877, quoted in Alexander, *Dangerous Dan Tucker*, 25).

15. Rose, "Dan Tucker."

16. Ibid.

17. *Grant County Herald*, January 5, 1878; Sonnichsen, *El Paso Salt War*, 1877, 58.

18. *Grant County Herald*, January 5, 1878.

19. Sonnichsen, *El Paso Salt War*, 1877, 59.

20. *Grant County Herald*, July 20, 1878.

21. Ibid., November 11, 1878; May 2, 1879.

22. January 3, 1880.

23. *Grant County Herald*, January 24, 1880.

24. Myres, *Pioneer Surveyor*, 152–53.

25. Russian Bill's true name has appeared in various publications as "Feador Telfin," "Bill Littenborn," "William Tatenbaum," "William Rogers Tettenborn," and "Waldemar Tethenborn," among others (Stanley, *Shakespeare, New Mexico, Story*; Bartholomew, *Wyatt Earp, The Man and the Myth*, 265; Hill, *Then and Now*, 39; Rasch, "AKA 'Russian Bill'"; Thrapp, *Encyclopedia of Frontier Biography*, 3:1411).

26. King's name has been given as "Ferguson" (Bartholomew, *Wyatt Earp, The Man and the Myth*, quoting a Deming newspaper of November 8, 1881).

27. *El Paso Lone Star*, November 16, 1881; Rasch, "AKA 'Russian Bill.'"

28. Hill, *Then and Now*, 38.

29. Ibid., quoting a Tucson paper.

30. Alexander, *Dangerous Dan Tucker*, 58–59.

31. Myres, *Pioneer Surveyor*, 188.

32. *Grant County Herald*, March 19, 1881.

33. Chase, *Editor's Run*, 127.

34. Rose, "Dan Tucker."

35. Bartholomew, *Wyatt Earp, The Man and the Myth*, quoting a Silver City newspaper, 264.

36. In his *Six Years with the Texas Rangers*, 198, Gillett remembered Peveler's name as "Len Peterson." In the *El Paso Lone Star* of November 23, 1881, he gave

it as "Pevely." The man is correctly identified as Chris Peveler in Metz, *Dallas Stoudenmire*, 46.

37. *Las Vegas Optic*, September 30, 1881.

38. Metz, *Dallas Stoudenmire*, quoting the *El Paso Daily Herald*, June 7, 1902.

39. Chase, *Editor's Run*, 127.

40. Ibid., 127–28.

41. November 2, 1881.

42. December 3, 1881.

43. *El Paso Lone Star*, February 22, 1882.

44. James Cook, *Fifty Years on the Old Frontier*, 139.

45. *Grant County New Southwest*, August 26, 1882.

46. Ibid.

47. Thurmond was the husband of Carlotta Thompkins Thurmond, who, under the name "Lottie Deno," had built a legend as one of the West's most mysterious and successful female gamblers.

48. *Grant County New Southwest*, September 9, 1882.

49. Ibid.

50. Ibid., August 26, 1882.

51. Ibid., September 9, 1882.

52. Ibid.

53. Ibid., September 2, 1882.

54. Ibid., September 9, 1882.

55. Ibid., September 16, 1882.

56. December 23, 1882.

57. *New Southwest and Grant County Herald*, October 7, 1882; *Southwest Sentinel*, March 17, April 7, 1883.

58. Rose, "Dan Tucker."

59. Ibid.; *Silver City Enterprise*, April 20, 1883; October 1, 1886.

60. Rose, "Dan Tucker."

61. *Santa Fe Weekly Democrat*, August 11, 1881; *El Paso Lone Star*, August 16, 1882; *Silver City Enterprise*, May 6, 1892.

62. *Silver City Enterprise*, October 1, 1886.

63. *El Paso Lone Star*, September 23, 1882.

64. *Silver City Enterprise*, December 21, 1882.

65. *New Southwest and Grant County Herald*, December 23, 1882.

66. Rose, "Dan Tucker."

67. Ibid.

68. *Silver City Enterprise*, November 30, 1883. See chapter 8.

69. Carolyn Lake, *Under Cover for Wells Fargo*, 53.

70. Alexander, *Dangerous Dan Tucker*, 136, quoting the *Silver City Enterprise*, April 25, 1884.

71. The 1885 New Mexico Territorial Census listed sixteen men boarding in the house of Dan and Maria Tucker, man and wife. But no record of Tucker's marriage has been found, and the union was probably a common-law arrangement (Ibid., 139, 147).

72. *El Paso Lone Star*, October 3, 1885.

73. Alexander, *Dangerous Dan Tucker*, 145, quoting the *Silver City Enterprise* of November 5, 1886.

74. *Southwest Sentinel*, November 17, 1885.

75. Quoted in the *Silver City Enterprise*, October 7, 1887.

76. Ibid., May 6, 1892.

77. Rose, "Dan Tucker." Researcher Bob Alexander has recently made an exhaustive effort to verify this report, without success (Alexander, *Dangerous Dan Tucker*, 156–57).

CHAPTER 6

1. Enumerated as "George C. Goodell" in the 1860 U.S. Census for Vermont on August 16, his age was given as seven, indicating an 1853 birth. For the 1880 U.S. Census taken at Dodge City, Kansas, on June 17, 1880, his age was given as twenty-six, indicating a birth in 1854.

2. 1860 U.S. Census.

3. In the summer of 1878 Dodge City was so tagged in derision by the *Kinsley Graphic*, but the editors of the Dodge City papers took pride in the alliterative phrase and repeated it often in their columns (Faulk, *Dodge City*, 90).

4. 1880 U.S. Census.

5. September 14, 1878.

6. September 17, 1878.

7. *Denver Post*, November 2, 1923.

8. See chapter 2.

9. Martin to author, January 9, 1981.

10. *Trinidad Daily Democrat*, June 25, 1882.

11. *Trinidad Daily News*, July 6, 1882.

12. July 15, 1882.

13. July 20, 1882.

14. August 6, 1882.

15. *Trinidad Daily News*, March 3, 1882.

16. *Trinidad Daily Democrat*, August 12, 1882.

17. *Trinidad Daily News*, August 15, 1882.

18. *Trinidad Daily Democrat*, August 16, 1882.

19. *Trinidad Daily News*, August 16, 1882.

20. *Trinidad Daily Democrat*, August 17, 1882.

21. Ibid., August 18, 1882.

22. *Trinidad Daily News*, August 18, 1882.

23. *Trinidad Daily Democrat*, August 22, 1882.

24. Ibid., October 18, 1882.

25. Ibid., October 20, 1882.

26. *Trinidad Daily Reporter*, February 6, 1883.

27. Green, *Green's City Directory for Leavenworth, Kansas*, 1886–1889; *Kansas City Star*, July 10, 1924.

28. *Leavenworth Times*, September 18, 1888.

29. *Leavenworth Times*, May 26, 1888.

30. *Kansas City Star*, July 10, 1924.

31. Lillie Black's testimony quoted in the *Leavenworth Times*, May 26, 1888.

32. Goodell's testimony quoted in ibid.

33. Ibid.

34. Ibid., May 30, 1888.

35. Ibid., May 26, 1888.

36. Ibid., May 30, 1888.

37. Ibid., September 29, 1888.

38. Martin to author, January 9, 1981.

39. *Denver Post*, November 2, 1923; *Kansas City Star*, July 10, 1924.

40. *History of the Tacoma Police Department*.

41. Gay, *History of Nowata County*, 22–24; Wardell, *Political History of the Cherokee Nation*, 320–21.

42. Bennett to McKinley, June 8, 1901, Petition for Pardon File, George Goodell.

43. Ibid.

44. Dooley to President McKinley, June 4, 1901, Petition for Pardon File, George Goodell.

45. Ibid. Goodell's appointment was announced in the *Fort Smith Elevator*, October 22, 1897.

46. The story of the Nowata shootings has been pieced together from very conflicting versions of the affair. Accounts highly critical of Goodell appeared in the *Vinita Indian Chieftain*, November 18, 1897, and the *Fort Smith Elevator*, November 26, 1897. Goodell gave his side of the affair in the *Denver Post*, November 2, 1923, and the *Kansas City Star*, July 10, 1924.

47. *Fort Smith Elevator*, December 3, 24, 1897.

48. November 18, 1897.

49. Campbell to McKinley, June 3, 1901, Petition for Pardon File, George Goodell.

50. Soper to Easby-Smith, September 22, 1901, Petition for Pardon File, George Goodell.

51. December 24, 1897.

52. November 25, 1898.

53. Register of Prisoners in Ohio State Penitentiary.

54. Jennings and Irwin, *Beating Back*, 185–88; Jennings, *Through the Shadows with O. Henry*, 109–10.

55. Coffin to McKinley, May 2, 1901, Petition for Pardon File, George Goodell.

56. Documents pertaining to the pardon are in the Records of the Pardon Attorney, Pardon Case File (U-247), George Goodell.

57. Martin to author, January 9, 1981.

58. "Veteran of Pioneer Days in Oklahoma Packs a 'Six' with Nineteen Notches." Clipping from a Bartlesville paper dated January 8, 1922, author's collection.

59. *Denver Post*, November 2, 1923.

60. *Kansas City Star*, July 10, 1924.

61. Post to Martin, May 1, 1991; Martin to author, June 14, 1991.

CHAPTER 7

1. Douglas, *Cattle Kings of Texas*, 306.

2. Black, *End of the Long Horn Trail*, 32.

3. The year of birth was either 1853 or 1854, according to conflicting census reports. The place of birth has been variously reported as Lampasas County (Douglas, *Cattle Kings of Texas*, 307) and as Bastrop or Burnet Counties (Jackson to author, August 18, 1991).

4. O'Neal, *Bloody Legacy of Pink Higgins*, 73.

5. Debo, *Burnet County History*, 301.

6. Douglas, *Cattle Kings of Texas*, 307.

7. Ibid.

8. Ibid., 311.

9. Ibid., 307–10. Douglas got this story from veteran cowboys he interviewed. Fogg Coffey, a cowman who worked that roundup, remembered the dead man's name as "McMahon," and that "he was shot and killed by a boy who worked for him, whom he had whipped" (Lanning and Lanning, *Texas Cowboys*, 25).

10. Douglas, *Cattle Kings of Texas*, 310.

11. Ibid., 311.

12. Hunter, *Trail Drivers of Texas*, 343–46.

13. Bill Meador was a tough customer himself. A former deputy sheriff of DeWitt County and city marshal of Cuero, he had faced a charge of murder in 1878, but came clear (Raymond, *Captain Lee Hall of Texas*, 70–75). He later served as a Texas Ranger in the company of Captain G. W. Arrington (Douglas, Cattle Kings of Texas, 314).

14. Douglas, *Cattle Kings of Texas*, 314–16.

15. Ibid., 311.

16. Ibid., 314.

17. Tise, *Texas County Sheriffs*, 137.

18. Cunningham, "Experiences of a Pioneer District Attorney," 126–35.

19. According to Douglas, *Cattle Kings of Texas*, 311, the incident happened the first evening after supper, but the *Lampasas Leader*, March 9, 1889, and George D. Harper, who was a cowboy in the area at the time (Harper, "Eighty Years of Recollections," 6), placed the time as early the next morning.

20. Stories of how Mrs. Neal was shot also vary. Douglas (*Cattle Kings of Texas*, 312) said the bullet that struck Quillen passed through, striking the woman. In Harper's version ("Eighty Years of Recollections"), Standifer shot at Brookins, missed, and hit Mrs. Neal.

21. Here again, versions of the story disagree. Standifer overpowered and handcuffed both outlaws, according to Douglas (*Cattle Kings of Texas*, 312). The *Lampasas Leader* (March 9, 1889) merely said the "two prisoners were recaptured." Harper ("Eighty Years of Recollections") remembered that one of Neal's cowboys, "Martin Morose . . . caught one of the horses and mounting bareback, overtook and captured the outlaws and brought them back chained together." This same Martin Morose (or Mroz) died at El Paso six years later, the victim in a controversial shooting by George Scarborough and other officers (DeArment, *George Scarborough*, 95–112).

22. Douglas, *Cattle Kings of Texas*, 312.

23. Ibid., 313.

24. Ibid.

25. Asbury, *Sucker's Progress*, 332.

26. Holden, *Rollie Burns*, 162–63.

27. Holden, "Problem of Stealing on the Spur Ranch," 31, quoting Horsbrugh's reports in the Spur Ranch records.

28. Sinise, *Pink Higgins*, 24.

29. Ibid., 36.

30. Ibid., 33.

31. Jay, "Bad Blood."

32. Ibid. Stock detective Jefferson Davis Hardin, eight years younger than his famous brother, was killed by John Snowden at Clairemont in November 1891. A quarrel over Hardin's earlier killing of a suspected cattle thief resulted in his death at the hands of Snowden, who claimed self-defense and never went to trial (Metz, *John Wesley Hardin*, 280; O'Neal, *Bloody Legacy of Pink Higgins*, 89–90).

33. Holden, "Problem of Stealing on the Spur Ranch," 35.

34. *State of Texas v. J. W. Standifer*, Cause No. 30, Kent County.

35. Holden, "Problem of Stealing on the Spur Ranch," 36.

36. Ibid., 36–37.

37. Gober, *Cowboy Justice*, 219.

38. Ibid., 220.

39. Sinise, *Pink Higgins*, 3.

40. Douglas, *Famous Texas Feuds*, 145.

41. O'Neal, *Encyclopedia of Western Gunfighters*, 140.

42. Webb, *Texas Rangers*, 334.

43. Holden, "Problem of Stealing on the Spur Ranch," 39.

44. Horsbrugh report of October 6, 1902, quoted in Douglas, *Cattle Kings of Texas*, 317.

45. Douglas, *Cattle Kings of Texas*, 316–17; O'Neal, *Bloody Legacy of Pink Higgins*, 80.

46. O'Neal, *Bloody Legacy of Pink Higgins*, 80.

47. Jones, "Pink Higgins"; Sinise, *Pink Higgins*, 24; O'Neal, *Bloody Legacy of Pink Higgins*, 80.

48. Sinise, *Pink Higgins*, 24.

49. Horsbrugh report of October 6, 1902, quoted in Douglas, *Cattle Kings of Texas*, 317.

50. Jones, "Pink Higgins," 88; O'Neal, *Bloody Legacy of Pink Higgins*, 81.

51. Jones, "Pink Higgins," 88; Fred Horsbrugh said that Standifer received two gunshot wounds (report of October 6, 1902, quoted in Douglas, *Cattle Kings of Texas*, 317).

52. Douglas, *Cattle Kings of Texas*, 317.

53. Ibid.

54. Sinise, *Pink Higgins*, 27; O'Neal, *Bloody Legacy of Pink Higgins*, 86.

55. Sinise, *Pink Higgins*, 27.

56. O'Neal, *Bloody Legacy of Pink Higgins*, 96.

57. Jones, "Pink Higgins," 89.

CHAPTER 8

1. Larry Ball, "Lawman in Disgrace," 125.

2. Burton, *Dynamite and Six-shooter*, 194.

3. Klasner, *My Girlhood among Outlaws*, 255.

4. King, "Pecos War," 21.

5. This is the date given by Cramer, *Pecos Ranchers*, 82, and King, "Pecos War," 22. Frederick Nolan in *Lincoln County War*, 121, cites March 28, 1877.

6. Cramer, *Pecos Ranchers*, 82; King, "Pecos War," 22.

7. Cramer, *Pecos Ranchers*, 85.

8. Larry Ball, "Lawman in Disgrace," 126, 127.

9. *Silver City Enterprise*, November 30, 1883; January 4, 18, 1884; DeArment, "Sheriff Whitehill."

10. *Silver City Enterprise*, January 25, 1884.

11. Ibid.

12. Ibid., March 14, 1884.

13. Ibid., March 28, November 28, 1884.

14. *Southern Pacific Railroad and Wells, Fargo & Company v. Harvey H. Whitehill, et al.*

15. Ibid.

16. Eve Ball, *Ma'am Jones of the Pecos*, 207.

17. Ed Harral, interview by Haley and Chesley, June 13, 1939.

18. Barbara Jones remembered that both men died that night (ibid., 208), but the *Eddy Argus* of January 18, 1890, in relating essentially the same story, reported that Kent lingered for three days, until the following Tuesday (January 14), and Berkely died the following day.

19. Klasner, *My Girlhood among Outlaws*, 221.

20. Ibid.

21. The identity of George Griffin's companion is not certain. The *Eddy Argus* of September 6, 1890 said he was James, the brother of George (Rasch, "Half Told Tales," 8). Judge Lea identified him as B. Champion, a Griffin cousin (Klasner, *My Girlhood among Outlaws*, 222).

22. Klasner, *My Girlhood among Outlaws*, 222.

23. Ibid., 223.

24. Ibid.

25. Ibid.; *Eddy Argus*, September 6, 1890; Rasch, "Half Told Tales."

26. Klasner, *My Girlhood among Outlaws*, 221.

27. Larry Ball, "Lawman in Disgrace," 126.

28. Shinkle, *Reminiscences of Roswell Pioneers*, 223, quoting the *Roswell Record*, March 3, 10, 1893.

29. Ibid., 225.

30. Rasch, "Half Told Tales," 8.

31. Larry Ball, "Lawman in Disgrace," 126–27.

32. Shirley, *Marauders of the Indian Nations*, 90, quoting the *Oklahoma State Capital*, January 15, 1895.

33. Telegram, Perry to Hall, January 12, 1895, quoted in Larry Ball, "Lawman in Disgrace," 127.

34. *New York Sun*, January 15, 1895; Larry Ball, "Lawman in Disgrace," 127; Shirley, *Marauders of the Indian Nations*, 90.

35. Sullivan, *Twelve Years in the Saddle*, 121.

36. Ibid., 124.

37. Shirley, *Marauders of the Indian Nations*, 93.

38. *New York Journal*, reprinted in *Santa Fe Daily New Mexican*, February 14, 1895, quoted in Larry Ball, "Lawman in Disgrace," 127.

39. Shirley, *Marauders of the Indian Nations*, 92.

40. Larry Ball, "Lawman in Disgrace," 128, quoting the *New York Sun*, January 14, 1895, and the *New York Herald*, January 27, 1895.

41. Harkey, *Mean as Hell*, 94.

42. Dee Harkey, interview by Haley, December 16, 1947.

43. Larry Ball, "Lawman in Disgrace," 129, quoting the *Santa Fe Daily New Mexican*, May 1, 1895.

44. *El Paso Daily Times*, November 18, 1896. This story had originally appeared in the *San Francisco Chronicle* of July 25, 1896 (Larry Ball, "Lawman in Disgrace," 134).

45. *El Paso Daily Herald*, May 24, 1895; *Memoranda of Court Cases*, D. Storms, 2:17–18; Larry Ball, "Lawman in Disgrace," 129–30; Harkey, *Mean as Hell*, 94–95; DeArment, *George Scarborough*, 117.

46. *El Paso Daily Times*, November 18, 1896.

47. Harkey, *Mean as Hell*, 95.

48. Ibid., 97; *Roswell Record*, June 21, 1895; Rasch, "Half Told Tales," 9.

49. Rasch, "Half Told Tales," 9.

50. *El Paso Daily Herald*, February 18, 1896; *El Paso Daily Times*, February 19, 1896.

51. Sullivan, *Twelve Years in the Saddle*, 180–81.

52. Larry Ball, "Lawman in Disgrace," 129.

53. Ibid., 132; Rasch, "Half Told Tales," 9; Burton, *Dynamite and Six-shooter*, 25, 27.

54. Harkey, *Mean as Hell*, 98–99.

55. Larry Ball, "Lawman in Disgrace," 132.

56. Ibid., 134, quoting Lea to Thornton, July 16, 1896.

57. Ibid.

58. *El Paso Daily Times*, November 18, 1896.

59. Larry Ball, "Lawman in Disgrace," 135.

60. *El Paso Daily Times*, November 17, 18, 1896; *Roswell Record*, November 20, 1896; Larry Ball, "Lawman in Disgrace," 135–36.

61. Shinkle, *Reminiscences of Roswell Pioneers*, 229–30.

62. Rasch, "Half Told Tales," 9.

63. *Roswell Record*, November 12, 1897.

64. Larry Ball, "Lawman in Disgrace," 136.

65. Ibid.

66. Ibid.

67. Shinkle, *Reminiscences of Roswell Pioneers*, 230.

CHAPTER 9

1. Williams, *Texas' Last Frontier*, 327. There has been some confusion over Riggs's birthplace. Philip J. Rasch, a careful researcher, wrote that Riggs was probably born at Emigrant Canyon, Cochise County, Arizona, around 1856 (Rasch, *Desperadoes of Arizona Territory*, 77). However, Clayton Williams was close to the Riggs family, and his statement that Barney was born in Arkansas is credible, although he never specified the location in that state.

2. Williams, *Texas' Last Frontier*, 327; James, *Barney Riggs*, 9.

3. September 5, 1875.

4. Williamson to Rasch, December 20, 1981.

5. De la Garza, *Story of Dos Cabezas*, 15, 21. Other young Riggs boys, cousins of Barney, cowboying in Cochise County during these years, included William Austin Riggs of the El Dorado Ranch, Thomas Jefferson Riggs of the Mendocino Ranch, and William Monroe Riggs of the Star Ranch (Guthrie, *Great Register*).

6. De la Garza, *Story of Dos Cabezas*, 15, 21.

7. *Tombstone Daily Epitaph*, February 27, 1882, quoting the *Dos Cabezas Gold Note*.

8. Tefertiller, *Wyatt Earp*, 242.

9. Williamson to Rasch, December 20, 1981.

10. *Arizona Daily Star*, October 5, 1886; Rasch, *Desperadoes of Arizona Territory*, 78.

11. *Arizona Daily Star*, October 5, 1886, quoting the *Wilcox Stockman*.

12. *Silver City Enterprise*, October 22, 1886.

13. Carolyn Lake, *Under Cover for Wells Fargo*, 68–70. The *Tombstone Democrat* reported simply that Henry Dial made the capture (Rasch, *Desperadoes of Arizona Territory*, 78).

14. Williamson to Rasch, December 20, 1981.

15. Carolyn Lake, *Under Cover for Wells Fargo*, 71–72.

16. Hancock, "Reminiscences of Judge James C. Hancock, 1933."

17. Williamson to Rasch, December 20, 1981; *Silver City Enterprise*, December 31, 1886.

18. Carolyn Lake, *Under Cover for Wells Fargo*, 73–74.

19. Prison Record of Barney K. Riggs. His place of birth was recorded as New Jersey, probably because of a flippant answer by Riggs to a question.

20. This was the same John Behan who, as sheriff of Cochise County, had played a major role in the Earp troubles five years earlier.

21. Riggs gave his account of the incident in a letter to the editor of the *Arizona Gazette*, dated April 18, 1895, and published April 30. Contemporary stories of the escape attempt were published in the *Arizona Sentinel* and the *Arizona Citizen* of October 29, 1887.

22. B. F. "Frank" Hartley was a veteran lawman who had helped capture Tiburcio Vasquez and other notorious California bad men. According to Frank King, who was also a guard at the Yuma prison at the time of the riot, Hartley was "a brave, cool-headed man and a fine shot" (King, *Wranglin' the Past*, 191).

23. *Arizona Gazette*, April 30, 1895.

24. Gates, "Gates Riot of 1887."

25. *Arizona Gazette*, April 30, 1895.

26. Gates, "Gates Riot of 1887."

27. *Arizona Gazette*, April 30, 1895.

28. Gates, "Gates Riot of 1887."

29. Jeffrey, *Adobe and Iron*, 92; King, *Wranglin' the Past*, 193.

30. *Arizona Sentinel*, October 29, 1887.

31. *Tombstone Daily Epitaph*, January 7, 1888.

32. Pardon of Barney K. Riggs.

33. Reprinted in the *Arizona Sentinel*, May 25, 1889.

34. Following Barney's death in 1902, Vennie F. Riggs filed a petition in Los Angeles County, California, claiming to be the "lawful and only surviving widow of B. K. Riggs" (Williams, *Texas' Last Frontier*, 330).

35. James, *Barney Riggs*, 11. The offspring of Barney and Annie Riggs were Barney, Jr. (born May 1892), Ernest (born June 8, 1894), Eva (born April 1896), and George (born February 15, 1898) (Browning, *Violence Was No Stranger*, 210).

36. Williams, *Texas' Last Frontier*, 308.

37. Ibid., 367; Hester to Lamborn, June 19, 1951; *State of Texas v. Barney Riggs*, Cause No. 140, Reeves County; James, *Barney Riggs*, 11.

38. Williams, *Texas' Last Frontier*, 366; Hester to Lamborn, June 19, 1951; *State of Texas v. Barney Riggs*, Cause No. 143, Reeves County.

39. Williams, *Texas' Last Frontier*, 367; Hester to Lamborn, June 19, 1951.

40. DeArment, *George Scarborough*, 56–57.

41. James, *Sheriff A. J. Royal*, 26.

42. Ibid., 27–30; James, *Barney Riggs*, 12; Williams, *Texas' Last Frontier*, 385.

43. Shirley, *Shotgun for Hire*, 49.

44. Williams, *Texas' Last Frontier*, 396.

45. One of these was Judge Charles R. Brice of Roswell, who told Lou Blachly in a June 29, 1953 interview: "Jim Miller was always afraid of Barney Riggs" (Lou Blachly interviews).

46. Harkey, *Mean as Hell*, 104–105; Brice to Blachly, June 29, 1953 (Lou Blachly interviews).

47. *State of Texas v. Barney Riggs*, Cause No. 240, Reeves County.

48. Ibid.

49. May 19, 1897.

50. May 19, 1897.

51. Special dispatch from Eastland to the *El Paso Daily Herald*, June 18, 1897.

52. Lanning and Lanning, *Texas Cowboys*, 158.

53. Bill Cope, interview by Williams, February 19, 1966.

54. Williams, *Texas' Last Frontier*, 398.

55. Will P. Rooney, interview by Williams.

56. Williams, *Texas' Last Frontier*, 399. Son Ernest Riggs, five years old at the time, told Clayton Williams many years later: "I . . . picked up a rock and made Daddy stop trying to put Mamma on that coal oil can and set it on fire."

57. Annie's attorney was Walter Gillis, "a former district judge that Jim Miller had once offered to kill for two hundred dollars" (James, *Barney Riggs*, 16).

58. Williams, *Texas' Last Frontier*, 402.

59. Rasch, *Desperadoes of Arizona Territory*, 86.

CHAPTER 10

1. U.S. Census, Hamilton County, Texas, 1880. His mother, D. B. Pierce, 48, was a widow, and headed a household that included her son, Daniel B. Bogan, 20, and daughters Emma Oldham, 16, and Minnie Pierce, 13. Bogan, his mother, and sisters were all born in Alabama.

2. Raine, *Guns of the Frontier*, 126, quoting the *Lusk Herald*, July 29, 1887.

3. Testimony of W. T. Cropper at trial of David Kemp, quoted in the *Gatesville Sun*, June 15, 1881.

4. "David Kemp v. The State," in Jackson and Jackson, *Cases Argued and Adjudged in the Court of Appeals of the State of Texas*, 181.

5. Ibid., 177.

6. Ibid., 178.

7. Ibid., 180.

8. Ibid., 178.

9. Harkey, *Mean as Hell*, 119, quoting letter from Hervey E. Chesley, attorney of Hamilton; J. Evetts Haley notes on Kemp, Haley Library.

10. *Galveston Daily News*, May 26, 1881; "David Kemp v. The State," in Jackson and Jackson, *Cases Argued and Adjudged*, 175.

11. Raine, *Guns of the Frontier*, 125; Harkey, *Mean as Hell*, 119; *Cheyenne State Leader*, November 7, 1931.

12. See chapter 11.

13. *List of Fugitives from Justice for 1900*.

14. This story appeared in the *Cheyenne Daily Sun*, July 22, 1887, and the *Buffalo Echo* of July 28, 1887. It was repeated in Raine, *Guns of the Frontier*, 125, and Carroll, "As an Outlaw and Escape Artist," 12.

15. Siringo, *Riata and Spurs*, orig. ed., 44.

16. Siringo, *Riata and Spurs*, rev. ed., 200.

17. Ibid.; McCarty, *Maverick Town*, 107–14.

18. Hunter, *Trail Drivers of Texas*, 928.

19. McCarty, *Maverick Town*, 125.

20. Hough, *Story of the Outlaw*, 299; Metz, *Pat Garrett*, 145.

21. McCarty, *Maverick Town*, 133.

22. Ibid.

23. Ibid., 131.

24. Ibid., 137–38; Metz, *Pat Garrett*, 144–45.

25. Metz, *Pat Garrett*, 145.

26. Raine, *Guns of the Frontier*, 126.

27. Carroll, "As an Outlaw and Escape Artist," 13.

28. Ibid., 12, 13.

29. Ibid., 10.

30. Griffith, *House of Blazes*, 20–21.

31. Carroll, "As an Outlaw and Escape Artist," 10; Raine, *Guns of the Frontier*, 126–27.

32. Carroll, "As an Outlaw and Escape Artist," 10–11, quoting the *Cheyenne Daily Sun*, February 11, 1887.

33. Raine, *Guns of the Frontier*, 126–27.

34. Griffith, *House of Blazes*, 20, quoting the *Lusk Herald* of September 24, 1886.

35. Ibid., 21, quoting the *Lusk Herald* of December 24, 1886.

36. This was Gunn's answer according to McCoy's testimony (Carroll, "As an Outlaw and Escape Artist," 14). Other witnesses said that he gave Gunn no opportunity to respond before firing (*Lusk Herald*, January 21, 1887).

37. Flannery, *John Hunton's Diary*, 229, quoting the *Cheyenne Daily Leader*.

38. Carroll, "As an Outlaw and Escape Artist," 11, citing witness testimony before Justice of the Peace Roe Kingman.

39. *Lusk Herald*, January 21, 1887; Raine, *Guns of the Frontier*, 127–28.

40. Carroll, "As an Outlaw and Escape Artist," 11, quoting the *Cheyenne Daily Sun*, January 23, 1887.

41. Ibid., quoting the *Cheyenne Daily Sun*, September 3, 1887.

42. Griffith, *House of Blazes*, 5–6.

43. Raine, *Guns of the Frontier*, 128.

44. Carroll, "As an Outlaw and Escape Artist," 11–12; Flannery, *John Hunton's Diary*, 165, quoting the *Cheyenne Daily Leader*.

45. Carroll, "As an Outlaw and Escape Artist," 12, citing the *Cheyenne Daily Sun*, February 5, 1887.

46. Ibid., citing the *Cheyenne Daily Sun*, February 6, 7, 10, 1887.

47. *Cheyenne Daily Leader*, October 5, 1887.

48. Carroll, "As an Outlaw and Escape Artist," 13; Woods, *Wyoming Biographies*, 69–70, 124, 162. W. R. Stoll would come to national attention sixteen years later as the prosecutor who got a conviction and death sentence for Tom Horn.

49. *Big Horn Sentinel*, September 3, 1887; Carroll, "As an Outlaw and Escape Artist," 13.

50. Ibid., citing the *Cheyenne Daily Sun*, July 22, 1887.

51. Ibid., 14, citing the *Cheyenne Daily Sun*, August 9 and 10, 1887; Flannery, *John Hunton's Diary*, quoting the *Cheyenne Daily Leader*.

52. Carroll, "As an Outlaw and Escape Artist," citing the *Cheyenne Daily Sun*, September 3, 1887.

53. Flannery, *John Hunton's Diary*, 229, quoting the *Cheyenne Daily Leader*.

54. Siringo, *Two Evil Isms*, 14. He was probably the G. F. Nickell who, with Bill Gatlin, signed the cowboy strike ultimatum (McCarty, *Maverick Town*, 110).

55. *Cheyenne Daily Leader*, October 5, 1887; *Big Horn Sentinel*, October 15, 1887; Carroll, "As an Outlaw and Escape Artist," 14; Siringo, *Riata and Spurs*, rev. ed., 201.

56. Carroll, "As an Outlaw and Escape Artist," 14–15. Teton Jackson, outlaw gang leader with whom Bogan is said to have worked, told a reporter five years later that Bogan had hidden out for two weeks in the ruins of old Fort Caspar, a "temporary hiding place of criminals for years" (David, *Malcolm Campbell*, 87). Another report (*Big Horn Sentinel*, November 19, 1887) was that Bogan was headed for "the British Possessions" (Canada).

57. Siringo, *Cowboy Detective*, 51–52; *Riata and Spurs*, orig. ed., 131.

58. *Big Horn Sentinel*, November 26, 1887; Siringo, *Cowboy Detective*, 60–65; *Riata and Spurs*, orig. ed., 132.

59. A. C. Campbell manuscript, T. A. Campbell Collection.

60. McCarty, *Maverick Town*, 140–55.

61. Siringo said he saw McCoy's letter to Hall while he was waiting to testify before the grand jury in Cheyenne (*Cowboy Detective*, 63). The rest of the story Lem Woodruff told him when they met in Hot Springs, Arkansas, in 1915. Siringo, *Riata and Spurs*, rev. ed., 200–203.

62. Siringo, *Lone Star Cowboy*, 165.

63. Quoted in Frye, *Atlas of Wyoming Outlaws*, 269.

64. Raine, *Guns of the Frontier*, 128.

65. *Cheyenne State Leader*, November 7, 1931.

CHAPTER 11

1. Bosque, Mason, and Coleman Counties have been mentioned as Kemp's place of birth (Rasch and Myers, "Les Dow," 251; McCown, "Despite Big Losses," 10), but family members say he was born in Hamilton County (O'Neal, "They Called Him Mister Kemp," 31). The year of birth has also been disputed. At the time of his death, a newspaper gave 1861 as the year of Kemp's birth (McCown, "Despite Big Losses," 14), but his gravestone, erected many years later, shows 1863. Census records also conflict. The birth date of March 1, 1862, provided by the family is in agreement, however, with Kemp's stated age of twenty-one when he entered prison in 1883 (Convict Record Ledger Data, Texas State Penitentiary).

When Kemp's mother died in 1900, the *Carlsbad Current* gave her name as "Mary." She was enumerated as "Jane" along with husband William and children Walker (14), David (7), Victoria (6), Mary (4), and Albert (1) in the 1870 Hamilton County census.

2. O'Neal, "They Called Him Mister Kemp," 31.

3. U.S. Census, Hamilton County, Texas, 1880. Interestingly, the census taker was M. S. Brunck, the jailer.

4. Raine, *Guns of the Frontier*, 126, citing the *Lusk Herald*, July 29, 1887.

5. *Cheyenne Daily Sun*, July 22, 1887, as cited in Carroll, "As an Outlaw and Escape Artist," 12; Grugg to Scott, October 24, 1945. Grugg was a child in Hamilton at the time and remembered Kemp well. He did, however, confuse the Snell killing with the Smith murder case.

6. Testimony of E. Shumaker, in "David Kemp v. The State" (Jackson and Jackson, *Cases Argued and Adjudged*, 185). The marriage may have taken place, for Kemp's prison record indicates that he was married when he entered the penitentiary in 1883 (Convict Record Ledger Data, Texas State Penitentiary). However, Kemp family members believe Kemp's first marriage was to Elizabeth King about 1888 (O'Neal, "They Called Him Mister Kemp," 31–32).

7. See chapter 10.

8. Cause No. 888, "David Kemp v. The State" (Jackson and Jackson, *Cases Argued and Adjudged*, 174–206).

9. Convict Record Ledger Data, Texas State Penitentiary.

10. Ibid.

11. Texas Department of State, File No. 538, Executive Clemency, Reasons For, *The State of Texas vs. David Kemp*, January 1, 1887. Coincidentally, January 15, 1887, the day Kemp was freed, was the day his old pal, Dan Bogan, gunned down Constable Charley Gunn in Lusk, Wyoming (see chapter 10).

12. O'Neal, "They Called Him Mister Kemp," 31–32. *Eddy Argus*, July 18, 1891.

13. O'Neal, "They Called Him Mister Kemp," 32. In December 1892 Elizabeth gave birth to another child, but it lived only a few hours (*Eddy Argus*, December 23, 1892).

14. Myers, "Pearl of the Pecos," ii–vii; Myers, "Experiment in Prohibition," 293–306; Howard, "Phenix and the Wolf."

15. *Eddy Argus*, March 15, 1890.

16. Ibid., March 29, 1890.

17. Ibid., June 14, 1890.

18. Ibid., July 12, 1890.

19. Ibid., July 19, 1890.

20. Ibid., August 16, 1890. "We can truthfully say of the late firm," remarked the paper, "that they conducted their business in a square and honorable manner."

21. Ibid., September 6, 1890.

22. Ibid., April 26, 1890.

23. Texas Department of State, File No. 1710, Executive Clemency, Reasons For, *The State of Texas vs. David Kemp*, September 8, 1890. Among those signing at Hamilton were G. N. Gentry, the sheriff at whom he had snapped his pistol before his arrest back in 1881 and evidently a very forgiving man. M. S. Brunck, the deputy and jailer who had guarded him in the Hamilton jail, also affixed his signature. Petitioners in Fisher County included the incumbent sheriff, C. E. Roy, County Judge John W. Deming, and Kemp's half brother, Walker Bush.

24. Erwin, *Southwest of John Horton Slaughter*, passim.

25. The editor of the *Eddy Argus* was Richard Rule, the same Richard Rule who, with Barney Riggs, had helped thwart the breakout attempt at Yuma prison in 1887 (see chapter 9).

26. August 2, 1890.

27. November 8, 1890.

28. December 13, 1890.

29. December 20, 1890.

30. Ibid., July 5, 1890.

31. Harkey, *Mean as Hell*, 51.

32. Chesley, *Adventuring with the Old-Timers*, 119–20.

33. *Eddy Argus*, December 13, 1890, March 28, 1891.

34. Ibid., September 5, 1891.

35. Ibid., March 3, 1893.

36. *Eddy Current*, April 24, 1895.

37. O'Neal, "They Called Him Mister Kemp," 32.

38. *Eddy Argus*, November 10, 1893; *Eddy Current*, November 10, 24, 1893.

39. *Eddy Argus*, May 9, 1891; *Eddy County Citizen*, May 28, 1892.

40. December 12, 1891.

41. *Eddy Argus*, June 8, 1894; *Eddy Current*, March 9, 1895 (see chapter 9).

42. *Pecos Valley Argus*, April 1, 1898. His true name was said to be William Rogers (Rasch and Myers, "Les Dow," 251).

43. *Eddy Argus*, April 7, 1893; *Eddy Current*, April 7, 1893.

44. August 4, 1893. "The experience so unnerved Waldie that he got religion and became an evangelist and a popular preacher around Eddy" (Rasch, "Life and Death of Lon Bass," 8).

45. *Eddy Argus*, December 21, 1894.

46. *Eddy Current*, March 9, 13, 1895; *Pecos Valley Argus*, March 15, 1895.

47. *Eddy Current*, August 15, 1895. Like his cousin Denson, Hardin after leaving Eddy did not have long to live. On August 19, 1895, Constable John Selman shot him to death in El Paso.

48. Harkey, *Mean as Hell*, 102.

49. January 27, 1893.

50. *Eddy Argus*, April 7, 1893.

51. *Eddy Current*, April 7, 1893; *Eddy Argus*, May 19, 1893.

52. *Eddy Current*, December 23, 1892. Since a municipal government was not established in Eddy until elections were held in April 1893, Sheriff Kemp seems to have been empowered to appoint local policemen and constables.

53. Reynolds, *Trouble in New Mexico*, 1:292.

54. *Eddy Argus*, September 8, 22, 1893; *Eddy Current*, September 22, October 13, 20, 1893.

55. Harkey, *Mean as Hell*, 58.

56. *Pecos Valley Argus*, November 8, 1895.

57. Harkey, *Mean as Hell*, 125.

58. *Pecos Valley Argus*, November 29, 1895.

59. Ibid., April 24, 1896.

60. *Eddy Argus*, May 11, 18, 1894.

61. Ibid., March 30, 1894.

62. Ibid., July 28, 1893.

63. *Eddy Current*, September 15, 1894.

64. Reynolds, *Trouble in New Mexico*, 1:126–27.

65. Myers, "Pearl of the Pecos," 149.

66. July 11, 1891.

67. Howard, "Phenix and the Wolf," 32.

68. *Eddy Argus*, February 20, March 26, 1892; January 13, 1893.

69. June 4, 1892.

70. Ibid.

71. Ibid., March 3, 1893.

72. March 9, 1894.

73. August 4, 1893.

74. *Eddy Argus*, June 25, 1892; September 15, 1893; *Eddy Current*, October 17, 1896; Myers, "How Hell-Raising Phenix," 18. Prior to his arrival in Phenix, Ed Lyell had led a checkered career. He was raised in Hays County, Texas, where he served as deputy sheriff before drifting west to Arizona Territory where he and his brother John ranched and rode at times with the notorious Curly Bill Brocius gang of outlaws. The Lyell brothers are said to have sided Curly Bill in his gun battle with Wyatt Earp's posse at Iron Springs, Arizona, in March 1882 during Earp's famous "Vendetta Ride," and to have ridden with the Sheriff John Behan posse searching for the Earp party (Stuart Lake, *Wyatt Earp*, 278, 340, 346). Later Ed Lyell reportedly threatened the life of Cochise County sheriff John Slaughter, who ran him out of the country (Erwin, *Southwest of John Horton Slaughter*, 236–38; Cunningham, *Triggernometry*, 303–304). In these

accounts the name is spelled "Lyle," but the correct spelling was "Lyell" (Hickey, *Death of Warren Baxter Earp*, 628). Lyell, like Walker Bush, may have been related to Kemp, whose middle name was Lyle, suggesting a possible family tie.

75. *Eddy County Citizen*, November 5, 12, 1892. Bennett died in San Antonio, Texas, at the age of thirty-six (*Pecos Valley Argus*, August 20, 1897).

76. *Eddy Argus*, October 21, 1892.

77. *Eddy Current*, November 21, 1896. Rhodes was forty-two years old when he was killed.

78. Ibid.

79. *Eddy Argus*, June 8, 1894.

80. Ibid., June 15, 1894.

81. *Eddy Current*, September 22, 1894.

82. Rasch, "Life and Death of Lon Bass," 8.

83. *Eddy Argus*, April 6, 1894; Howard, "Phenix and the Wolf," 46.

84. Rasch and Myers, "Les Dow," 243; Harkey, *Mean as Hell*, 58–60.

85. *Eddy Current*, January 16, 1895.

86. *Pecos Valley Argus*, April 5, 1895.

87. *Eddy Argus*, October 10, 1891.

88. Ibid., February 20, 1892.

89. October 15, 1892.

90. November 5, 1892.

91. July 7, 1893.

92. August 4, 1893.

93. March 16, 1894.

94. *Eddy Argus*, April 6, June 1, 1894.

95. *Eddy Current*, March 19, 1896.

96. August 31, 1894.

97. *Eddy Argus*, September 21, 1894.

98. Ibid., January 25, 1895.

99. Ibid., December 23, 1892.

100. *Eddy Current*, May 5, June 23, 1893.

101. Ibid., November 17, 1893.

102. *Eddie Argus*, August 3, 1894.

103. *Pecos Valley Argus*, November 15, 1895.

104. Ibid., October 30, 1896.

105. *Pecos Valley Argus*, April 26, December 20, 1895; *Eddy Current*, April 27, July 11, 1895.

106. *Pecos Valley Argus*, March 22, 1895; *Eddy Current*, March 23, 1895.

107. *Pecos Valley Argus*, September 25, 1896; *Eddy Current*, September 26, 1896.

108. Issues of April 7 and June 16, 1893.

109. *Eddy Argus*, March 22, 1895; *Eddy Current*, March 23, 1895.

110. DeArment, *George Scarborough*, 103–12.

111. *Eddy Current*, May 16, 1895; *Pecos Valley Argus*, May 17, 1895.

112. *Eddy Current*, October 3, 1895.

113. Ibid.; *Pecos Valley Argus*, October 4, 1895.

114. October 24, 1895.

115. Ibid., August 8, 1896. This latest setback seems to have brought an end to the Kemp-Lyell partnership. Ed and Nellie Lyell later operated restaurants in Tucson, a hotel in Agua Caliente, Arizona, and kept a corral and dining room on the road to Cananea, Mexico. According to newspaper reports, Nellie died at Douglas, Arizona, in August 1902, and Ed followed her in death a few days later (*Arizona Daily Star*, August 12, 28, 1902). Michael Hickey, in his book *The Death of Warren Baxter Earp*, makes the case that, as a continuation of the Earp-Clanton feud of two decades earlier, Ed Lyell conspired with others to assassinate Warren, youngest of the Earp brothers, at Willcox, Arizona, on July 6, 1900, and was subsequently hunted down and killed in Mexico by Wyatt Earp.

116. August 11, 1893.

117. *Eddy Current*, October 24, 31, 1895; *Pecos Valley Argus*, October 25, 1895.

118. *Pecos Valley Argus*, May 8, 1896.

119. *Pecos Valley Argus*, April 24, 1896.

120. Dee Harkey, interview by Haley, December 16, 1947.

121. See chapter 8.

122. Harkey, *Mean as Hell*, 120.

123. Bonney, *Looking Over My Shoulder*, 104.

124. Quoted in the *Eddy Current*, August 21, 1896.

125. Rasch and Myers, "Les Dow," 245.

126. Ibid.; *Pecos Valley Argus*, January 8, 1897.

127. Harkey, *Mean as Hell*, 120–21.

128. Ibid., 123; *Eddy Current*, February 20, 1897; Rasch and Myers, "Les Dow," 246–47.

129. Harkey, *Mean as Hell*, 122–23.

130. *Eddy Current*, October 16, 23, 1897; *Pecos Valley Argus*, October 22, November 19, 1897.

131. April 2, 1898.

132. *Eddy Current*, March 26, April 2, 1898; *Pecos Valley Argus*, April 1, 1898; Howard, "Phenix and the Wolf," 68; Myers, "Pearl of the Pecos," 150–51; Rasch and Myers, "Les Dow," 248.

133. Bonney, *Looking Over My Shoulder*, 105.

134. Harkey, *Mean as Hell*, 124.

135. Carroll, "As an Outlaw and Escape Artist," 28.

136. A. C. Campbell manuscript, T. A. Campbell Collection.

137. Ibid.

138. *Pecos Valley Argus*, December 25, 1896.

139. *Pecos Valley Argus*, April 8, 1898; *Eddy Current*, April 9, 1898. According to the *Argus*, the bride's name was Mary, but O'Neal, in "They Called Him Mister Kemp," 37, gives it as Ada Patti. Family tradition is that Kemp, following his divorce from Elizabeth, courted a girl named Clara. He

gave her a "lovely jewel box lined with pink satin" and a black pony she named "Dave" after him (ibid). McCown ("Despite Big Losses," 12, 16) says that this marriage failed also, and that Kemp married at least four times. "D. L. was the marrying kind," Kate Blau, who claimed to know him well, told McCown.

140. *Pecos Valley Argus*, June 10, 1898.

141. *Pecos Valley Argus*, July 8, 1898; *Eddy Current*, October 22, 1898.

142. *Pecos Valley Argus*, August 26, 1898.

143. *Carlsbad Current*, February 24, 1900; O'Neal, "They Called Him Mister Kemp," 37.

144. Arizona Ranger Captain Tom Rynning described Bush as "a hard hombre who had at least seven notches on the handle of his .45" (Rynning, *Gun Notches*, 210.

145. Rasch, "Life and Death of Lon Bass," 10–11; Rynning, *Gun Notches*, 207; O'Neal, *Arizona Rangers*, 40–41.

146. Harkey, *Mean as Hell*, 126.

147. Haley, *Jeff Milton*, 230.

148. McCown, "Despite Big Losses," 12, quoting *History of Lipscomb County*, 468.

149. Rasch and Myers, "Les Dow," 249–50; Shirk, *Oklahoma Place Names*, 121.

150. Rasch and Myers, "Les Dow," 250.

151. McCown, "Despite Big Losses," 12, 16.

152. Harkey, *Mean as Hell*, 128.

153. Rasch and Myers, "Les Dow," 250; O'Neal, "They Called Him Mister Kemp," 37.

CHAPTER 12

1. Haley, *Jeff Milton*, 364.

2. "After He Fell Kidder Killed Three Bandits," unidentified clipping, "Special to the Tribune," datelined Vermillion, South Dakota, April 22, in Jeff Kidder file.

3. *Dakota Republican*, October 11, 1883; Schell, *History of Clay County*, 49.

4. Thrapp, *Encyclopedia of Frontier Biography*, 2:778–79.

5. Moses, *Clay County Place Names*.

6. Schell, *History of Clay County*; Schell to author, December 30, 1981. A Western gunfighter with college training was certainly unusual, but Kidder was not unique. The famous gunman John H. "Doc" Holliday was an 1872 graduate of Philadelphia's Pennsylvania College of Dental Surgery.

7. O'Neal, *Arizona Rangers*, 44.

8. Raine, *Famous Sheriffs and Western Outlaws*, 15.

9. O'Neal, *Arizona Rangers*, 43.

10. Ibid., 70.

11. *Douglas American*, July 7, 1904.

12. July 6, 1904.

13. Miller, *Arizona Rangers*, 76–77.

14. Arcus Reddoch in the *Border Vidette*, quoted in O'Neal, *Arizona Rangers*, 70.

15. Coolidge, *Fighting Men of the West*, 287.

16. Haley, *Jeff Milton*, 364–65.

17. *Border Vidette*, quoted in O'Neal, *Arizona Rangers*, 71.

18. Ibid., 195–96.

19. Rynning, *Gun Notches*, 288.

20. Unidentified newspaper clippings in Jeff Kidder file.

21. W. A. Old to Mrs. Silas Kidder, Jeff Kidder file.

22. "Kidder Was Victim of Plot Says Rankin," unidentified newspaper clipping, Jeff Kidder file.

23. Pearce and Summers, "Joe Pearce—Manhunter," 250, 257.

24. Kelly, "Last of the Arizona Rangers," 16.

25. Coolidge, *Fighting Men of the West*, 288.

26. Donoho, "Death of an Arizona Ranger," 24–25.

27. *Arizona Citizen*, April 6, 1908; quoted in the *Dakota Republican*, April 23, 1908.

28. Rynning, *Gun Notches*, 286–88.

29. Ibid., 223–24.

30. "Kidder Was Victim of Plot Says Rankin," Jeff Kidder file.

31. Ibid.

32. Miller, *Arizona Rangers*, 117, quoting the *Bisbee Review*.

33. *Border Vidette*, December 8, 1906.

34. Miller, *Arizona Rangers*, 127–28, quoting the *Bisbee Review*; O'Neal, *Arizona Rangers*, 109–10.

35. Miller, *Arizona Rangers*, 128–31, quoting the *Bisbee Review*; O'Neal, *Arizona Rangers*, 110.

36. Quoted in Miller, *Arizona Rangers*, 139.

37. Coolidge, *Fighting Men of the West*, 288.

38. *Border Vidette*, November 23, 1907, quoted in O'Neal, *Arizona Rangers*, 123–24.

39. February 15, 1908.

40. March 28, 1908.

41. O'Neal, *Arizona Rangers*, 140.

42. Miller, *Arizona Rangers*, 190–91, quoting unspecified copy of the *Bisbee Review*.

43. Ibid.

44. Captain Harry Wheeler to Governor Joseph H. Kibbey, April 8, 1908, Jeff Kidder file.

45. Miller, *Arizona Rangers*, 192; *Bisbee Evening Miner*, April 6, 1908.

46. Wheeler to Kibbey, April 8, 1908, Jeff Kidder file. The situation was further complicated by a dispute over whether Kidder was a ranger or a private citizen at the time of the shooting. His commission had officially expired on March 31, but Wheeler argued that he knew Kidder had every

intention of re-enlisting and only formal dismissal could terminate a ranger's active service.

47. Ibid. In his report to the governor, Wheeler said that the undertaker told him Kidder's injuries from the beating were horrific, his "head must have been almost jelly, he could not keep the embalming fluid from running out the ears and nose."

48. Kidder is buried in Inglewood Park Cemetery, Inglewood, California. The grave marker incorrectly gives 1910 as the year of his death (Browning, *Violence Was No Stranger*, 130).

49. Unidentified clippings in the Jeff Kidder file.

50. "Kidder Was Victim of Plot Says Rankin," Jeff Kidder file.

51. Wheeler to Kibbey, April 8, 1908, Jeff Kidder file.

52. "Commissions Lifted from Mexicans," unidentified clipping, datelined Naco, April 24, in the Jeff Kidder file.

53. O'Neal, *Arizona Rangers*, 176; Rynning, *Gun Notches*, 288.

AFTERWORD

1. McKanna, *Homicide, Race, and Justice*, 43.

Bibliography

GOVERNMENT DOCUMENTS

Certificate of Death, John Edwin Bull. Division of Vital Statistics, Ministry of Health, Victoria, B.C., Canada.

U.S. Census, Windham County, Vermont, 1860; Hamilton County, Texas, 1870, 1880; Ford County, Kansas, 1880; Grant County, New Mexico Territory, 1880.

COURT AND PRISON RECORDS

Convict Record Ledger Data, Texas State Penitentiary. Texas State Archives, Austin.

Memoranda of Court Cases, D. Storms, County Attorney, El Paso County. El Paso Public Library, El Paso, Texas.

Pardon of Barney K. Riggs. Arizona Department of Library, Archives and Public Records, Phoenix.

Petition for Pardon File, George Goodell. National Archives, Washington, D.C.

Prison Record of Barney K. Riggs. Territorial Prison, Yuma, Arizona.

Record of Convicts Received in Colorado State Penitentiary, Canon City. Division of State Archives and Public Records, Denver, Colorado.

Records of the Pardon Attorney. Pardon Case File (U-247), George Goodell. National Archives, Washington, D.C.

Register of Prisoners in Ohio State Penitentiary. Ohio Historical Society, Columbus.

Southern Pacific Railroad and Wells, Fargo & Company v. Harvey H. Whitehill, et al. New Mexico State Records and Archives, Santa Fe.

State of Texas v. Barney Riggs, Cause No. 140, Reeves County, "Assault with intent to murder Augustin Palanco." Reeves County Courthouse, Pecos, Texas.

State of Texas v. Barney Riggs, Cause No. 143, Reeves County, "Unlawfully carrying a pistol." Reeves County Courthouse, Pecos, Texas.

State of Texas v. Barney Riggs, Cause No. 240, Reeves County, "Murder of John Denson." Reeves County Courthouse, Pecos, Texas.

State of Texas v. Barney Riggs, Cause No. 244, Reeves County, "Murder of William Earhart." Reeves County Courthouse, Pecos, Texas.

State of Texas vs. J. W. Standifer, Cause No. 30, Kent County, Murder. Kent County Courthouse, Clairemont, Texas.

Territory of New Mexico agt Milton J. Yarberry, Cause No. 935, District Court, Bernalillo County. New Mexico State Records and Archives, Santa Fe.

Texas Department of State, File No. 538, Executive Clemency, Reasons for. *The State of Texas vs. David Kemp*, January 1, 1887. Texas State Archives, Austin.

Texas Department of State, File No. 1710, Executive Clemency, Reasons for. *The State of Texas vs. David Kemp*, September 8, 1890. Texas State Archives, Austin.

ARCHIVES

Arizona Historical Society, Tucson. Files of undated newspaper clippings.

Lou Blachly interviews. Zimmerman Library, University of New Mexico, Albuquerque.

A. C. Campbell manuscript. T. A. Campbell Collection. Wyoming State Historical Publications Division, Cheyenne.

Jim East manuscript file. Historical Research Center, Panhandle-Plains Historical Museum, Canyon, Texas.

J. Evetts Haley Collections. Nita Stewart Haley Memorial Library, Midland, Texas.

Jeff Kidder file. Arizona Historical Society, Tucson.

E. P. Lamborn Collection. Kansas State Historical Society, Topeka.

Robert M. Marks. Riggs family collection, Seattle, Washington.

MANUSCRIPTS

Duggan, Martin. "Dictation Taken from Mr. Martin Duggan, Leadville, Colorado, September 4th, 1885." H. H. Bancroft Collection. Bancroft Library, University of California, Berkeley.

Gates, Thomas. "The Gates Riot of 1887." Unpublished manuscript in Arizona Historical Society, Tucson.

———. "Notes on an Interview with Hon. Thomas Gates." Eugene J. Trippel Papers. Arizona Pioneers' Historical Society Collections, Tucson.

Hancock, James C. "Reminiscences of Judge James C. Hancock." Arizona Historical Society, Tucson.

Harper, George D. "Eighty Years of Recollections." WPA Interviews, Panhandle-Plains Historical Society, Canyon, Texas.

Howard, Jed. "Phenix and the Wolf: The Saloon Battles of Eddy and the Dave Kemp Saga." Unpublished manuscript in author's collection.

Myers, Lee. "The Pearl of the Pecos." Unpublished manuscript in author's collection.

Riggs, William Carroll. "Autobiography of William Carroll Riggs." Unpublished manuscript provided by Robert M. Marks, Seattle, Washington.

LETTERS

Ron Donoho to author, May 27, 1980.

Dave Grubb to Zelma Scott, October 20, 1945. Gatesville Public Library, Gatesville, Texas.

Vannie I. Hester, Clerk of District Court, Reeves County, Texas, to E. P. Lamborn, June 19, 1951. Lamborn Collection. Kansas State Historical Society, Topeka.

Jeff Jackson to author, July 15, August 18, 1991.

Robert M. Marks to author, December 10, 1982.

Gene Martin to author, October 12, 1980; January 9, 1981; June 14, 1991.

Randy Post to Gene Martin, May 1, 1991. Author's collection.

Herbert S. Schell to author, July 16, 1980; December 10, 15, 30, 1981.

Lionel A. Sheldon, Governor, Territory of New Mexico, to Amado Chavez, Speaker, House of Representatives, re reward for Milton Yarberry. New Mexico State Records and Archives, Santa Fe.

Lionel A. Sheldon, Governor, Territory of New Mexico, to Sheriff of county of Bernalillo, January 25, 1883 (Milton J. Yarberry death warrant). New Mexico State Records and Archives, Santa Fe.

Glenn Shirley to author, February 3, 1981.

Captain Harry Wheeler to Governor Joseph H. Kibbey, April 8, 1908. Jeff Kidder file, Arizona Historical Society, Tucson.

Joe W. Williamson to Philip J. Rasch, December 20, 1981. Copy provided by Robert M. Marks, Seattle, Washington.

INTERVIEWS

Bill Cope. Interview by Clayton W. Williams, February 19, 1966. Clayton Williams Papers, Fort Stockton, Texas.

Dee Harkey. Interview by J. Evetts Haley. December 16, 1947. Nita Stewart Haley Memorial Library, Midland, Texas.

Ed Harral. Interview by J. Evetts Haley and Hervey Chesley, June 13, 1939. Nita Stewart Haley Memorial Library, Midland, Texas.

Will P. Rooney. Interview by Clayton W. Williams, "in the early 1950s." Clayton Williams Papers, Fort Stockton, Texas.

Cicero Stewart. Interview by Lou Blachly. Carlsbad, New Mexico, December 20, 1953. Zimmerman Library, University of New Mexico, Albuquerque.

NEWSPAPERS

Albuquerque Morning Journal, May 21, 1882; February 8, 9, 10, 11, 1883.

Albuquerque Review, September 2, 1882.

Albuquerque Tribune, December 14, 17, 1953; January 15, 1959; February 8, 10, 15, 1966; February 8, 1973; February 9, 1978.

Albuquerque Weekly Journal, May 25, 1882.

Anaconda Standard (Butte, Mont.), April 28, 1894; January 11, 1899.

Arizona Citizen (Tucson), October 29, November 29, 1887; April 18, 1889; April 6, 1908.

Arizona Daily Star (Tucson), October 5, 1886; August 12, 28, 1902; April 21, 1909; August 12, 1923; March 22, 1936.

Arizona Gazette (Phoenix), January 17, April 30, 1895.

Arizona Sentinel (Yuma), October 29, November 5, 1887; May 25, 1889; April 23, 1902.

Austin Democratic Statesman, September 5, 1875.

Bartlesville (Okla.) Magnet, November 19, 1897.

Big Horn Sentinel (Buffalo, Wyo.), September 3, October 15, 29, November 19, 26, 1887; June 16, 1888.

Bisbee Evening Miner, April 6, 1908.

Bisbee Review, July 6, 1904.

Border Vidette (Nogales, Ariz.), December 8, 1906; November 23, 1907; February 15, March 28, 1908.

Buffalo (Wyo.) Echo, July 28, August 8, 1887.

Carlsbad Argus, January 15, 1925.

Carlsbad Current, February 24, 1900.

Cherokee Advocate (Tahlequah, I.T.), June 21, 1902.

Cheyenne Daily Leader, August 18, September 8, October 5, 1887.

Cheyenne Daily Sun, February 5, 6, 7, 10, 11, July 22, 23, August 9, 10, September 3, 1887.

Cheyenne State Leader, November 7, 1931.

Chicago Sunday Chronicle, October 16, 1898.

Colorado Chieftain (Pueblo), January 15, February 8, 28, March 7, 11, 12, 14, April 2, May 20, June 5, 12, July 2, 8, 1879; March 31, 1881; February 15, 16, 17, 19, 21, 22, 24, 25, March 1, 7, 8, 9, 10, 20, 24, 30, April 6, 7, 8, 11, 19, 20, 22, 25, 27, 30, May 6, 14, 17, 25, 30, 31, June 6, 23, 24, July 2, 4, 7, 21, August 3, 8, 10, 17, September 13, October 10, November 18, 22, 25, 26, 29, 30, December 6, 1882; February 10, 22, March 1, October 4, 23, 1883; January 2, 7, 24, 1884; June 4, 11, September 17, 1885; March 3, 1887; January 12, December 20, 1888; July 25, 1889; March 6, 1890.

Dakota Republican (Vermillion, S.Dak.), October 4, 11, 1883; April 23, May 7, 1908.

Denver Post, March 6, 1895; February 2, 1912; June 6, 1917; November 2, 1923.

Denver Republican, June 17, 1881; March 1, 1890; June 24, 1892.

Denver Times, May 26, 1904.

Dodge City Times, September 14, 1878; February 2, 1882.

Douglas (Ariz.) American, July 7, 1904.

Eddy (N.Mex.) Argus, January 18, 25, March 15, 29, April 16, June 14, July 5, 12, 19, August 2, 16, September 6, November 8, December 13, 1890; March 3, 28, May 9, July 11, 18, September 5, October 10, December 12, 1891; February 20, March 26, June 4, 25, October 21, December 23, 1892; January 13, March 3, April 7, May 19, July 7, 28, August 11, September 8, 15, 22, November 10, December 29, 1893; March 9, 16, 30, April 6, May 11, 18, June 1, 8, 15, August 3, 31, September 21, December 21, 1894; January 25, March 22, 1895.

Eddy County (N.Mex.) Citizen, May 28, October 15, November 5, 12, 1892.

Eddy (N.Mex.) Current, December 23, 1892; January 27, April 7, May 5, June 16, 23, August 4, September 22, October 13, 20, November 10, 17, 24, 1893; March 19, September 15, 22, 1894; January 16, March 9, 23, April 24, 27, May 16, July 11, October 3, 24, 31, 1895; August 8, 21, September 26, November 21, 1896; February 20, October 16, 23, 1897; March 26, April 2, 9, October 22, 1898.

El Paso Daily Herald, March 5, May 24, August 15, 1895; February 18, October 17, 1896; February 23, May 19, June 18, 1897; June 7, 1902.

El Paso Daily Times, February 19, November 17, 18, 1896; May 19, 1897.

El Paso Lone Star, November 2, 16, 23, December 3, 1881; February 22, August 16, September 23, December 23, 1882; October 3, 1885.

Ford County Globe (Dodge City), September 17, 1878.

Fort Smith (Ark.) Elevator, October 22, November 20, 26, December 3, 24, 1897; December 25, 1898.

Galveston Daily News, May 26, 1881.

Gatesville (Tex.) Sun, June 15, 1881.

Grant County Herald (Silver City, N.Mex.), August 8, 18, 1877; January 1, 5, March 28, April 11, July 20, November 11, 23, 1878; May 2, October 11, 1879; January 3, 24, March 16, 20, 1880; March 19, 1881.

Grant County New Southwest (Silver City, N.Mex.), March 19, October 29, 1881; February 25, August 26, September 2, 9, 16, 1882.

Kansas City Star, July 10, 1924.

Kinsley Valley (Kans.) Republican, February 2, 1878.

Lampasas (Tex.) Leader, March 9, 1889; October 10, 1902; December 26, 1913.

Las Vegas (N.Mex.) Gazette, May 19, June 21, 1881.

Las Vegas (N.Mex.) Optic, September 30, 1881.

Leavenworth Times, May 26, 30, September 18, 19, 29, 1888.

Lusk (Wyo.) Herald, September 24, December 24, 1886; January 21, July 29, 1887.

National Police Gazette, December 21, 1889.

New Southwest and Grant County Herald (Silver City, N.Mex.), September 2, 16, October 7, December 23, 1882; March 17, April 7, 1883.

New York Herald, January 27, 1895.

New York Sun, January 14, 15, 1895.

Ogden Standard, March 2, 5, 6, April 5, June 25, 26, 27, 28, July 1, 1890.

Omaha Daily Bee, July 14, 28, 29, 1873.

Pecos Valley Argus (Eddy, N.Mex.), March 15, 22, April 5, 26, May 17, October 4, 25, November 8, 15, 29, December 20, 1895; April 24, May 8, September 25, October 30, December 25, 1896; January 8, August 20, October 22, November 19, 1897; April 1, 8, June 10, July 8, August 26, 1898.

Rocky Mountain News (Denver, Colo.), February 20, 1877; January 4, 1879; October 15, November 30, 1880; June 17, 1881; August 8, 1883; March 1, 1890; May 27, 1904.

Roswell Record, March 3, 10, 1893; June 21, 1895; November 20, 1896; November 12, 1897.

San Francisco Chronicle, July 25, 1896.

Santa Fe Daily New Mexican, June 22, 1881; May 29, September 10, 12, 14, 1882; February 9, 10, 11, 19, 1883; February 14, May 1, 1895.

Santa Fe Weekly Democrat, April 7, June 23, August 11, 1881; February 5, 1883.

Silver City (N.Mex.) Enterprise, December 14, 21, 1882; April 20, November 30, 1883; January 4, 18, 25, March 14, 28, November 28, 1884; October 1, 22, December 31, 1886; October 7, 1887; May 6, 1892; October 27, 1949.

Silver City (N.Mex.) Independent, September 11, 1906; September 22, 1931.

Southwest Sentinel (Silver City, N.Mex.), March 17, April 7, 11, 1883; May 31, September 27, 1884; November 17, 1885.

Spokane Daily Chronicle, December 28, 1921.

Stillwater Advance, June 19, 1902.

Tombstone Daily Epitaph, February 27, 1882; January 7, 1888.

Trinidad (Colo.) Daily Democrat, June 25, July 15, 20, August 12, 16, 17, 18, 20, 22, October 18, 20, 1882.

Trinidad (Colo.) Daily News, January 25, March 3, July 6, August 6, 11, 15, 16, 17, 18, 1882.

Trinidad (Colo.) Daily Reporter, February 6, 1883.

Tucson Post, July 27, 1907.

Vancouver (B.C.) Sun, September 10, 1929.

Vinita (I.T.) Indian Chieftain, November 18, 1897; November 25, 1898.

BOOKS AND PAMPHLETS

Adams, Ramon. *Burs Under the Saddle*. Norman: University of Oklahoma Press, 1964.

———. *More Burs Under the Saddle*. Norman: University of Oklahoma Press, 1979.

———. *Six-Guns and Saddle Leather*. Norman: University of Oklahoma Press, 1969.

Alexander, Bob. *Dangerous Dan Tucker: New Mexico's Deadly Lawman*. Silver City, N.Mex.: High-Lonesome Books, 2001.

Asbury, Herbert. *Sucker's Progress: An Informal History of Gambling in America from the Colonies to Canfield*. New York: Dodd, Mead, 1938.

Ball, Eve. *Ma'am Jones of the Pecos*. Tucson: University of Arizona Press, 1968.

Bancroft, Caroline. *Tabor's Matchless Mine and Lusty Leadville*. Boulder, Colo.: Johnson, 1960.

Bartholomew, Ed. *The Biographical Album of Western Gunfighters*. Houston, Tex.: Frontier Press of Texas, 1958.

———. *Western Hard-Cases, or, Gunfighters Named Smith*. Ruidoso, N.Mex.: Frontier Book Co., 1960.

———. *Wyatt Earp, 1879 to 1882. The Man and the Myth*. Toyahville, Tex.: Frontier Book Co., 1964.

Benedict, John D. *Muskogee and Northeastern Oklahoma*. Chicago: S. J. Clarke Publishing Co., 1922.

Black, A. P. (Ott). *The End of the Long Horn Trail.* Selfridge, N.Dak.: Selfridge Journal, [1936?].

Blair, Edward. *Leadville, Colorado's Magic City.* Boulder, Colo.: Pruett Publishing Co., 1980.

Blair, Edward, and E. Richard Churchill. *Everybody Came to Leadville.* Leadville, Colo.: Timberline Books, 1971.

Boessenecker, John. *Badge and Buckshot: Lawlessness in Old California.* Norman: University of Oklahoma Press, 1988.

Bonney, Cecil. *Looking Over My Shoulder: Seventy-Five Years on the Pecos Valley.* Roswell, N.Mex.: Hall-Poorbaugh Press, 1971.

Breakenridge, William M. *Helldorado: Bringing the Law to the Mesquite.* 1928. Glorieta, N.Mex.: Rio Grande Press, 1970.

Brent, William and Milarde. *The Hell Hole.* Yuma, Ariz.: Southwest Printers, 1962.

Bristow, David L. *A Dirty, Wicked Town: Tales of 19th Century Omaha.* Caldwell, Idaho: Caxton Press, 2000.

Brown, Richard Maxwell. *No Duty to Retreat: Violence and Values in American History and Society.* Norman: University of Oklahoma Press, 1994.

Browning, James A. *Violence Was No Stranger: A Guide to the Graves of Famous Westerners.* Stillwater, Okla.: Barbed Wire Press, 1993.

———. *The Western Reader's Guide: A Selected Bibliography of Nonfiction Magazines, 1953–91.* Stillwater, Okla.: Barbed Wire Press, 1992.

Bryan, Howard. *Robbers, Rogues, and Ruffians: True Tales of the Wild West in New Mexico.* Santa Fe, N.Mex.: Clear Light Publishers, 1991.

Buffum, George T. *Smith of Bear City and Other Frontier Sketches.* New York: Grafton Press, 1906.

Burke, John. *The Legend of Baby Doe: The Life and Times of the Silver Queen of the West.* New York: G. P. Putnam's Sons, 1974.

Burton, Jeff. *Dynamite and Six-shooter.* Santa Fe, N.Mex.: Press of the Territorian, 1970.

Chase, C. M. *The Editor's Run in New Mexico and Colorado.* 1882. Fort Davis, Tex.: Frontier Book Co., 1968.

Chesley, Hervey E. *Adventuring with the Old-Timers: Trails Traveled—Tales Told.* Midland, Tex.: Nita Stewart Haley Memorial Library, 1979.

Clark, Walter van Tilburg, ed. *The Journals of Alfred Doten.* Reno: University of Nevada Press, 1973.

Collier, William Ross, and Edwin Victor Westrate. *Dave Cook of the Rockies: Frontier General, Fighting Sheriff, and Leader of Men.* New York: Rufus Rockwell Wilson, 1936.

Cook, General D. J. *Hands Up; or, Twenty Years of Detective Life in the Mountains and the Plains.* 1882. Norman: University of Oklahoma Press, 1958.

Cook, James H. *Fifty Years on the Old Frontier as Cowboy, Hunter, Guide, Scout, and Ranchman.* 1923. Norman: University of Oklahoma Press, 1957.

Coolidge, Dane. *Fighting Men of the West.* New York: E. P. Dutton & Co., 1932.

Courtwright, David T. *Violent Land: Single Men and Social Disorder from the Frontier to the Inner City.* Cambridge: Harvard University Press, 1996.

Cramer, T. Dudley. *The Pecos Ranchers in the Lincoln County War.* Oakland: Branding Iron Press, 1996.

Cunningham, Eugene. *Triggernometry: A Gallery of Gunfighters.* 1934. Caldwell, Idaho: Caxton Printers, 1962.

Dary, David. *True Tales of the Old-Time Plains.* New York: Crown Publishers, 1979.

David, Robert B. *Malcolm Campbell, Sheriff.* Casper, Wyo.: S. E. Boyer & Co., 1932.

DeArment, Robert K. *Bat Masterson: The Man and the Legend.* Norman: University of Oklahoma Press, 1979.

———. *George Scarborough: The Life and Death of a Lawman on the Closing Frontier.* Norman: University of Oklahoma Press, 1992.

———. *Knights of the Green Cloth: The Saga of the Frontier Gamblers.* Norman: University of Oklahoma Press, 1982.

Debo, Darrell, *Burnet County History.* Vol. 2. N.p., 1979.

De la Garza, Phyllis. *The Story of Dos Cabezas.* Tucson, Ariz.: Westernlore Press, 1995.

DeMattos, Jack. *Mysterious Gunfighter: The Story of Dave Mather.* College Station, Tex.: Creative Publishing Co., 1992.

Devol, George H. *Forty Years a Gambler on the Mississippi.* 1892. Austin, Tex.: Steck-Vaughn Co., 1967.

Douglas, C. L. *Cattle Kings of Texas.* 1939. Austin, Tex.: State House Press, 1989.

———. *Famous Texas Feuds.* 1936. Austin, Tex.: State House Press, 1988.

Dugan, Mark. *Knight of the Road: The Life of Highwayman Ham White.* Athens: Ohio University Press, 1990.

Erwin, Allen A. *The Southwest of John Horton Slaughter.* Glendale, Calif.: Arthur H. Clark Co., 1965.

Faulk, Odie B. *Dodge City: The Most Western Town of All.* New York: Oxford University Press, 1977.

Fergusson, Erna. *Albuquerque.* Albuquerque, N.Mex.: Merle Armitage Editions, 1947.

Flannery, L. G. (Pat), ed. *John Hunton's Diary, Wyoming Territory, Volume 6, 1885–1889.* Glendale, Calif.: Arthur H. Clark Co., 1970.

Fleischer, Nat. *The Flaming Ben Hogan: Pugilist, Pirate, Gambler, Civil War Spy, Oil Magnate, Evangelist.* New York: Ring Magazine, 1941.

Foy, Eddie, and Alvin F. Harlow. *Clowning Through Life.* New York: E. P. Dutton & Co., 1928.

Frye, Elnora L. *Atlas of Wyoming Outlaws at the Territorial Penitentiary.* Laramie, Wyo: Jelm Mountain Publications, 1990.

Gay, Felix M. *History of Nowata County.* Stillwater, Okla.: Redlands Press, 1957.

Gillett, James B. *Six Years with the Texas Rangers, 1875 to 1881.* 1921. Lincoln: University of Nebraska Press, 1976.

Gober, Jim. *Cowboy Justice: Tale of a Texas Lawman*. Lubbock: Texas Tech University Press, 1997.

Gottesman, Ronald, ed. *Violence in America: An Encyclopedia*. New York: Scribner, 1999.

Green, Edwin. *Green's City Directory of Leavenworth, Kansas, 1886, 1887, 1888, 1889.*

Griffith, Elizabeth T. *The House of Blazes: The Story of Johnny Owens*. Newcastle, Wyo.: News Letter Journal, 1990.

Guthrie, J. *Great Register of the County of Cochise, Territory of Arizona, for the Year 1884*. Tombstone, Ariz.: Tombstone Commemorative Enterprises, n.d.

Haley, J. Evetts. *Jeff Milton, A Good Man with a Gun*. Norman: University of Oklahoma Press, 1948.

Harkey, Dee. *Mean as Hell*. Albuquerque: University of New Mexico Press, 1948.

Harrison, Fred. *Hell Holes and Hangings*. Clarendon, Tex.: Clarendon Press, 1968.

Hening, H. B., ed. *George Curry, 1861–1947*. Albuquerque: University of New Mexico Press, 1958.

Henry, Stuart. *Conquering Our Great American Plains*. New York: E. P. Dutton & Co., 1930.

Hickey, Michael M. *The Death of Warren Baxter Earp: A Closer Look*. Honolulu: Talei Publishers, 2000.

Hicks, John Edward. *Adventures of a Tramp Printer, 1880–1890*. Kansas City, Mo.: Midamerican Press, 1950.

Hill, Rita. *Then and Now, Here and Around Shakespeare*. Lordsburg, N.Mex.: Pyramid Printing, 1963.

A History of Lipscomb County, Texas, 1876–1976. Lipscomb, Tex.: Lipscomb County Historical Survey Committee, 1976.

History of the Tacoma Police Department. Tacoma, Wash.: Patrolmen's Benevolent Association, 1908.

Holden, W. C. *Rollie Burns: An Account of the Ranching Industry on the South Plains*. 1932. College Station: Texas A&M University Press, 1986.

Hough, Emerson. *The Story of the Outlaw: A Study of the Western Desperado*. New York: Grosset & Dunlap, 1905.

Hoyt, William R. *A Frontier Doctor*. Boston: Houghton Mifflin Co., 1929.

Hunter, J. Marvin. *The Trail Drivers of Texas*. Austin: University of Texas Press, 1985.

Hunter, J. Marvin, and Noah H. Rose. *The Album of Gunfighters*. Bandera, Tex.: n.p., 1951.

Jackson and Jackson. *Cases Argued and Adjudged in the Court of Appeals of the State of Texas, 11*. St. Louis: Gilbert Book Co., 1882.

James, Bill C. *Barney Riggs, A West Texas Gunman*. Carrollton, Tex.: n.p., 1982.

James, Bill C., and Mary Kay Shannon. *Sheriff A. J. Royal, Fort Stockton, Texas*. N.p., 1984.

Jeffrey, John Mason. *Adobe and Iron.* LaJolla, Calif.: Prospect Avenue Press, 1969.

Jennings, Al. *Through the Shadows with O. Henry.* New York: H. K. Fly Co., Publishers, 1921.

Jennings, Al, and Will Irwin. *Beating Back.* New York: D. Appleton and Co., 1914.

Jessen, Kenneth. *Colorado Gunsmoke: True Stories of Outlaws and Lawmen on the Colorado Frontier.* Boulder, Colo.: Pruett Publishing Co., 1986.

King, Frank M. *Wranglin' the Past.* 1935. Pasadena, Calif.: Trail's End Publishing Co., 1946.

Klasner, Lily. *My Girlhood among Outlaws.* Tucson: University of Arizona Press, 1972.

Lake, Carolyn, ed. *Under Cover for Wells Fargo: The Unvarnished Recollections of Fred Dodge.* Boston: Houghton Mifflin Co., 1969.

Lake, Stuart N. *Wyatt Earp, Frontier Marshal.* Boston: Houghton Mifflin Co., 1931.

Langford, Nathaniel Pitt. *Vigilante Days and Ways: The Pioneers of the Rockies.* 1890. New York: A. L. Burt, 1912.

Lanning, Jim and Judy, eds. *Texas Cowboys: Memories of the Early Days.* College Station: Texas A&M University Press, 1984.

Lavash, Donald R. *Wilson and the Kid.* College Station, Tex.: Creative Publishing Co., 1990.

Lindsey, Ellis and Gene Ripps. *Barney K. Riggs, the Yuma and Pecos Avenger.* N.p.: Xlibris Corporation, 2002.

A List of Fugitives from Justice for 1900. Austin: Texas State Library, 1900.

Lundwall, Helen J., ed. *Pioneering in Territorial Silver City: H. B. Ailman's Recollections of Silver City and the Southwest, 1871–1892.* Albuquerque: University of New Mexico Press, 1983.

McCarty, John L. *Maverick Town: The Story of Old Tascosa.* Norman: University of Oklahoma Press, 1946.

McIntire, Jim. *Early Days in Texas: A Trip to Hell and Heaven.* 1902. Norman: University of Oklahoma Press, 1992.

McKanna, Clare V., Jr. *Homicide, Race, and Justice in the American West, 1880–1920.* Tucson: University of Arizona Press, 1997.

Metz, Leon C. *Dallas Stoudenmire, El Paso Marshal.* Austin, Tex.: Pemberton Press, 1969.

———. *John Wesley Hardin: Dark Angel of Texas.* El Paso, Tex.: Mangan Books, 1996.

———. *Pat Garrett: The Story of a Western Lawman.* Norman: University of Oklahoma Press, 1974.

———. *The Shooters.* El Paso, Tex.: Mangan Books, 1976.

Miller, Joseph, ed., *The Arizona Rangers.* New York: Hastings House, 1972.

Miller, Nyle H., and Joseph W. Snell. *Why the West Was Wild.* Topeka: Kansas State Historical Society, 1963.

Monaghan, Jay. *Last of the Bad Men: The Legend of Tom Horn.* Indianapolis: Bobbs-Merrill Co., 1946.

Moses, Lloyd R., ed. *Clay County Place Names*. Vermillion, S.Dak.: Clay County Historical Society, 1976.

Myers, Lee. "An Experiment in Prohibition." *New Mexico Historical Review*. N.d.

Myres. S. D., ed. *Pioneer Surveyor, Frontier Lawyer: The Personal Narrative of O. W. Williams, 1877–1902*. El Paso: Texas Western College Press, 1966.

Nash, Jay Robert. *Encyclopedia of Western Lawmen and Outlaws*. New York: Paragon House, 1992.

Nelson, Susan and David, eds. *Silver City Book*. Vol. 1, *Wild and Wooly Days*. Silver City, N.Mex.: Silver City Publications, 1978.

Nolan, Frederick. *The Lincoln County War: A Documentary History*. Norman: University of Oklahoma Press, 1992.

O'Neal, Bill. *The Arizona Rangers*. Austin, Tex.: Eakin Press, 1987.

———. *The Bloody Legacy of Pink Higgins*. Austin, Tex.: Eakin Press, 1999.

———. *Encyclopedia of Western Gunfighters*. Norman: University of Oklahoma Press, 1979.

———. *Fighting Men of the Indian Wars*. Stillwater, Okla.: Barbed Wire Press, 1991.

Otero, Miguel A. *My Life on the Frontier, 1864–1882*. New York: Press of the Pioneers, 1935.

———. *My Life on the Frontier, 1882–1897*. Albuquerque: University of New Mexico Press, 1939.

Parkhill, Forbes. *The Wildest of the West*. New York: Henry Holt & Co., 1951.

Raine, William MacLeod. *Famous Sheriffs and Western Outlaws*. Garden City, N.Y.: Doubleday, Doran & Co., 1929.

———. *Guns of the Frontier*. Boston: Houghton Mifflin Co., 1940.

Rasch, Philip J. *Desperadoes of Arizona Territory*. N.p.: National Association for Outlaw and Lawman History, 1999.

———. *Warriors of Lincoln County*. N.p.: National Association for Outlaw and Lawman History, 1998.

Raymond, Dora Neill. *Captain Lee Hall of Texas*. Norman: University of Oklahoma Press, 1940.

Reynolds, Bill. *Trouble in New Mexico: The Outlaws, Gunmen, Desperados, Murderers, and Lawmen for Fifty Turbulent Years*. Vol. 1, *The A's & B's*. Bakersfield, Calif.: Kinko's Copies, 1994.

———. *Trouble in New Mexico: The Outlaws, Gunmen, Desperados, Murderers, and Lawmen for Fifty Turbulent Years*. Vol. 2, *The C's*. Bakersfield, Calif.: Kinko's Copies, 1994.

———. *Trouble in New Mexico: The Outlaws, Gunmen, Desperados, Murderers, and Lawmen for Fifty Turbulent Years*. Vol. 3, *The D's & E's*. Bakersfield, Calif.: Kinko's Copies, n.d.

Rickards, Colin. *Charles Littlepage Ballard, Southwesterner*. El Paso: Texas Western Press, 1966.

———. *How Pat Garrett Died*. Santa Fe, N.Mex.: Press of the Territorian, 1970.

Robinson, Doane. *History of South Dakota*. Vol. 1. N.p.: B. F. Bowen & Co., 1904.

Rosa, Joseph G. *The Gunfighter: Man or Myth?* Norman: University of Oklahoma Press, 1969.

Rynning, Captain Thomas H., as told to Al Cohn and Joe Chisholm. *Gun Notches: The Life Story of a Cowboy-Soldier.* New York: Frederick A. Stokes Co., 1931.

Sanders, Helen Fitzgerald, ed. *X. Beidler: Vigilante.* Norman: University of Oklahoma Press, 1957.

Sandoz, Mari. *The Cattlemen, from the Rio Grande across the Far Marias.* New York: Hastings House, 1958.

Sawey, Orlan. *Charles A. Siringo.* Boston: Twayne Publishers, 1981.

Schell, Herbert S. *History of Clay County, South Dakota.* Vermillion, S.Dak.: Clay County Historical Society, 1976.

Shinkle, James D. *Reminiscences of Roswell Pioneers.* Roswell, N.Mex.: Hall-Poorbaugh Press, 1966.

Shirk, George H. *Oklahoma Place Names.* Norman: University of Oklahoma Press, 1965.

Shirley, Glenn. *Marauders of the Indian Nations: The Bill Cook Gang and Cherokee Bill.* Stillwater, Okla.: Barbed Wire Press, 1994.

———. *Shotgun for Hire.* Norman: University of Oklahoma Press, 1970.

———. *Temple Houston: Lawyer with a Gun.* Norman: University of Oklahoma Press, 1980.

Simmons, Marc. *When Six-Guns Ruled: Outlaw Tales of the Southwest.* Santa Fe, N.Mex.: Ancient City Press, 1990.

Sinise, Jerry. *Pink Higgins, the Reluctant Gunfighter, and Other Tales of the Panhandle.* Quanah, Tex.: Nortex Press, 1974.

Siringo, Charles A. *A Cowboy Detective: A True Story of Twenty-Two Years with a World-Famous Detective Agency.* Lincoln: University of Nebraska Press, 1988.

———. *A Lone Star Cowboy.* Santa Fe, N.Mex.: n.p., 1919.

———. *Riata and Spurs.* Orig. ed. Boston: Houghton Mifflin Co., 1927.

———. *Riata and Spurs.* Rev. ed. Boston: Houghton Mifflin Co., 1927.

———. *Two Evil Isms: Pinkertonism and Anarchism.* 1915. Austin, Tex.: Steck-Vaughn Co., 1967.

Slotkin, Richard. *Gunfighter Nation: The Myth of the Frontier in Twentieth-Century America.* New York: Atheneum, 1992.

Sonnichsen, C. L. *The El Paso Salt War, 1877.* El Paso, Tex.: Texas Western Press, 1961.

Sorenson, Alfred. *The Story of Omaha from the Pioneer Days to the Present Time.* Omaha: National Printing Co., 1923.

Spikes, Nellie Witt, and Temple Ann Ellis. *History of Crosby County, Texas.* San Antonio, Tex.: Naylor Co., 1952.

Stanley, F. *The Shakespeare, New Mexico, Story.* Panten, Tex., 1961.

Stuart, Granville. *Prospecting for Gold: From Dogtown to Virginia City, 1852–1864.* 1925. Lincoln: University of Nebraska Press, 1977.

Sullivan, W. J. L. *Twelve Years in the Saddle for Law and Order on the Frontiers of Texas.* 1909. New York: Buffalo-Head Press, 1966.

Tefertiller, Casey. *Wyatt Earp: The Life Behind the Legend*. New York: John Wiley & Sons, 1997.

Thrapp, Dan L. *Encyclopedia of Frontier Biography in Three Volumes*. Glendale, Calif.: Arthur H. Clark Co., 1988.

Tise, Sammy. *Texas County Sheriffs*. Albuquerque, N.Mex.: Oakwood Printing, 1989.

Twain, Mark. *Roughing It*. Hartford, Conn.: American Publishing Co., 1872.

Vickers, C. L. ed., *History of the Arkansas Valley, Colorado*. Chicago: O. L. Baskin & Co., Historical Publishers, 1881.

Wardell, Morris L. *A Political History of the Cherokee Nation, 1838–1907*. Norman: University of Oklahoma Press, 1977.

Webb, Walter Prescott. *The Texas Rangers*. Boston: Houghton Mifflin Co., 1935.

Williams, Clayton W. *Texas' Last Frontier: Fort Stockton and the Trans-Pecos, 1861–1895*. College Station: Texas A&M University Press, 1982.

Willison, George F. *Here They Dug the Gold*. New York: Reynol and Hitchcock Co., 1946.

Wilson, Rufus Rockwell. *Out of the West*. New York: Wilson-Erickson, 1936.

Woods, Lawrence M. *Wyoming Biographies*. Worland, Wyo.: High Plains Publishing Co., 1991.

ARTICLES

Ball, Larry D. "Lawman in Disgrace: Sheriff Charles C. Perry of Chaves County, New Mexico." *New Mexico Historical Review* 61, no. 2 (April 1986).

Bartlett, G. W. "Mart Duggan, Fighter." *Rocky Mountain Magazine*, December 1903.

Blachly. Lou. "I'll Never Forget. . . ." *Silver City Enterprise*, October 27, 1949.

Blair, Edward. "Leadville's Marshal Who Knew No Fear." *Empire Magazine, Denver Post*, May 16, 1971.

Callaghan, James. "The Bold Fenian Men." *National Tombstone Epitaph*, November–December, 1982.

Carroll, Murray L. "As an Outlaw and Escape Artist Dan Bogan Was the Real McCoy." *Journal of the Western Outlaw-Lawman History Association* 2, no. 1 (spring–summer 1992).

Carson, Xanthus. "Shoot-Out in Number 11 Saloon." *Pioneer West*, April 1971.

Cowan, E. D. "Memories of the Happy Bad Man of the West." *Chicago Sunday Chronicle*, October 16, 1898.

Cunningham, J. F. "Experiences of a Pioneer District Attorney." *West Texas Historical Association Year Book*, June 1932.

DeArment, R. K. "Barney Riggs—Man of Violence." *Old West*, fall 1983.

———. "The Blood-Spattered Trail of Milton J. Yarberry." *Old West*, fall 1985.

———. "Cole Belmont, Barfly Witness." *Quarterly of the National Association for Outlaw and Lawman History*, spring 1990.

————. "Deadly Deputy." *True West*, November 1991.

————. "The Fatal Defect of Charley Perry." *Old West*, winter 1991.

————. "A Forgotten Gunfighter of the Indian Territory." *Oklahombres: The Journal of Lawman and Outlaw History of Oklahoma*, winter 1995.

————. "George 'Red' Goodell, Forgotten Gunfighter." *Quarterly of the National Association and Center for Outlaw and Lawman History* 12, no. 4 (1989).

————. "Gunman Ambushes Sheriff, Is Acquitted." *National Tombstone Epitaph*, February 9, 1991.

————. "Jeff Kidder, Arizona Ranger." *Quarterly of the National Association and Center for Outlaw and Lawman History*, winter 1982–83.

————. "John Bull, Gunman, Gambler: A Frontier Odyssey." *True West*, March 1986.

————. "Mart Duggan: Leadville Lawman." *Frontier Times*, February 1985.

————. "The Outlaw Trail of Dan Bogan." *True West*, January 1984.

————. "The Protection Man." *Old West*, spring 1991.

————. "Sheriff Whitehill and the Kit Joy Gang." *Old West*, winter 1994.

————. "Tough Irish Lawman." *True West*, June 1992.

Donoho, Ron. "Death of an Arizona Ranger." *Arizona Sheriff*, November–December 1971.

"Duggan's Slayer Met Same Fate." *Rocky Mountain News*, May 27, 1904

Freeman, Frank M. "The Meanest So-And-So in Colorado." *Real West*, September 1981.

"George Evans, The Slayer of Duggan." *Denver Times*, May 26, 1904.

Greenfield, Charles D. "There Was Something about Him." *The West*, February 1967.

Gregg, Andy. "The Day They Hung Marshal Yarbery." *Real West*, November 1961.

Griffith, Elizabeth. "Johnny Owens: Gambler, Whoremaster, Rancher, Killer—Sheriff." *Journal of the Western Outlaw-Lawman History Association* 1, no. 1 (spring–summer 1991).

Guinn, Jack. "The Timely End of Jim Moon." *Empire Magazine*, Denver Post, April 30, 1967.

Holden, W. C. "The Problem of Stealing on the Spur Ranch." *West Texas Historical Year Book* 8 (June 1932).

Hunt, Robert V., Jr. "Big Ed Burns, Leadville Badhat." *True West*, April 1995.

Jay, Don M. "Bad Blood." *Frontier Times*, December–January, 1967.

Jones, Charles A. "Pink Higgins, the Good Bad Man." *Atlantic Monthly*, July 1934.

Kelly, Bill. "The Last of the Arizona Rangers." *Real West*, January 1977.

King, David. "The Pecos War." *True West*, December 1996.

Lewis, Alfred Henry. "The King of the Gun-Players, William Barclay Masterson." *Human Life*, November 1907.

Masterson, W. B. "Famous Gun Fighters of the Western Frontier: Ben Thompson." *Human Life*, January 1907.

———. "Wyatt Earp." *Human Life*, February 1907.

———. "Luke Short." *Human Life*, April 1907.

———. "Doc Holliday." *Human Life*, May 1907.

———. "Billy Tilghman." *Human Life*, July 1907.

McCown, Dennis. "'Despite Big Losses . . .': The Last Shooting of the Old West." *Quarterly of the National Association and Center for Outlaw and Lawman History* 24, no. 4 (October–December 2000).

Myers, Lee. "How Hell-Raising Phenix Dug Its Own Grave." *The West*, July 1964.

O'Neal, Bill. "They Called Him Mister Kemp." *True West*, April 1991.

Owen, James. "Reminiscences of Early Pueblo." *Colorado Magazine*, May 1945.

Pearce, Joe, and Richard Summers. "Joe Pearce—Manhunter: Some Adventures of an Arizona Ranger," *Journal of Arizona History*, autumn 1978.

Rasch, Philip J. "AKA 'Russian Bill.'" *Branding Iron, Los Angeles Corral of the Westerners*, no. 86 (March 1968).

———. "Half Told Tales: Charles C. Perry and John B. Legg." *English Westerners' Brand Book* 13, no. 3 (April 1971).

———. "John Kinney: King of the Rustlers." *English Westerners Brand Book*, 1961.

———. "The Life and Death of Lon Bass." *Quarterly of the National Association for Outlaw and Lawman History* 14, nos. 3 and 4 (1990).

Rasch, Philip J., and Lee Myers. "Les Dow, Sheriff of Eddy County." *New Mexico Historical Review* 49, no. 3 (July 1974).

Robbins, Lance. "The Killer Who Succeeded at Dying." *Real West*, fall 1965.

Roberts, Gary L. "Gunfighters and Outlaws, Western." In Ronald Gottesman, ed., *Violence in America: An Encyclopedia*, vol. 2. New York: Scribner, 1999.

Rose, Dan. "Dan Tucker, The Killer." *Silver City Independent*, September 22, 1931.

Secrest, William B. "The Last Ride." *True West*, January–February 1967.

Spring, Agnes Wright. "Twenty Notches on His Gun." *True West*, April 1970.

Index

Simpson, Pete, 117–19
Siringo, Charles A. ("Charlie"), 152, 156, 165–67, 230n.61
Slaughter, C. C., 101
Slaughter, Charles Holmes, 173–74
Slaughter, John H., 173, 233n.74
Smith, Carrie, 89
Smith, Charley, 137
Smith, Dick, 116
Smith, Erastus ("Rackety"), 118–19
Smith, F. A. ("Doll"), 153–54, 164, 169, 170, 173, 191, 231n.5
Smith, F. W., 65
Smith, Lance D., 179
Smith, Marcus A. ("Mark"), 137, 139
Smith, Thomas J. ("Bear River Tom"), 21, 213n.7
Smith, W. H. ("Bill"), 176, 181–82, 186, 190
Smyth, R. P., 105
Snell, Addison, 12
Snell, William, 170, 231n.5
Snyder, Tex., 102
Socorro, N.Mex., 117, 118
"Socorro Stranglers," 117
Soldiers' Home, Leavenworth, Kans., 88
Sonora Rurales, 201
Soper, P. L., 94, 96
Sosa, Crispin, 143
Sosa, Pablo, 143
South Africa, 132
South Munster, Ireland, 20
South Pueblo, Colo., 21–24, 27, 30–31
Spanish-American War, 196
Sparks, Bill, 201–202
Spillman, C. W., 6–7
Spokane, Wash., 18
Springer, N.Mex., 88
Springer, William M., 91–92, 94, 96
Spur ranch, 106, 107–12, 114
Stalcup, William K., 181, 185
Standifer, J. William ("Bill"), 99–114, 222n.20, 223n.21, 224n.51
Standifer, Mary E. Lawhon, 100
Standifer, Mrs. J. William, 111
Standifer, Sarah M. Wolf, 100
Standifer's Thicket, 114
Stanford, Tip, 201, 204, 206
State University of Dakota, 195

Steary, William C., 165
Stevenson, R. M., 24, 28
Stewart, M. Cicero, 188, 191, 192
Stewart, Patrick, 45
Stilwell, Frank, 135
Stockton, Ike, 59
Stoll, Walter R., 164, 166, 191, 230n.48
Stores: Blackmore's Drugs, Eddy, N.Mex., 189; Bradford Drugs, Leadville, Colo., 50; Castlebaum's, Nogales, Ariz., 199
Street, Webster, 137, 139
Stringfellow, R. R., 185
Stuart, Granville, 7
Stuart, James, 6
Sughrue, Mike, 19
Sughrue, Pat, 19
Sullivan, Jack, 13
Sullivan, W. J. L., 124, 126, 129–30
Sulphur Springs Valley, Ariz., 135, 137, 138, 141
Sutherland, John, 204
Sweeney, Peter, 163
Swift, H. L., 185

Tabletop cattle brand, 157, 158
Tabor, H. A. W. ("Haw"), 39–42
Tacoma, Wash., 91, 98
Taggart, Frank, 117–19
Talbot, W. E., 65
Tampico, Mexico, 132
Tarango, Francisco, 177
Tarbeau, Frank, 16
Tascosa, Tex., 156, 157, 158, 159, 162, 167
Teel, Newt, 148
Tercero, Florentine, 144
Tercero, Ramon, 144
Tercero, Tainas, 144
Texarkana, Tex., 53
"Texas George" (gambler), 88
Texas House, Leadville, Colo., 49–50
"Texas Jack" (Leadville rowdy), 43
Texas Rangers, 53, 54, 69, 72, 101, 124, 126, 129, 130, 144, 147, 194, 222n.13
Texas State Court of Appeals, 170
Thams, Peter, 45
Thayer, John M., 44–45
Thomas, T. J., 124